This is the first practical guide to *small* antiques for collectors with limited space and for enthusiasts wanting to start a collection.

Two hundred different objets d'art, each with a section to itself, are concisely described and illustrated with drawings and photographs. Each description is followed by relevant countrywide addresses and details of the following:

Collectors' clubs, societies and associations
Specialist dealers, for advice and purchases
Museums and famous collections, for closer study
Books recommended for further reading

James Mackay has written many books on antiques, stamps, coins and general collecting, and is the *Financial Times* Antiques Correspondent. In this book he has included many less well known antiques which merit the attention of collectors; these include barge teapots, caudle cups, cow creamers, door knockers, étagère, kakiemon, locks and keys, pomade tops, posset pots, stump work and wax fruit.

This book is published by Garnstone Press, London, who issue a wide range of attractive non-fiction titles in the fields of communications, history, philosophy, hobbies, literature, London information and travel. Their catalogue is always available free on request.

AN INTRODUCTION TO
Small Antiques

by James Mackay
Drawings by Diane Dancklefsen

GARNSTONE PRESS

An Introduction to Small Antiques
is published by
THE GARNSTONE PRESS LIMITED
59 Brompton Road, London SW3

SBN 900391 33 2

Contents

Contents

Foreword

The past few years have witnessed a tremendous boom in the hobby of antique collecting. In these troubled times of Freeze and Squeeze more and more people are turning from traditional forms of investment and seeking some assurance from the possession of tangible objects. The acquisitive hobbies such as stamps and coins have been enjoying a widespread upsurge in popularity but undoubtedly it is in the field of objets d'art that the increase in interest has been most general. While the museums are undoubtedly playing a major role in creating the interest of collectors and aggravating the demand for antiques, the growing interest in the private sector would have been inevitable anyway. The higher level of general prosperity and higher standards of education are but two of the factors which have made the public not only more appreciative of all that is best from times past but also given them the money and leisure to indulge their tastes. Without a doubt the devaluation of sterling in November 1967 acted as a stimulus on the antique market. In the year following devaluation few items in the field of antiques did not increase in value by less than 20 per cent and in some cases the increase was nearer 100 per cent. Although there is a dearth of really fine material there seem to be more and more antique shops with a surprising range of goods covering every conceivable aspect of collecting. Many objects have been promoted in status merely on account of their age; not so long ago these would have been beneath the notice of the collector. There is also a tendency to advance the age criterion and to regard anything produced in the 19th century as antique. At one time the term antique was only applied to the remains of the classical cultures of Greece and Rome but gradually the decorative arts of all past eras came to be considered antique. The British Antique Dealers' Association still adhere to the date line of 1830 which was originally stipulated in the British and United States customs and tariff laws of 1930. The legal definition for the purposes of exemption from payment of duty on import is rather more flexible and for all practical purposes any object which is over 100 years old may be regarded as an antique.

There is a very real need for a general introductory work such as this divided into various classes of objects and arranged for convenience in alphabetical order. Thousands of new collectors take up the absorbing subject of antiques each year and this book is primarily designed for their enlightenment. As this book is designed merely to outline briefly the scope of antique collecting, the way to further study is signposted by listing, where appropriate, general reference books and specialised monographs which the reader may consult for more detailed information. To read about a subject is not enough and a knowledge of antiques can only be gained by looking at collections. While it may not be practicable for the collector to gain direct access to reference collections and acquire expertise which can only come from handling the objects concerned, the museums in the United Kingdom have made enormous strides in recent years in the display of their collections. Wherever possible the museums which contain good examples of the various objects are listed at the end of each section. The practicality of the contents of this book necessitates the mentioning of specialist dealers for each object. I must hasten to add, however, that they are, of course, not the only such dealers and it should not be inferred that if no dealers are mentioned they do not exist. Many objects, while not meriting dealers specialising solely or largely in them, may be found in the general stock in trade of most antique dealers. All the objects in the book can be acquired through the London and provincial auctioneers listed at the beginning of the book. I cannot emphasise too strongly the value of the auction rooms in this country. Not only does the cream of antique material pass through the sale rooms where the collector and dealer are in friendly competition but the facilities for viewing lots prior to auction enables the collector and student to examine rare objects at close quarters in circumstances which are usually denied to visitors in museums.

The exigencies of space have meant that I have had to be selective in choosing the 200 subjects for this book. In selecting these objects I have borne in mind that one of the most pressing problems facing the collector today is lack of house room. For this reason I have placed emphasis on objects which are small and do not take up much space. Bearing in mind also the financial position of the average collector I have concentrated on objects in a price range which should seldom exceed £100 and in the great majority of cases should be very much below that figure. Many beginners are overawed by antique dealers and auctioneers in the erroneous belief that one has to be a Rothschild or a Mellon to indulge one's tastes in antiques. It is important to remember that a fairly large proportion of the turnover in Christie's and Sothebys and the other principal auction houses consists of lots which fetch £20 or less. Antique collecting is a hobby which can be tailored to suit even the most modest purse.

When I began compiling notes for this book I found that I could think of at least 500 categories of antique. For practical purposes I have had to whittle this down to 200. My choice is essentially a personal one and if this book is found to meet a need a further selection will be published in due course.

In the compilation of a reference work of this nature I have been indebted to private collectors, museum curators, antique dealers and auctioneers. It would be invidious of me to single out any person in

Mid 17th century Dutch
silver sweetmeat box

particular but without their assistance this book would not have been possible. I must, however, record my thanks to Judy Allen of Garnstone Press for compiling the lists of dealers, museums and reference works appended to each section.

James Mackay

Museums

mentioned in the book

IN LONDON

BETHNAL GREEN MUSEUM, Cambridge Heath Road, E2

BRITISH MUSEUM, Great Russell Street, WC1

BRITISH PIANO MUSEUM, 368 High Street, Brentford, Middlesex

MUSEUM OF BRITISH TRANSPORT, Clapham High Street, SW4

COURTAULD INSTITUTE GALLERIES, Woburn Square, WC1

FENTON HOUSE, Hampstead Grove, Hampstead, NW3

GEFFRYE MUSEUM, Kingsland Road, Shoreditch, E2

GUILDHALL MUSEUM, Gillett House, EC3

HORNIMAN MUSEUM, London Road, Forest Hill, SE23

LONDON MUSEUM, Kensington Palace, The Broadwalk, Kensington Gardens, W8

NATIONAL MARITIME MUSEUM, Romney Road, Greenwich, SE10

NATIONAL PORTRAIT GALLERY, St Martin's Place, Trafalgar Square, WC2

PERCIVAL DAVID FOUNDATION OF CHINESE ART, 53 Gordon Square, WC1

PHARMACEUTICAL SOCIETY'S MUSEUM, 17 Bloomsbury Square, WC1

POLLOCK'S TOY MUSEUM, 44 Monmouth Street, WC2

ROYAL COLLEGE OF MUSIC, Prince Consort Road, South Kensington, SW7

SCIENCE MUSEUM, Exhibition Road, South Kensington, SW7

SIR JOHN SOANE'S MUSEUM, 13 Lincoln's Inn Fields, WC2

TOWER OF LONDON, Tower Hill, EC3

VICTORIA AND ALBERT MUSEUM, Cromwell Road, South Kensington, SW7

WALLACE COLLECTION, Hertford House, Manchester Square, W1

WELLINGTON MUSEUM, Apsley House, Hyde Park Corner, W1 [P.T.O.]

OUTSIDE LONDON

THE HAWORTH ART GALLERY, Manchester Road, Accrington

WADDESDON MANOR, Waddesdon Village, Near Aylesbury, Bucks

MUSEUM OF WELSH ANTIQUITIES, University College of North Wales, College Road, Bangor

THE BOWES MUSEUM, Barnard Castle, Durham

HOLBOURNE OF MENSTRIE MUSEUM OF ART, Great Pulteney Street, Bath

VICTORIA ART GALLERY, Bridge Street, Bath

ULSTER FOLK MUSEUM, Cultra Manor, Graigavad, Belfast

CITY MUSEUM AND ART GALLERY, Department of Art, Congreve Street, Birmingham

CITY MUSEUM AND ART GALLERY, Department of Science and Industry, Newhall Street, Birmingham

ACTON ROUND HALL, Bridgnorth, Salop

ART GALLERY AND MUSEUM, Church Street, Brighton

THE GRANGE ART GALLERY AND MUSEUM, Rottingdean, Brighton

THE ROYAL PAVILION, Brighton

BLAISE CASTLE FOLK MUSEUM, Henbury, Bristol

CITY MUSEUM AND ART GALLERY, Queen's Road, Bristol

TOLSEY MUSEUM, High Street, Burford

GAWTHORPE HALL, Nr Burnley, Lancashire

GERSHOM-PARKINGTON MEMORIAL COLLECTION OF CLOCKS AND WATCHES, Bury St Edmunds, Suffolk

NATIONAL ARMY MUSEUM, Camberley, Surrey

FITZWILLIAM MUSEUM, Trumpington Street, Cambridge

WHIPPLE MUSEUM OF THE HISTORY OF SCIENCE, Cambridge

NATIONAL MUSEUM OF WALES, Cathays Park, Cardiff

PUBLIC LIBRARY AND MUSEUM, Carlton Street, Castleford, Yorks

MUSEUM AND ART GALLERY, Clarence Street, Cheltenham   [P.T.O.]

ASTLEY HALL, Astley Park, Chorley, Lancs
CLEVEDON COURT, Near Clevedon, Somerset
MINORIES ART GALLERY, High Street, Colchester
ART GALLERY AND MUSEUM, Coventry, Warks
BOROUGH MUSEUM, The Butterwalk, Dartmouth, Devon
MUSEUM AND ART GALLERY, The Strand, Derby
CORPORATION MUSEUM, Ladywell, Dover
NATIONAL MUSEUM OF IRELAND, Kildare Street, Dublin
GULBENKIAN MUSEUM OF ORIENTAL ART AND ARCHAEOLOGY, Elvet Hill, Durham
UPTON HOUSE, Near Edgehill, Warks
NATIONAL MUSEUM OF THE ANTIQUITIES OF SCOTLAND, Queen Street, Edinburgh
ROYAL SCOTTISH MUSEUM, Chambers Street, Edinburgh
ALMONRY MUSEUM, Vine Street, Evesham, Worcs
WILLMER HOUSE MUSEUM, 38 West Street, Farnham, Hants
ART GALLERY AND MUSEUM, Kelvingrove, Glasgow
CITY MUSEUM AND ART GALLERY, Broad Street, Hereford
HONITON AND ALL HALLOWS PUBLIC MUSEUM, High Street, Honiton, Devon
MUSEUM, Causeway House, Horsham, Sussex
TRANSPORT MUSEUM, 36 High Street, Hull
WILBERFORCE HOUSE, 25 High Street, Hull
LITTLECOTE HOUSE, Near Hungerford, Berks
ART GALLERY AND MUSEUM, Cliffe Castle, Keighley, Yorks
TEMPLE NEWSAM HOUSE, Nr Leeds
MUSEUM AND ART GALLERY, New Walk, Leicester
ANNE OF CLEVES HOUSE, High Street, Lewes, Sussex
GLYNDE PLACE, Near Lewes, Sussex
CITY AND COUNTY MUSEUM, Broadgate, Lincoln
USHER GALLERY, Lindum Road, Lincoln
WERNHER COLLECTION, Luton Hoo, Luton   [P.T.O.]

MUSEUM AND ART GALLERY, Llandarth Street, Newport, Mon.

CENTRAL MUSEUM AND ART GALLERY, Guildhall Road, Northampton

CITY MUSEUM AND ART GALLERY, the Castle, Nottingham

THE ASHMOLEAN MUSEUM OF ART AND ARCHAEOLOGY, Beaumont Street, Oxford

MUSEUM OF THE HISTORY OF SCIENCE, Broad Street, Oxford

PITT RIVERS MUSEUM, Parks Road, Oxford

SCONE PALACE, Near Perth, Scotland

LADY LEVER ART GALLERY, Port Sunlight, Cheshire

HARRIS MUSEUM AND ART GALLERY, Preston, Lancs

MUSEUM AND ART GALLERY, Blagrave Street, Reading, Berks

MUSEUM AND ART GALLERY, Rotherham, Yorks

MUSEUM OF CHILDHOOD AND COSTUME, Blithfield Hall, Rugeley, Staffs

SALISBURY AND SOUTH WILTSHIRE MUSEUM, St Ann Street, Salisbury, Wilts

PILKINGTON GLASS MUSEUM, St Helen's, Lancs

CITY MUSEUM, Weston Park, Sheffield

ANNE HATHAWAY'S COTTAGE, Shottery, Warks

MARTINWARE POTTERY COLLECTION, Public Library, Osterley Park Road, Southall, Middlesex

CITY MUSEUM AND ART GALLERY, Broad Street, Hanley, Stoke-on-Trent

SPODE–COPELAND MUSEUM AND ART GALLERY, Church Street, Stoke-on-Trent

WEDGWOOD MUSEUM, J Wedgwood and Sons Limited, Barlaston, Stoke-on-Trent

SOMERSET COUNTY MUSEUM, Taunton Castle, Taunton, Somerset

ELIZABETHAN HOUSE, Fore Street, Totnes, Devon

ROYAL TUNBRIDGE WELLS MUSEUM AND ART GALLERY, Civic Centre, Tunbridge Wells, Kent

THE ASHWORTH MUSEUM, Turton Tower, Chapletown Road, Turton, Lancs   [P.T.O.]

DOLL MUSEUM, Oken's Street, Castle Hill, Warwick, Warks

WINDSOR CASTLE, High Street, Windsor, Berks

BANTOCK HOUSE, Bantock Park, Wolverhampton

BLENHEIM PALACE, Woodstock, North of Oxford, Oxon

CITY MUSEUM AND ART GALLERY, Foregate Street, Worcester

DYSON PERRINS MUSEUM OF PORCELAIN, The Royal Porcelain Works, Severn Street, Worcester

SNOWSHILL MANOR, Broadway, Worcester

THE YORKSHIRE MUSEUM, Museum Street, York, Yorkshire

Principal auctioneers

IN LONDON

W & F BONHAM AND SONS, Montpelier Galleries, Montpelier Street, SW7

CHRISTIE, MANSON AND WOODS, 8 King Street, St James's, SW1

W E COE AND SONS, South Kensington Auction Rooms, 79–85 Old Brompton Road, SW7

DRUCE AND CO., 54–56 Baker Street, W1

GLENDINING AND CO., Blenstock House, 7 Blenheim Street, New Bond Street, SW1

HALLETTS, 280/282 Holloway Road, N7

H R HARMER, 41 New Bond Street, W1

HARRODS AUCTION GALLERIES, Arundel Terrace, SW13

HODGSONS ROOMS, 115 Chancery Lane, WC2

KNIGHT, FRANK AND RUTLEY, 20 Hanover Square, W1

PHILLIPS, SON AND NEALE, Blenstock House, 7 Blenheim Street New Bond Street, W1

PUTTICK AND SIMPSON, Blenstock House, 7 Blenheim Street, New Bond Street, W1

SOTHEBY AND CO, 34 and 35 New Bond Street, W1

OUTSIDE LONDON

JOLLY AND SON, The Auction Rooms, Old King Street, Bath, Somerset

RIDDETT AND ADAMS SMITH, The Auction Rooms, 24 Richmond Hill, The Square, Bournemouth

WELLER AND DUFTY, The Fine Art Salerooms, 141 Bromsgrove Street, Birmingham 5

GRAVES, SON AND PILCHER, 42 Church Road, Hove 3, Sussex (Office at 51 Old Steyne, Brighton 1)

CAVENDISH HOUSE, Cambray Galleries, 26 Cambray Place, Cheltenham, Glos

DOWALL'S, 65 George Street, Edinburgh, Scotland

LYON AND TURNBULL, 51 George Street, Edinburgh, Scotland

MORRISON, MCCHLERY AND CO, 98 Sauchiehall Street, Glasgow, Scotland

WYLIE AND LOCKHEAD, 100 Kent Road, Glasgow C3, Scotland

FRASER'S, 28/30 Church Street, Inverness, Scotland

WALLIS AND WALLIS, 210 High Street, Lewes, Sussex

LOVE, THOMAS, AND SONS, St John's Place, Perth, Scotland

KING AND CHASEMORE, Station Road, Pulborough, Sussex

SPENCER, HENRY, AND SONS, 20 The Square, Retford, Nottinghamshire

BEARNE'S SALEROOMS, Warren Road, Torquay, Devon

BUTTON, MENHENITT AND MUTTON, Belmont Auction Rooms, Wadebridge, Cornwall

Recommended books

Recommended general antiques reference books

ANTIQUES IN BRITAIN
Published annually by Antique and General Advertising
Limited, 13 High Street, Wendover, near Aylesbury, Bucks.

BRITISH ANTIQUES YEARBOOK
and
INTERNATIONAL ANTIQUES YEARBOOK
Published annually by Apollo Magazine and distributed by
Collins
BUYING ANTIQUES REFERENCE BOOK *and* BUYING ANTIQUES
GENERAL GUIDE
David and Charles Limited, The Railway Station, Newton
Abbott, Devon

THE CONNOISSEUR'S HANDBOOK OF ANTIQUE COLLECTING
and
THE CONNOISSEUR PERIOD GUIDES
(*Tudor Period—Stuart Period—Early Georgian Period—Late
Georgian Period—Regency Period—Victorian Period*)
The Connoisseur, Chestergate House, Vauxhall Bridge Road,
London SW1

For Eleanor and Gordon

Acknowledgements

The author and publishers would like to thank the following for lending photographs or blocks for the illustration secton: Christie, Manson & Woods London (Figures 1, 2, 4 5, 6, 7, 9, 10, 11, 12, 14, 15, 16, 17, 20, 21, 22), Harvey & Gore, London (Figures 3 & 13), J and E D Vandekar, London (Figure 8 and cover illustrations) and St Ouens, London (Figure 18).

China Marks

Page

Bow

25

Chelsea

46

Derby

73

Coalport

60

Doulton

79

Longton Hall

133

Lowestoft

135

Minton
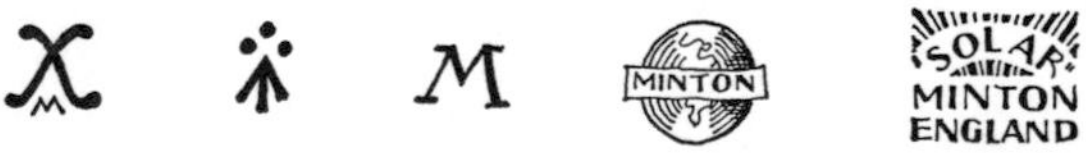

151

Spode

227

Worcester
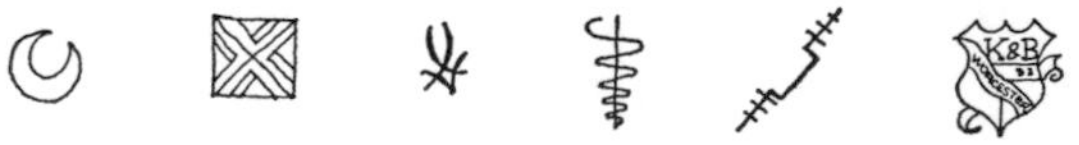

266

Apostle spoons

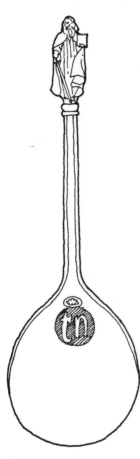

Silver Apostle's Spoon
(St. Paul), 1536

Sets of silver spoons in groups of twelve, their handles embellished with tiny figures representing the Twelve Apostles, are known as Apostle Spoons. They seem to have come into favour in the 16th century, though they were probably in existence before then. Among the wealthier classes it was customary to present sets of Apostle Spoons to children at their christenings; hence the expression "to be born with a silver spoon in one's mouth."

Early examples of Apostle Spoons are now extremely rare but, from the time of the Restoration in 1660 onwards they became gradually more plentiful. Price depends largely on the date and the silversmith, both of which can usually be identified from the hall-marks.

READING
Apostle Spoons, C G Rupert (OUP)

TO VIEW
London Museum, London. Victoria and Albert Museum, London. Holbourne of Menstrie Museum, Bath. City Museum and Art Gallery, Birmingham. Fitzwilliam Museum, Cambridge. National Museum of Wales, Cardiff. Royal Scottish Museum, Edinburgh. Wilberforce House, Hull. Salisbury and South Wiltshire Museum, Salisbury. City Museum, Sheffield.

DEALERS
London Silver Vaults, Chancery House, Chancery Lane, London WC2. S J Shrubsole Limited, 45 Museum Street, London WC1. Antiques and Crafts, Tanderagee, County Armagh, Ireland. Charles T Gilmer Limited, 16 Old Bond Street, Bath, Somerset. Ellis and Co Limited, 16 Constitution Hill, Hockley 19, Birmingham. The Antique Shop, 21 Academy Street, Cork. William Bruford and Son Limited, 60–62 Terminus Road, Eastbourne, Sussex.

Apothecaries' jars

These earthen ware vessels, with their mysterious abbreviations for wholly forgotten drugs and remedies, illustrate the development of ceramics in Europe from the Middle Ages onwards. The science of medicine was highly developed in the countries of the Arab world, whence it was imported via Spain into Europe. Thus it is not surprising that apothecaries' jars followed the same route, originating in the exotic *albarelli* of the Near East and coming to Europe as Hispano-Mauresque ware, out of which developed the maiolica, faience and delft ware of Italy, France and the Netherlands. These jars were often embellished in bright colours and ornamented with angels, putti and birds. They vary greatly in value; genuine tin-glazed earthen ware jars of the 16th to 18th centuries are in great demand, but more recent examples which probably graced a 19th century chemists' shop or drug-store are more plentiful and should not be too expensive.

A more modern counterpart of the apothecaries' jars is the medicine bottle and a surprisingly varied collection can be formed at little cost of unusual bottles containing the patent medicines – and quack remedies – of the recent past.

Late 17th century
Apothecaries' Jar.
English (Lambeth)

READING
Early English Drug Jars, G E Howard

TO VIEW
Guildhall Museum, London. London Museum, London. Pharmaceutical Society's Museum, London. Victoria and Albert Museum, London. Wallace Collection, London. City Museum and Art Gallery, Bristol. National Museum of Wales, Cardiff. Royal Scottish Museum, Edinburgh. Museum and Art Gallery, Leicester. The Wernher Collection, Luton Hoo. Central Museum and Art Gallery, Northampton. Museum of the History of Science, Oxford. Salisbury and South Wiltshire Museum, Salisbury.

City Museum, Sheffield. City Museum and Art
Gallery, Stoke-on-Trent. City Museum and Art
Gallery, Worcester.

DEALERS
Phoenix Antiques, 6 Market Street, Fordham,
Cambridgeshire. Durstons Antiques, Petersfield,
Hants. Quinneys Antiques, Sawbridgeworth, Herts.

Barge tea pots

Occasionally one will find in antique shops, particularly in the Midlands and the Cotswold areas, large brown earthen ware tea pots, usually covered with extravagant decoration and invariably surmounted by a miniature tea pot set on the lid. The capacity of these tea pots is enormous, up to two gallons being not uncommon. They derive their name from the fact that they were used by the 'water gipsies', the folk who lived on and worked the barges which plied along the inland waterways of England from Regent's Park in London to Llangollen in Wales.

Most of these pots were produced by the smaller potteries in the district round Burton-on-Trent. They are particularly interesting on account of the personalised inscriptions on them, often giving the name and address of the owner and the date. Some commemorate weddings, christenings and other family events.

Barge tea pots seem to have died out round about the First World War, while the earliest examples do not date back beyond about 1850. As examples of a vanished folk art they are now highly prized, particularly in the Midlands, and a good example would fetch £50 to £75 today, though smaller, more modern items should be obtainable for less.

READING
Talking about Tea Pots, John Bedford (Cassell)

TO VIEW
Victoria and Albert Museum, London. City Museum and Art Gallery, Bristol (1 example). City Museum, Gloucester. Museum and Art Gallery, Leicester. Central Museum and Art Gallery, Northampton. City Museum, Sheffield. City Museum and Art Gallery, Stoke-on-Trent.

DEALERS
General antique shops, particularly in the Midlands and Cotswold areas.

Barometers

These instruments for measuring atmospheric pressure were developed in the 17th century, following an experiment by Torricelli in 1643 to demonstrate the notion that "the atmosphere had weight". The earliest stick barometers used a mercury column which was known as a Torricelli tube. These mercurial barometers vary considerably in style, according to the system adopted of indicating the different levels in the mercury column, either a U-tube or a tube ending in a small reservoir being used. The Fortin's barometer, on the latter principle, with a reservoir adjustable to the zero of a fixed scale, was invented in the early years of the 19th century and is still in use. Alternatively the scale itself may be adjustable: this type, devised by Newman in 1840 is comparatively rare. In more recent times, aneroid barometers incorporating a vacuum box instead of a mercury column have become very popular. This is the type which terminates in a large dial whose needle points alternatively to "Fair", "Changeable", "Rain" and so on. Since barometers have long been favourite subjects as wedding presents or presentations to employees on retirement the dial type are fairly plentiful and not very highly rated by collectors. Much preferable are the early stick barometers which often exhibit fine craftsmanship in their construction.

READING
English Barometers 1680–1860, Nicholas Goodison (Cassell)
The History of the Barometer, W E K Middleton (Oxford)

TO VIEW
National Maritime Museum, London. Science Museum, London. Victoria and Albert Museum, London. Wallace Collection, London. Waddesdon

Manor, Aylesbury. City Museum and Art Gallery, Birmingham. National Museum of Wales, Cardiff. Royal Scottish Museum, Edinburgh. Gloucester City Museums, Gloucester. Hampton Court. Museum and Art Gallery, Leicester. History of Science Museum, Oxford. Salisbury and South Wiltshire Museum, Salisbury. City Museum, Sheffield. County Museum, Stafford. Windsor Castle, Windsor.

DEALERS

D. Boulstridge Limited, 47 Lower Belgrave Street, London sw1. Aubrey Brocklehurst, 124 Cromwell Road, London sw7. Daniel Desbois and Sons, 51 Carey Street, London wc2. E Hollander, 80 Fulham Road, London sw3. E A J Parker, 23 and 74a Tranquil Vale, Blackheath, London se3. Gordon Partridge, 10 Davies Street, London w1. Charles Stewart Limited, 67 Wigmore Street, London w1. John Walker, 1 South Molton Street, London w1. Park Street Antiques, Berkhamsted, Herts. Peter Carmichael, 13–14 Ship Street Gardens, Brighton. Douglas Strong, 52 Thistle Street, Edinburgh. "55 Antiques", Spring Bank, Hull, Yorks. J S Horwood, Hungerford, Berks. The Old Carpenter's Arms, Littlebury, Essex. Maurice H King, Eynsham, Oxford. B Ogleby, 36 The Green, Thirsk, Yorks. Richard J Piner Limited, 51 High Street, Windsor, Berks. G H Bell, 32a The Square, Winchester, Hants.

Bartolozzi prints

Francesco Bartolozzi (1727–1815), a Florentine engraver, popularised the red chalk manner of engraving which was actually originated in France by Demortenu. He came to England in 1764 and became engraver to King George III, a position which he held for nearly 40 years. He engraved a large number of prints from the works of his friends Cipriani and Angelica Kauffman as well as reproductions from the Old Masters. In his later years many of the engravings which emanated from his London studio were only finished by him and were really the work of his pupils.

True Bartolozzi prints are characterised by the coloured dots which make up the composition – a sort of forerunner of the "screen" used in half-tone blocks today.

READING
Graphic Art of the Eighteenth Century, J Adheman (Thames and Hudson)
Bartolozzi and His Works, A Tuer (Leadenhall Press)

TO VIEW
Victoria and Albert Museum, London. National Museum of Wales, Cardiff. Central Museum and Art Gallery, Northampton. Windsor Castle, Windsor.

DEALERS
Baynton-Williams, 70 Old Brompton Road, London sw7. Craddock and Barnard, 32 Museum Street, London wc1. John McMaster, 15–16 Royal Opera Arcade, Pall Mall, London sw1. Willow Tree Antiques, Amersham, Bucks. Pat Stone, South John Street, Liverpool. Antiques of Newport, Monmouthshire. Josephine's Antiques, Needingworth, Hunts. C H & D Burrows, Scarborough, Yorks. Also, those dealers specialising in prints – often the same ones deal in maps (q.v.)

Basaltes

This jet black pottery with a matt surface was invented by Josiah Wedgwood and named by him from a fancied resemblance to the basalt columns forming the Giant's Causeway in Ireland. It is often found with decoration applied in relief in a light contrasting colour or in white, and most effective it looks too. It was used primarily for vases and similar ornamental items. Under the name "Egyptian Black" this type of pottery was copiously imitated in the late 18th century, though it was not very popular with succeeding generations. Even today it is relatively cheap, though its popularity, as with everything antique, is increasing.

READING

The Makers of Black Basaltes, M H Grant (Holland)

TO VIEW

Victoria and Albert Museum, London. Museum and Art Gallery, Birmingham. City Museum and Art Gallery, Bristol. National Museum of Wales, Cardiff. Royal Scottish Museum, Edinburgh. Central Museum and Art Gallery, Northampton. City Museum and Art Gallery, Nottingham. City Museum, Sheffield. City Museum and Art Gallery, Stoke-on-Trent. Wedgwood Museum, Stoke-on-Trent.

DEALERS

Peerage Antiques, 29 Thayer Street, London w1. Alfred Spero, 4 Park Mansions Arcade, Knightsbridge, London sw1. Joseph Clough, 70 South Parade, Cleckheaton, Yorks. S M Collins, 105 Leeds Road, Ilkley, Yorks. Evaline Winter, 1 Wolesley Road, Rugeley, Staffs.

Battersea enamels

Among the bijouterie which was exceedingly popular with the English middle classes in the late 18th century, the enamelled boxes produced at Battersea, and subsequently in Birmingham and certain towns in South Staffordshire, were probably the most highly prized. These objects satisfied a need for objects of vertu of the not so wealthy. Snuff-boxes, patch-boxes, etuis and bonbonnières were produced in enamelled copper in imitation of the expensive gold and jewelled articles which French craftsmen manufactured for the very rich.

The term "Battersea enamel" is a misnomer since only a small percentage of these enamels were produced there. The technique of enamelling on copper was invented in Geneva and was certainly being used in London by 1747. It was through the factory of Stephen Theodore Janssen, established at Battersea in 1753, that English enamel ware rose to new heights. Battersea enamels far surpassed their predecessors in quality and design and, indeed, outclassed the later products of Birmingham, Bilston and Wednesbury. The Battersea enterprise at York House unfortunately went bankrupt in 1756 and thus its brilliant career was comparatively short-lived – which largely explains the great value attached to enamel ware which can be definitely assigned to this factory. Battersea enamels are noticed for their lustrous milk-white background and pale colours with an almost ethereal quality. Aesthetically they closely imitated in decoration the finest contemporary work from Meissen and were strongly influenced by the engravings of Simon-François Ravenet and the paintings of Watteau. It would be difficult to buy a genuine Battersea enamel box for under £100 today – and usually considerably more has to be paid. Even trinkets and wine labels in this material are sought after by collectors.

9

READING
Battersea Enamels, E Mew (Medici)

TO VIEW
London Museum, London. Victoria and Albert
Museum, London. Waddesdon Manor, Aylesbury.
City Museum and Art Gallery, Bristol. Royal
Scottish Museum, Edinburgh. Central Museum and
Art Gallery, Northampton. Salisbury and South
Wiltshire Museum, Salisbury. City Museum, Shef-
field. Windsor Castle, Windsor.

DEALERS
M Ekstein Limited, 90 Jermyn Street, London sw1.
House of Gadany, 152 Walton Street, London sw3.
Gerald Kerin Limited, 9 Mount Street, Berkeley
Square, London w1. J Lipitch, 10a, 25 & 26 St
Christopher's Place, Wigmore Street, London w1.
D & M Davis Limited, 3 Livery Street, Birmingham.
Victor Needham Limited, 119 Old Christchurch
Road, Bournemouth. Denys Cowell, 60 Middle
Street, Brighton. Scott Cooper Limited, 52 The
Promenade, Cheltenham Spa, Gloucestershire.

Baxter prints

George Baxter (1804–1867) pioneered colour printing in England by the aquatint and mezzotint processes, anything up to 20 blocks being used to build up the colouring in a single picture. Considering the work involved in the more complicated pictures it is hardly surprising that the best Baxter prints have always been expensive. Extremely popular and not so costly are the monochrome Baxterotypes which depicted scenes of a religious or sentimental nature. Subjects for Baxter prints ranged from reproductions of Old Masters to portraits of Queen Victoria and the Royal Family, dancing girls and fairytale scenes.

From the middle of the century onwards Baxter sold licences for his process to other printers; thus many so-called Baxter prints are, in fact, the work of Mansell, Le Blond, Dickes and others. These are also of interest to collectors though the products of Baxter himself are worth a premium.

READING
Baxter Colour Prints: Their History and Production, H G Clarke (Maggs Brothers)
George Baxter: His Life and Work, C T Lewis (Sampson Low)
The Picture Printer of the Nineteenth Century: George Baxter, C T Lewis (Sampson Low).

TO VIEW
British Museum, London. Victoria and Albert Museum, London. National Museum of Wales, Cardiff. Museum and Art Gallery, Reading (almost a complete collection). City Museum and Art Gallery, Worcester.

DEALERS
Baynton-Williams, 70 Old Brompton Road, London SW7. Craddock & Barnard, 32 Museum Street, London WC1. John McMaster, 15–16 Royal Opera

Arcade, Pall Mall, London SW1. Willow Tree Antiques, Amersham, Bucks. Pat Stone, South John Street, Liverpool. Antiques of Newport, Monmouthshire. Josephine's Antiques, Needingworth, Hunts. C H & D Burrows, Scarborough, Yorks. Also those dealers specialising in prints – often the same ones deal in maps (q.v.)

Bead work

Beads have been used in the manufacture of dress ornaments for thousands of years and, in more recent times, have been used to decorate all manner of articles from table mats to curtains, from chair backs to ladies' hand bags. The bazaar craftsmen of the Middle East still specialise in the production of articles covered with bead work, arranged into attractive geometric patterns or even pictures. English bead work of the 18th and early 19th century – samplers and cushion covers worked on satin – are very difficult to find in good condition and now fetch high prices.

TO VIEW
British Museum, London. Geffrye Museum, London. London Museum, London. Victoria and Albert Museum, London. Waddesdon Manor, Aylesbury. Art Gallery and Museum, Brighton. National Museum of Wales, Cardiff. Royal Scottish Museum, Edinburgh. City Museum, Hereford. Museum and Art Gallery, Leicester. Salisbury and South Wiltshire Museum, Salisbury. City Museum, Sheffield. City Museum and Art Gallery, Stoke-on-Trent. Elizabethan House, Totnes. City Museum and Art Gallery, Worcester.

DEALERS
Many junk shops stock articles covered in beadwork, particularly handbags and belts. Chelsea and Kensington Markets should be explored.

Bellarmines

The notorious Cardinal Roberto Francesco Bellarmino (1542–1621), one of the greatest Catholic controversialists of all time, gave his name to a type of stone ware jug or bottle, which was certainly in production before he gained an unenviable reputation as a persecutor of heretics in the Netherlands. These vessels, known in Germany as Bartmannkruge, in France as Barbmans and in England as Greybeards, derive their name from the effigy of a bearded man which is usually found on the neck. They were extensively produced in the Rhineland, the Low Countries and England from the middle of the 16th century onwards. These ugly jugs have a peculiar fascination and a rising value – a group of them made £120 at Christie's in 1966.

READING

Das Rheinische Steinzeug, O van Falke (Munich)

TO VIEW

Geffrye Museum, London. Guildhall Museum, London. London Museum, London. Victoria and Albert Museum, London. Wallace Collection, London. Art Gallery and Museum, Brighton. City Museum and Art Gallery, Bristol. National Museum of Wales, Cardiff. Royal Scottish Museum, Edinburgh. Museum and Art Gallery, Leicester. Central Museum and Art Gallery, Northampton. Salisbury and South Wiltshire Museum, Salisbury. City Museum, Sheffield. City Museum and Art Gallery, Stoke-on-Trent. Royal Tunbridge Wells Museum and Art Gallery, Tunbridge Wells. The Yorkshire Museum, York.

DEALERS

General antique dealers.

Belleek

Ireland's only pottery was founded in the 1860s at Belleek in County Fermanagh. A businessman visiting the district was intrigued by the distinctive appearance of the white wash used on the cottages and, on further investigation, discovered a great quantity of material in the surrounding hills suitable for the manufacture of porcelain. Belleek china varies from the finest eggshell to solid basket-weave. Until comparatively recently Belleek wares were uncoloured, ornamentation being confined to relief modelling and applied decoration.

Belleek ware has a most distinctive glaze with a pearly lustre. Pieces are marked BELLEEK and a combination of symbols consisting of an Irish wolfhound, a round tower, a harp or a shamrock.

TO VIEW
Victoria and Albert Museum, London. Royal Scottish Museum, Edinburgh. City Museum, Sheffield.

Bells

Ignoring those small mounted bells produced in brass with polished wooden hammers which are to be found on sale in any tourist resort, this subject is capable of wide interpretation, from the large standing bells of ancient China and the brass gongs of India, to Swiss cow bells, town criers' hand bells, ship's bells etc.

READING
Little Book of Bells, Eric Hatch (New York)
Bells: Their History and Romance, G Morrison (California).

TO VIEW
British Museum, London. London Museum, London. Victoria and Albert Museum, London. Wallace Collection, London. Art Gallery and Museum, Brighton. Borough Museum, Dartmouth (Ships' Bells). City Museum, Hereford. Museum and Art Gallery, Leicester. Salisbury and South Wiltshire Museum, Salisbury. City Museum, Sheffield. Elizabethan House, Totnes. Windsor Castle, Windsor.

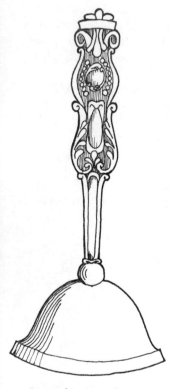

Late 17th century silver call bell

Bidri ware

This attractive technique of inlaid metalwork seems to have originated in Bidar, one of the native states of India. Silver was inlaid on a base composed of an alloy similar to pewter. When the work of damascening (as the inlay is known) was completed the object was blackened by chemical action and the silver areas then polished up brightly in contrast. A wide variety of smaller objects, domestic utensils and vessels, vases and boxes, were produced in this silver and black ware. A popular motif on these items was the saracenic leaf pattern, introduced by the Mughals who invaded India from the north in the 11th century.

TO VIEW
Wallace Collection, London. City Museum, Sheffield.

DEALERS
As so often, small antique and 'junk' shops should be explored for bidri ware.

Black jacks

These large leather vessels with a metal rim and enormous looped handles were popular in Shakespeare's time (as the guide at Anne Hathaway's Cottage is at pains to point out) and were surprisingly effective for keeping liquids without loss. Not so long ago leather bottles and jugs could be picked up in farm and country house sales but now they are something of a rarity, being infrequently met with in antiques shops.

TO VIEW
Guildhall Museum, London. London Museum, London. Victoria and Albert Museum, London. Art Gallery and Museum, Brighton. Blaise Castle Folk Museum, Bristol. City Museum, Hereford. Museum and Art Gallery, Leicester. Central Museum and Art Gallery, Northampton. Salisbury and South Wiltshire Museum, Salisbury. Anne Hathaway's Cottage, Stratford-on-Avon.

Blanc de chine

This white porcelain was evolved at Te-Hua in the Fukien province of China during the Ming dynasty. It varies considerably from a mellow creamy colour to a hard bluish white. It was used invariably for the production of figures which were either left undecorated or were painted in enamel colours for European consumption. The majority of pieces were exported in the white, to be decorated in Europe.

READING
Chinese Porcelain, Anthony de Boulay (Weidenfeld & Nicholson)
Wares of the Ming Dynasty, R L Hobson (Prentice Hall)

TO VIEW
British Museum, London. London Museum, London. Percival David Foundation of Chinese Art, London. Victoria and Albert Museum, London. Art Gallery and Museum, Brighton. City Museum and Art Gallery, Bristol. Gulbenkian Museum of Oriental Art, Durham. Royal Scottish Museum, Edinburgh. Museum and Art Gallery, Leicester. Central Museum and Art Gallery, Northampton. City Museum and Art Gallery, Stoke-on-Trent. Windsor Castle, Windsor.

DEALERS
Bluett and Sons, 48 Davies Street, London W1. John Day Limited, 53 Buckingham Court, Kensington Park Road, London W11. Brian Johnson, 45 Beauchamp Place, London SW3. David Newbon, 56 Beauchamp Place, London SW3. John Sparks Limited, 128 Mount Street, London W1. Andrew Dando, 4 Wood Street, Queen Square, Bath. Denys Cowell, 60 Middle Street, Brighton, Sussex. Michael Brett, Picton House, Broadway, Worcs. Collins & Clark, 81 Regent Street, Cambridge. F C Dixon, 54 Bridgegate, Retford, Notts.

Blue and white

By far the commonest form of decoration on early
pottery and porcelain consists of blue colour on a
white ground, the reason being that the blue pigment
was almost the only one available to the potters
which could withstand the terrific heat of the kiln
during firing. The patterns and decorations used by
European potters were copied from Chinese models,
the willow pattern being the best known. Views of
European landmarks were another popular subject
for treatment in blue and white. The best English
blue and white came from Worcester (q.v.), with the
products of Caughley (q.v.), Liverpool and Lowestoft (q.v.) in descending order of merit and quality
in craftsmanship.

READING
Oriental Blue and White, H Garner (Faber)

TO VIEW
British Museum, London. Geffrye Museum, London.
London Museum, London. Percival David Founda-
tion of Chinese Art, London. Victoria and Albert
Museum, London. Art Gallery and Museum,
Brighton. City Museum and Art Gallery, Bristol.
National Museum of Wales, Cardiff. Museum and
Art Gallery, Derby. Royal Scottish Museum,
Edinburgh. City Museum, Hereford. Museum and
Art Gallery, Leicester. Central Museum and Art
Gallery, Northampton. City Museum and Art
Gallery, Stoke-on-Trent. Spode-Copeland Museum
and Art Gallery, Stoke-on-Trent. Wedgwood
Museum, Stoke-on-Trent. Windsor Castle, Windsor.
Dyson Perrins Museum of Porcelain, Worcester.

CLUBS
The English Ceramic Circle, 8 Church Row,
Hampstead, London NW3.
The Oriental Ceramic Society, 31b Torrington
Square, London WC1.

DEALERS
See under porcelain.

Bonbonnières

Small boxes containing the sort of sweets or "bonbons" sucked in the 18th century to sweeten the breath. They come in a variety of materials, gold, silver, enamel or tortoise shell being the most frequently used. Examples produced in Battersea or Staffordshire enamels on a copper base are now beyond the purses of most of us, though plainer silver or tortoise shell bonbonnières may still be found occasionally at a reasonable price.

READING

All Kinds of Small Boxes, J Bedford (Cassell)
Antique Gold Boxes, H & S Berry-Hill (Abelard-Shuman)
Silver Boxes, Eric Delieb (Jenkins)
Eighteenth-Century Gold Boxes of Europe, Snowman (Faber)

TO VIEW

London Museum, London. Wallace Collection, London. Victoria and Albert Museum, London. City Museum and Art Gallery, Bristol. Royal Scottish Museum, Edinburgh. City Museum, Sheffield. City Museum and Art Gallery, Stoke-on-Trent. Windsor Castle, Windsor.

DEALERS

Antiques Corner Limited, 104 Mount Street, London w1. Harvey and Gore Limited, 4 Burlington Gardens, London w1. House of Gadany, 152 Walton Street, London sw3. Garrard and Co Limited, 112 Regent Street, London w1. Spink and Son Limited, 5–7 King Street, St James', London sw1. Tessiers Limited, 26 New Bond Street, London w1. Thomas Hudson, 4 Dollar Street, Circenester, Glos. Richard H Everard, Woodhouse Eaves, Nr Loughborough, Leics.

Bonheur du jour

Literally the "happiness of the day", this is an apt name for a small writing desk at which elegant young ladies in pre-Revolution France would sit and compose their *billets doux*. The table is surmounted by a tiny cabinet containing drawers for writing materials, a small bookcase and 'pigeon holes'. The most attractive examples were beautifully inlaid in kingwood and satinwood. Like all elegant but small pieces of good antique furniture, bonheurs du jour are now exceedingly expensive.

READING
Paris Furniture, 1710–1810, C Packer (Ceramic)
French 18th Century Furniture, G Souchal (Weidenfeld and Nicholson)
French Furniture and Interior Decoration of the 18th century, P Verlet (Barrie and Rockcliffe)
Louis XVI Furniture, F J B Watson (Tiranti)

TO VIEW
Victoria and Albert Museum, London. Wallace Collection, London. Waddesdon Manor, Aylesbury. City Museum and Art Gallery, Birmingham. Royal Pavilion, Brighton. Royal Scottish Museum, Edinburgh. Scone Palace, Perth. Windsor Castle, Windsor.

CLUB
The Furniture History Society, Department of Furniture and Woodwork, Victoria and Albert Museum, London sw7.

DEALERS
H Blairman and Sons Limited, 36 New Bond Street, London w1. Spink and Son Limited, King Street, St James', London sw1. Leslie Davey Antiques, 286 High Street, Bangor, North Wales. The Galleries, 27 Preston New Road, Blackburn, Lancs.

Russells Antiques Limited, 9 Richmond Hill, Bournemouth. Trevor-Antiques of Brighton, 14-15 Ship Street, Brighton, Sussex. Bodmin Antiques, Cornwall. Hill-Mayo Antiques, The Malt House, 59 Market Place, Henley-on-Thames. Yellow Lantern Antiques, Hove, Sussex. Charles Jackson, 48 & 68 Market Jew Street, Penzance, Cornwall. Jackson's Antiques, 308-310 London Road, Sheffield, Yorks. Hall's Antiques, Ash Priors, Near Taunton, Somerset. Robinson Limited, 9 Church Street, Warwick. Woodstock Galleries, Woodstock, Northants.

Boulle

Charles Andre Boulle (1642–1732) is often credited with the invention of tortoiseshell and ivory inlaid work, but it was in fact originated by a Neopolitan named Laurentini and was already popular in Paris when Boulle began to work at the Louvre in 1672. As a craftsman at the court of King Louis XV, however, Boulle rose to eminence for his inlaid work using brass and tortoiseshell. The materials, inlaid into the other, were usually cut out at a single operation. Brass inlaid on tortoiseshell is known as boulle or *première partie* while the converse of tortoiseshell inlaid on brass is called *contre-boulle* or *contre-partie*.

The term was borrowed by English cabinet makers to describe wood inlays used in furniture making. In this guise it is often found as "buhl".

TO VIEW
London Museum, London. Victoria and Albert Museum, London. Wallace Collection, London. Waddesdon Manor, Aylesbury. Central Museum and Art Gallery, Northampton. Scone Palace, Perth. County Museum, Stafford. Windsor Castle, Windsor.

DEALERS
Tortoiseshell and Ivory House Limited, 24 Chiltern Street, London W1.

Bow

Compared with the other pioneer porcelain works in England the Bow factory was surprisingly long-lived. It was founded in or around 1744 by Thomas Frye and Edward Heylyn and survived as late as 1776. The product of Bow is characterised by its heavy, opaque appearance. Bow has the credit of having introduced transfer printing and applying it to porcelain. This pottery is probably best remembered for its figures, which were second only in quality to those of Chelsea, and which are now in extremely high favour with collectors.

READING
Bow, Chelsea & Derby Porcelain, W Bembrose (Bembrose)
Old Bow Porcelain, M Egan (Jack)
Bow Porcelain, F Hurlbutt (Bell)
Chelsea, Bow & Derby Porcelain Figures (Ceramic)

TO VIEW
Fenton House, London. London Museum, London. Victoria and Albert Museum, London. Art Gallery and Museum, Brighton. National Museum of Wales, Cardiff. Royal Scottish Museum, Edinburgh. City Museum, Hereford. Temple Newsam House, Leeds. The Wernher Collection, Luton Hoo. Central Museum and Art Gallery, Northampton. Salisbury and South Wiltshire Museum, Salisbury. City Museum and Art Gallery, Stoke-on-Trent. Windsor Castle, Windsor.

CLUB
The English Ceramic Circle, 8 Church Row, Hampstead, London NW3.

DEALERS
Albert Amor Limited, 37 Bury Street, St James', London SW1. Newman & Newman Limited,

156 Brompton Road, London sw3. Bradstone House Antiques, Alvington, Glos. Andrew Dando, 4 Wood Street, Queen Square, Bath. Trimmers, Burnham Market, Norfolk. Mrs Araxie Love, Newbiggin, Richmond, Yorks. Collectors Treasures Limited, 8–9 Church Street, Windsor.

NOTE

See the illustration of Bow china marks on page xx at the beginning of the book.

Brass ware

A vast array of objects have been produced in brass at some time or another – candle sticks and skimmers, meat-jacks and fire-dogs, trays and letter-racks, horse-brasses (q.v.), gongs and door-knockers. Although many antique shops now tend to specialise in non-ferrous metal wares, brass ware will be found in every shop which deals with the antique or merely the second-hand. Many items of brass ware are still surprisingly cheap – though the effort of keeping brass objects shining brightly may militate against their popularity.

READING

Chats on Old Copper and Brass, F W Burgess (Benn)
The English Brass and Copper Industries to 1880, H Hamilton (Frank Cass)
Iron and Brass Instruments of the English House, J S Lindsay (Tiranti)
Collecting Copper and Brass, G Wills (Arco)

TO VIEW

London Museum, London. Victoria and Albert Museum, London. Museum, Berwick-on-Tweed. City Museum and Art Gallery, Birmingham. Art Gallery and Museum, Brighton. City Museum and Art Gallery, Bristol. Royal Scottish Museum, Edinburgh. City Museum, Hereford. Central Museum and Art Gallery, Northampton. Salisbury and South Wiltshire Museum, Salisbury. City Museum, Sheffield. Elizabethan House, Totnes. Ashworth Museum, Turton. City Museum and Art Gallery, Worcester.

DEALERS

Gordon Hand and Co, 18 Chepstow Mansions, Westbourne Grove, London w2. Jans Antiques, 69 Portobello Road, London w11. The Antique Shop, Broadway, Amersham, Bucks. Quality Antiques,

Meeting House Lane, Brighton. Millhouse Antiques, The Old Mill, Clophill, Beds. J Feather, 120 Gledhow Valley Road, Leeds. Peter Bromley, 72 King Richards Road, Leicester. Desmond Antiques, Welford Road, Leicester. C H and D Burrows, 15 St Thomas Street, Scarborough. Turpins Antiques, Thaxted, Essex. Woburn Antique Galleries, Woburn, Nr. Bletchley, Bucks.

Bristol glass

The city of Bristol was famous in the second half of the 18th century for its glass manufacture, in particular the special type of blue glass which, though also made elsewhere, is always associated with Bristol. The cobalt oxide necessary in the production of this blue glass had to be imported from Silesia. The merchants of Bristol secured for themselves a concession from the Elector of Saxony by which they were given a virtual monopoly of cobalt oxide. This substance was mixed with powdered glass to produce "smalt" which was then carefully added to molten flint glass in order to produce blue glass of the desired shade. Bristol blue glass was expensive to produce and items have always been quite costly, though highly desired by collectors. In particular demand are wine glasses (q.v.), decanters (q.v.) and scent bottles (q.v.).

READING

Bristol and Other Coloured Glass, John Bedford (Cassell)
Paperweights and other Glass Curiosities, E M Elville (Spring Books)
Nineteenth Century British Glass, Hugh Wakefield (Faber)

Late 18th century Bristol Glass, blue with gold

TO VIEW

Victoria and Albert Museum, London. Art Gallery and Museum, Brighton. Museum and Art Gallery, Bristol. National Museum of Wales, Cardiff. Borough Museum, Dartmouth. Royal Scottish Museum, Edinburgh. Gloucester City Museums, Gloucester. City Museum, Hereford. Central Museum and Art Gallery, Northampton. Pilkington Glass Museum, St Helens, Lancs. Salisbury and South Wiltshire Museum, Salisbury. City Museum, Sheffield. City Museum and Art Gallery, Worcester.

The Glass Circle, 50a Fulham Road, London SW3.

DEALERS
Arthur Churchill Limited, Marjorie Parr Galleries, 285 Kings Road, London SW3.
Regency Galleries, 72 Park Row, Bristol.

Britannia metal

The name given to an alloy of copper, antimony and tin, somewhat resembling pewter and popular in the early part of the 19th century. It was devised in the late 18th century by John Vickers who gave it the name Vickers Metal and used it in the manufacture of tea and coffee pots, etc., in imitation of silver and Sheffield plate. Like pewter, however, it did not retain its bright, shiny appearance for long so it was customary at one time to have items electro-plated; look for the tell-tale initials stamped on the base – EPBM (electro-plated Britannia Metal).

Britannia Metal should not be confused with British Plate – an alloy of copper, nickel and zinc (known as German Silver) which was then coated with silver in the same way as Sheffield Plate (q.v.) The main advantage of British Plate over Sheffield Plate was that if the silver wore thin the material underneath it resembled it sufficiently for the worn patch not to matter unduly.

TO VIEW
Victoria and Albert Museum, London. Central Museum and Art Gallery, Northampton. City Museum, Sheffield.

Bronzes

Bronze statuary, despised not so long ago, is now very much in the fashion. Figures of animals, allegorical studies and groups of humans have been neglected until recently, though those of them which escaped from the scrapyards of yesterday are now often highly prized as garden ornaments (q.v.) or for conversion into table lamps.

Particularly prized are the tiny bronzes, about six inches high, known as animalier bronzes after the group of late 19th century French artists who specialised in animal studies. Bronze items range in time from the prehistoric figures excavated in northern China, and the intriguing bronze weights used in the medieval wool industry of England, to the bronze busts, figures and plaques (q.v.) from Ife and Berin in Nigeria and the elegant bronzes of the Italian Renaissance. The books listed below give an insight into the varied and fascinating world of bronze.

READING
Old English Bronze Wool-Weights, H Dent.
Early Chinese Bronzes, A J Koop (Ceramic)
Bronzes, J Montague (Weidenfeld and Nicholson)
European Bronze Statuettes, A Radcliffe (Connoisseur & Michael Joseph)

TO VIEW
British Museum, London. London Museum, London. Victoria and Albert Museum, London. Wallace Collection, London. Waddesdon Manor, Aylesbury. Museum and Art Gallery, Birmingham. Art Gallery and Museum, Brighton. National Museum of Wales, Cardiff. Royal Scottish Museum, Edinburgh. Art Gallery and Museum, Glasgow. Museum and Art Gallery, Leicester. The Wernher Collection, Luton Hoo. Central Museum and Art Gallery, Nottingham. City Museum, Sheffield. Windsor Castle, Windsor.

George Cohn, 112 Crawford Street, London w1. Copper and Adams, 181 Green Lane, Norbury, London sw16. Cecil Davis Limited, 3 Grosvenor Street, London w1. A & F Gordon, 221 Kensington Church Street, London w8. Felix Hilton, 45 St John's Wood High Street, London nw8. Desmond Thomas, 183 Westbourne Grove, London w11. Wm Williams, The Doll's House, 27a Kensington Church Street, London w8. Balcombe Galleries, Balcombe, Sussex. Park Street Antiques, Berkhamsted, Herts. W & J Turner, 22 Montpellier Walk, Cheltenham, Glos.

Brown ware

This salt-glazed brown stone ware makes up in its intriguing appearance what it lacks aesthetically. It was used in the manufacture of all manner of objects from tankards to Toby Jugs, (q.v.) from tea pots (q.v.) to tobacco jars (q.v.). The majority of brown ware objects were made in the Chesterfield district in the late 18th century and early 19th, though it was enthusiastically copied in Victorian times.

READING
The ABC of English Saltglaze Stoneware, J F Blacker (S Paul)
More Small Decorative Antiques, Therle Hughes (Lutterworth).

TO VIEW
London Museum, London. Victoria and Albert Museum, London. Art Gallery and Museum, Brighton. Royal Scottish Museum, Edinburgh. City Museum, Hereford. City Museum, Nottingham. Salisbury and South Wiltshire Museum, Salisbury. City Museum, Sheffield. City Museum and Art Gallery, Stoke on Trent.

DEALERS
Most antique shops dealing in pottery.

Buttons

These tiny but indispensable objects have been used for as long as man has needed clothing. Consequently volumes could be written on the subject. Military buttons came into use in the 17th century and quite a sizeable collection could be formed at little cost, showing the emblems and insignia of different units and formations. Attractive buttons were die-stamped in silver or brass in the 19th century and were produced in sets showing different subjects, hunting and sporting scenes being the most popular. Then there are political buttons, fashionable in the United States, where they were worn by supporters of presidential candidates. Pictorial buttons enjoyed great popularity in the 19th century and it is possible to concentrate on certain subjects – animals, flowers, even fairy tales were depicted in this way. Glass-topped buttons containing tiny coloured pictures were invented about 1775 and enjoyed a brief vogue at the end of the 18th century. Glass paste cameos (q.v.) were set on mounts and used as buttons, while the Italians specialised in the manufacture of cameo buttons from laminated shells, such as cowry, smoky oyster pearl or queen's conch. Wedgwood produced attractive buttons in jasper ware, while porcelain and coloured glass buttons are readily available.

Tin glazed earthenware livery button, 1650, and French silk embroidered button, 1730

READING

The Complete Button Book, L S Albert & K Kent (World's Work)
Button Classics, L E Couse and M Maple (Lightner Pub. Co., USA).

TO VIEW

British Museum, London. Guildhall Museum, London. London Museum, London. Victoria and Albert Museum, London. Waddesdon Manor, Aylesbury. National Museum of Wales, Cardiff. Royal Scottish Museum, Edinburgh. City Museum, Hereford. Museum and Art Gallery, Leicester. Central Museum and Art Gallery, Northampton. Salisbury and South Wiltshire Museum, Salisbury. City Museum, Sheffield. Windsor Castle, Windsor.

CLUB

National Button Society, 7940 Montgomery Avenue, Elkins Park, Philadelphia, Pennyslvania 19117, U.S.A.

DEALERS

The Button Queen, 5 Marlborough Court, Carnaby Street, London W1.

Cameos

Cameos are items of jewellery carved from shell or precious stones, as many as a dozen layers being skilfully carved away to reveal the subject in high relief. These attractive, ivorine-looking ornaments were exceedingly popular as brooches in Victorian times and, after the inevitable period in unfashionable oblivion, have now come back into vogue. As a result cameo brooches, which a few years ago could be purchased for a few shillings, now rate as many pounds.

Cameos have been produced in artificial substances such as glass paste (q.v.) and Wedgwoods have for two centuries made a speciality of them in their famous jasper ware (q.v.). The current range includes miniaturised cameos formed into rings, ear rings, tie pins and cuff links.

READING

English Victorian Jewellery, E Bradford (Spring Books)
Victorian Jewellery, M Flower (Cassell)
More Small Decorative Antiques, Therle Hughes (Lutterworth)

TO VIEW

British Museum, London. Victoria and Albert Museum, London. Royal Scottish Museum, Edinburgh. City Museum, Hereford. Central Museum and Art Gallery, Northampton. Salisbury and South Wiltshire Museum, Salisbury. City Museum, Sheffield. City Museum and Art Gallery, Stoke-on-Trent. Wedgwood Museum, Stoke-on-Trent. Windsor Castle, Windsor. City Museum and Art Gallery, Worcester.

DEALERS

Asprey and Co Limited, 165/169 New Bond Street, London w1. N Bloom and Son Limited, 39–40 Albemarle Street, Piccadilly, London w1. Cameo Corner, 26 Museum Street, London wc1. Mayflower Antiques, 5 St Christopher's Place, London w1. S J Phillips Limited, 139 New Bond Street, London w1.

Candle stands

Tall slender wood stands, usually on tripod feet, are known as torchères or, to give them their English equivalent, candle stands. Originally they were used to provide illumination from oil lamps rather than candles; today they make rather elegant stands for potted plants or flower arrangements. Generally speaking the smaller and more slender examples are earlier and more expensive than the later, larger and much more solid types.

TO VIEW
British Museum, London. Geffrye Museum, London. Guildhall Museum, London. Victoria and Albert Museum, London. Wallace Collection, London. Waddesdon Manor, Aylesbury. Art Gallery and Museum, Brighton. Royal Pavilion, Brighton. National Museum of Wales, Cardiff. Royal Scottish Museum, Edinburgh. City Museum, Hereford. Temple Newsam House, Leeds. Museum and Art Gallery, Leicester. Central Museum and Art Gallery, Northampton. Salisbury and South Wiltshire Museum, Salisbury. City Museum and Art Gallery, Stoke-on-Trent. Elizabethan House, Totnes. Windsor Castle, Windsor. City Museum and Art Gallery, Worcester.

DEALERS
Yellow Lantern Antiques, Brighton, Sussex. Halls Antiques, Ash Priors, Nr Taunton, Somerset. Also furniture dealers and even junk shops.

Mahogany candle stand of the late 18th century

Cane ware

This unusual type of pottery was an early speciality of Wedgwood and the Turners. It takes its name from the use of bamboo and cane motifs in pottery, arranged in the form of baskets and bowls. They were ideal pie dishes and flower holders and were popular in the late 18th and early 19th century.

READING
The Turners of Lane End, B Hillier (Evelyn, Adams and McKay)

TO VIEW
Victoria and Albert Museum, London. National Museum of Wales, Cardiff. Royal Scottish Museum, Edinburgh. Central Museum and Art Gallery, Northampton. City Museum, Sheffield. City Museum and Art Gallery, Stoke-on-Trent. Spode-Copeland Museum and Art Gallery, Stoke-on-Trent. Wedgwood Museum, Stoke-on-Trent.

DEALERS
Peerage Antiques, 29 Thayer Street, London w1. Andrew Dando, 4 Wood Street, Queen Square, Bath. Joseph Clough, 70 South Parade, Cleckheaton, Yorks. Arthur West Antiques, Dawlish, Devon. Runnymede Galleries, Egham, Surrey. S M Collins, Leeds Road, Ilkley, Yorks. Evaline Winter, Wolseley Road, Rugeley, Staffs. Tunnicliffe's Antiques, Stoke-on-Trent, Staffs.

Canton ware

During the 19th century China developed a considerable trade in export porcelain which was shipped to Europe and America via the great entrepôt of Canton. It was deliberately manufactured to suit Victorian European taste and is often regarded nowadays as being over-ornamented. It is still plentiful, though not quite as cheap as it used to be, and is obviously coming back into favour.

READING
Later Chinese Poreclain, S Jenyns (Faber)
Chinese Export Art, M Jourdain & S Jenyns (Spring Books)

TO VIEW
British Museum, London. Victoria and Albert Museum, London. City Museum and Art Gallery, Bristol. National Museum of Wales, Cardiff. Royal Scottish Museum, Edinburgh. Central Museum and Art Gallery, Northampton. City Museum and Art Gallery, Stoke-on-Trent.

CLUB
The Oriental Ceramic Society, 31b Torrington Square, London WC1.

DEALERS
John Day Limited, 53 Buckingham Court, Kensington Park Road, London W11. Bluett and Sons, 48 Davies Street, London W1. David Newbon, 56 Beauchamp Place, London SW3. John Sparks Limited, 128 Mount Street, London W1. Andrew Dando, 4 Wood Road, Queen Square, Bath. Denys Cowell, 60 Middle Street, Brighton. Collins and Clark, 81 Regent Street, Cambridge. F C Dixon, 54 Bridgegate, Retford, Notts. Michael Brett, Picton House, Broadway, Worcs.

Card cases

In the 18th and 19th centuries, when the ritual of calling and leaving one's card was strictly observed, ladies and gentlemen carried their visiting cards in small flat cases. The habit of leaving cards derived from writing one's name on the back of a playing card. Hence the earliest visiting cards were quite large, in the format of a playing card, and it is only in fairly recent times that cards have been reduced to their present size where they can conveniently be fitted into one's wallet or handbag.

Card cases were at the height of their popularity from the end of the 18th century till the beginning of the present century. They may be found in silver, wood, mother of pearl, bone, ivory, papier maché (q.v.) or leather and vary considerably from severely utilitarian examples to highly decorative ones. They are still quite plentiful and most antique shops carry a comprehensive stock of them at prices from a few shillings upwards.

READING
All Kinds of Small Boxes, J Bedford (Cassell)
Silver Boxes, Eric Delieb (Herbert Jenkins)
Small Antiques for the Collector, Therle Hughes (Lutterworth)

TO VIEW
London Museum, London. Victoria and Albert Museum, London. Royal Scottish Museum, Edinburgh. City Museum, Hereford. Museum and Art Gallery, Leicester. Central Museum and Art Gallery, Northampton. Harris Museum and Art Gallery, Preston. Salisbury and South Wiltshire Museum, Salisbury. City Museum, Sheffield. Elizabethan House, Totnes, Devon. Royal Tunbridge Wells Museum and Art Gallery, Tunbridge Wells. City Museum and Art Gallery, Worcester. Snowshill Manor, Worcester.

Castleford

The firm of David Dunderdale and Co of Castleford in Yorkshire were largely responsible for putting this town on the ceramics map. They specialised in attractive stoneware crockery, especially teapots and jugs, which are characterised by decorated panels in relief. Comparatively little is known about Castleford ware and this somewhat neglected aspect of British pottery would well repay the interested collector.

READING
Yorkshire Potteries, Pots and Potters, O Grabham (Yorkshire Philosophical Society)

TO VIEW
Victoria and Albert Museum, London. Art Gallery and Museum, Brighton. Public Library and Museum, Castleford. Royal Scottish Museum, Edinburgh. Salisbury and South Wiltshire Museum, Salisbury. City Museum, Sheffield. City Museum and Art Gallery, Stoke-on-Trent.

CLUB
The English Ceramic Circle, 8 Church Row, Hampstead, London NW3.

DEALERS
Beauchamp Galleries, 8 Beauchamp Place, London SW3. D M and P Manheim, 69 Upper Berkeley Street, Portman Square, London W1. Andrew Dando, 4 Wood Street, Queen Square, Bath.

Caudle cups

Warm gruel made with spice, sugar, oatmeal and wine was favoured in ancient times as a pick-me-up for invalids and expectant mothers. It was originally served in a posset pot (q.v.) but later a two handled cup with a saucer and cover were used. Caudle cups are often found in pairs or sets, or as part of a coffee or tea service.

French 18th century pewter caudle cup

TO VIEW

Guildhall Museum, London. London Museum, London. Victoria and Albert Museum, London. Art Gallery and Museum, Brighton. National Museum of Wales, Cardiff. Royal Scottish Museum, Edinburgh. Temple Newsam House, Leeds. Central Museum and Art Gallery, Northampton. Salisbury and South Wiltshire Museum, Salisbury. Spode-Copeland Museum and Art Gallery, Stoke-on-Trent. City Museum and Art Gallery, Worcester.

Caughley

Thomas Turner, 1749–1809, purchased the Caughley earthen ware pottery in 1772 and turned it over to the production of steatite porcelain not unlike that produced at Worcester, though of somewhat inferior quality. The factory survived him by barely five years. Most of its useful wares were decorated in blue and white while the ever popular Willow Pattern was originated there.

READING
Caughley and Coalport Porcelain, F A Barrett (F. Lewis)
Caughley and Worcester Porcelain, G A Godden (Jenkins)

TO VIEW
British Museum, London. Victoria and Albert Museum, London. Art Gallery and Museum, Brighton. National Museum of Wales, Cardiff. Royal Scottish Museum, Edinburgh. City Museum, Hereford. Museum and Art Gallery, Leicester. Central Museum and Art Gallery, Northampton. Salisbury and South Wiltshire Museum, Salisbury. City Museum, Sheffield. Central Museum and Art Gallery, Stoke-on-Trent. City Museum and Art Gallery, Worcester.

CLUB
The English Ceramic Circle, 8 Church Row, London NW3.

DEALERS
Antique Porcelain Co Limited, 149 New Bond Street, London W1. Andrew Dando, 4 Wood Street, Queen Square, Bath. The Tetbury Furniture Company, 6 Long Street, Tetbury, Glos.

Celadon

This term describes the coloured glaze used by the Chinese from the 10th century onwards in the decoration of porcelain. It is often a shade of green, but delicate hues of grey and olive brown are also found. The origin of the name is obscure but some authorities derive it from Saladdin the Saracen king who is said to have been very partial to this kind of ware.

READING
Chinese Celadon Wares, G M Gompertz (Faber)

TO VIEW
British Museum, London. Percival David Foundation of Chinese Art, London. Victoria and Albert Museum, London. Wallace Collection, London. Waddesdon Manor, Aylesbury. National Museum of Wales, Cardiff. Museum and Art Gallery, Cheltenham. Royal Scottish Museum, Edinburgh. Museum and Art Gallery, Leicester. Central Museum and Art Gallery, Northampton. City Museum, Sheffield. City Museum and Art Gallery, Stoke-on-Trent. Windsor Castle, Windsor.

DEALERS
William Clayton Limited, 38 Bury Street, St James', London SW1. Gordon Hand and Co, 18 Chepstow Mansions, Westbourne Grove, London W2. Andrew Dando, 4 Wood Street, Queen Square, Bath. Denys Cowell, 60 Middle Street, Brighton, Sussex. Michael Brett, Picton House, Broadway, Worcester. Collins and Clark, 81 Regent Street, Cambridge. F C Dixon, 54 Bridgegate, Retford, Notts.

Chelsea

The earliest porcelain factory in England was probably that established at Chelsea in or about 1754. Among the earliest products was the famous 'goat and bee' jug and the entrancing 'girl on a swing' figures. The phases of the Chelsea factory are usually divided according to the marks found on porcelain: Triangle (1745–49), Raised Anchor (1750–53), Red Anchor (1753–8), and Gold Anchor (1758–70). Work of the Raised and Red Anchor periods is that most highly prized by collectors. Prices from these periods are characterised by their creamy texture, spotted by transparent glass specks. Although Meissen and Sèvres wares were often copied, Chelsea evolved many distinctive styles of its own. Chelsea, in turn, was extensively copied and even forged (by Coalport in the 19th century) so it pays to consult an expert when purchasing Chelsea porcelain.

The Chelsea factory changed hands in 1770 when it was taken over by William Duesbury and John Heath of Derby. From then until its closure in 1784 its products closely resembled those of Derby. The Chelsea factory was demolished in 1784 and some of the surviving moulds were transferred to Derby.

READING

The Cheyne Book of Chelsea China and Pottery, R Blunt (Bles)

Chelsea Porcelain Toys, G E Bryant (Medici Society)

Chelsea and Other English Porcelain, Pottery and Enamel, Hackenbroch (Thames and Hudson).

Chelsea China, F Hurlbutt (Hodder and Stoughton)

Chinese Porcelain, W King (Benn)

Chelsea Porcelain Gold Anchor Wares, F S McKenna (F Lewis)

Chelsea Porcelain Red Anchor Wares, F S McKenna (F Lewis)

Chelsea Porcelain, Triangle and Raised Anchor Wares, F Severne McKenna (F Lewis)

Chelsea, Bow and Derby Porcelain Figures, F Stoner (Ceramic)

TO VIEW
British Museum, London. Fenton House, London. London Museum, London. Victoria and Albert Museum, London. Waddesdon Manor, Aylesbury. Art Gallery and Museum, Brighton. National Museum of Wales, Cardiff. Upton House, Edgehill. Royal Scottish Museum, Edinburgh. Temple Newsam House, Leeds (Only complete tea and coffee service, Red Anchor, in existence). Museum and Art Gallery, Leicester. The Wernher Collection, Luton Hoo. Central Museum and Art Gallery, Northampton. Scone Palace, Perth. City Museum and Art Gallery, Stoke-on-Trent. Windsor Castle, Windsor. City Museum and Art Gallery, Worcester.

CLUB
The English Ceramic Circle, 8 Church Row, Hampstead, London NW3.

DEALERS
Antique Porcelain Co Limited, 149 New Bond Street, London W1. Albert Amor Limited, 37 Bury Street, London SW1. D M & P Manheim, 69 Upper Berkeley Street, Portman Square, W1. Spink and Son Limited, King Street, London SW1. Bradstone House, Alvington, Gloucestershire. Andrew Dando, 4 Wood Street, Queen Square, Bath. Mrs Araxie Love, Newbiggin, Richmond, Yorks.

NOTE
See the illustration of Chelsea china marks on page xx at the beginning of the book.

Chessmen

The origins of chess are obscure and various scholars have claimed as its inventors the Greeks, Romans, Chinese, Babylonians, Persians, Hindus and even the Welsh! Most experts, however, now agree that the game probably originated in India early in the Christian era. It was a four-handed dice game known as *chaturanga* (the four soldiers), but when it was exported to Persia it changed to *shatranj* and somehow this became corrupted and confused with the word *shah*. The expression "Check-mate" comes from the Arabic *Shah mat* (the King is dead). The names of the pieces were also of Arabic or Sanskrit origin; the bishop was originally called the *alphyn*, (from Hindu *aleph-hind* – the Indian ox or elephant) and the rooks derived from *rukh* – a warrior. The game came to Europe via Arabia and appears to have been established by the 11th century. One of the most famous sets of chessmen was the group of walrus-tusk pieces discovered at Ness in the Outer Hebrides. These Norse chessmen are now in the British Museum.

READING
A Book of Chessmen, A Hammond (A Barker)
Chessmen, A E J Mackett Beeson (Weidenfeld & Nicholson)
Chess, H & S Wichmann (Hamlyn)

TO VIEW
British Museum, London. Sir John Soane's Museum, London. Guildhall Museum, London. London Museum, London. Victoria and Albert Museum, London. The Wernher Collection, Luton Hoo. Central Museum and Art Gallery, Northampton. Blithfield, Rugeley, Staffs. Salisbury and South Wiltshire Museum, Salisbury. City Museum, Sheffield. City Museum and Art Gallery, Stoke-on-Trent. Wedgwood Museum, Stoke-on-Trent. The Yorkshire Museum, York.

Mackett Beeson, 22 Lansdowne Road, Berkeley Square, London w1. Crafts and Curios, 7 Bruntsfield Place, Edinburgh.

China fairings

These small porcelain groups of figures in various cosy domestic situations were very popular a century ago as souvenirs and prizes at fairgrounds, hence their name. Although designed specifically for the British market they were nearly all made by the German firm of Conta & Boehme.

The commonest types show a couple getting into bed; the inscription usually reads "The last in bed to put out the light." Others are entitled "An awkward interruption", "The landlord in love", and "Alone at last" – courtship and marriage scenes were the most popular. These somewhat bawdy groups gave way, about 1850, to more sentimental subjects – children or humanised animals. Relatively scarce are fairings with historical and political subjects. The early examples are comparatively solid and heavy, with the decoration carefully applied. Later examples, often produced by rivals of Conta & Boehme, are hollow, lighter and more slipshod in decoration as mass-production came into vogue. Oddly enough, china fairings showing Welsh tea parties emanated from Japan at the beginning of this century. Prices are still reasonable, from £3 to £30 in most cases.

READING
Victorian China Fairings, W S Bristowe (Black)
Antique China and Glass Under £5, G Godden (Barker)

TO VIEW
Victoria and Albert Museum, London. Central Museum and Art Gallery, Northampton. City Museum and Art Gallery, Stoke-on-Trent. Elizabethan House, Totnes.

CLUB
The English Ceramic Circle, 8 Church Row, London NW3.

Chinoiserie

This word was coined to describe a European craze for anything "in the Chinese style". The fashion for chinoiserie was introduced by the merchants of the East India companies in Britain and the Netherlands at the beginning of the 17th century. Although the demand was originally satisfied by genuine imports from the Far East, by the beginning of the 18th century the vogue for chinoiseries had grown to such a size that European craftsmen were trying to emulate the elusive art forms of China. The result would undoubtedly have surprised any Chinese who happened to visit Western Europe at that time, since most of the artists and craftsmen engaged in the production of chinoiserie had only a vague idea of Oriental art. It was very fashionable in the mid-18th century, but by 1765 had begun to give way to the baroque styles introduced from France. In cabinet-making the greatest exponent of chinoiserie was Chippendale, but most media, from silver and porcelain to papier maché (q.v.) became vehicles for the cult of chinoiserie while it lasted. Nowadays these pictures of Europeanised Chinamen and bookcases with pagoda-like pediments have a curious appeal, with a consequent rise in prices of even the most mundane items.

READING

Chinoiserie, H Honour (Murray)

TO VIEW

British Museum, London. Victoria and Albert Museum, London. Wallace Collection, London. Waddesdon Manor, Aylesbury. The Royal Pavilion, Brighton. City Museum and Art Gallery, Bristol. Royal Scottish Museum, Edinburgh. City Museum, Hereford. Central Museum and Art Gallery, Northampton. City Museum, Sheffield. County Museum,

Stafford. City Museum and Art Gallery, Stoke-on-Trent. Dyson Perrins Museum of Porcelain, Worcester. Snowshill Manor, Broadway, Worcester. Windsor Castle, Windsor.

DEALERS

Most general antique dealers.

Chip carving

Trays, boxes, letter-racks and picture frames are occasionally found decorated in this distinctive style and so, of course, is oak furniture. Chip-carving consists of the removal of shallow triangular "chips" of wood from the surface of an object, usually in a geometrical pattern. It seems to have been very popular with "do-it-yourself" enthusiasts about the turn of the century.

READING
Treen, W T James (Pitman)

TO VIEW
Victoria and Albert Museum, London. Royal Scottish Museum, Edinburgh. Temple Newsam House, Leeds.

DEALERS
Coxson Antiques Limited, 63 Cadogan Place, London sw1. Brian R Verrall, 48 Maddox Street, London w1. Trinkets and Treasures, 29 Barns Street, Ayr. J Hutton, 108 High Street, Berkhamsted, Herts. Avon Antiques, 26–27 Market Street, Bradford-on-Avon, Wilts. Jan Struther, 13 Randolph Place, Edinburgh. Charles Toller, 51 High Street, Eton. Wilkinson's Cottage Antiques, 27–28 Charnham Street, Hungerford, Berks. The Cottage Shop, High Street, Lechlade-on-Thames, Glos. John Eddy, Etnam Street, Leominster. Vincent Wood, Audley House, Osbournby, Nr Sleaford, Lincs. Market Hall Antiques, Towyn, Merionethshire.

Christmas cards

The Christmas greetings card was an English invention, making its dèbut at Christmas 1843. It was inspired by Sir Henry Cole and the first commercial design was produced by J C Horsley (who, on account of his antipathy to the use of nude models by artists of the Royal Academy, was later nicknamed "Clothes Horsley"). The Horsley design showed a typical Victorian middle-class family grouped round a table groaning with food and drink (the design was severely criticised at the time by temperance workers). About 1,000 of these cards were sold at a shilling each. Ten years ago it might have been possible to buy one for £10, but today five times that sum would be asked – if a Horsley card could be found at all.

The idea was slow to catch on, though the advent of second-class postage in 1870 helped to stimulate its popularity. Many of the early cards were overlaid with layers of lace. Others were richly embroidered or garnished with tinsel. The changing patterns of artistic styles are reflected in Christmas cards, from the Arts and Crafts movement as exemplified by William Morris and Kate Greenaway, via the sinewy lines of Art Nouveau, to modern 'pop' art. Generally speaking only cards before the First World War are automatically regarded as collectors' pieces, though some scarce modern items, such as hand-painted cards or those containing fine etchings and engravings would be worth buying, as their print runs are frequently short and the art considerable.

READING

The History of the Christmas Card, G Buday (Spring Books)
The Romance of Greeting Cards, E D Chase (US)
Small Antiques for the Collector, Therle Hughes (Lutterworth)

British Museum, London. London Museum, London. Victoria and Albert Museum, London. City Museum and Art Gallery, Birmingham. Blaise Castle Folk Museum, Bristol. National Museum of Wales, Cardiff. City Museum, Hereford. Museum and Art Gallery, Leicester. City Museum, Sheffield. Elizabethan House, Totnes. Royal Tunbridge Wells Museum and Art Gallery, Tunbridge Wells. City Museum and Art Gallery, Worcester.

DEALERS
John Hall & David MacWilliams, 17 Harrington Road, London sw7. Pleasures of Past Times, 11 Cecil Court, Charing Cross Road, London wc2.

Cigar cases

Cigars were introduced to Europe from America via Portugal and Spain during the latter part of the 17th century though they did not become widely popular till about 1740. Cigar-smoking became fashionable in France and Britain during the Peninsular War, though some years elapsed before the habit became socially acceptable in polite circles. It was not until then that the cigar case could evolve as an item which no well-equipped gentleman would be without.

Cigar cases are found in a great variety of styles and shapes, much attention being devoted to their decoration. The majority of them were made of wood, treated in various ways such as marquetry, japanning or mother-of-pearl inlay. The earliest cases are usually those in which the interior is divided into a number of separate compartments so that the cigars did not rub together. From about the middle of the 19th century onwards, however, these small partitions were invariably dispensed with as the demand for greater output increased.

TO VIEW
London Museum, London. Victoria and Albert Museum, London. City Museum, Hereford. City Museum, Sheffield. Royal Tunbridge Wells Museum and Art Gallery, Tunbridge Wells. City Museum and Art Gallery, Worcester.

DEALERS
General antique dealers.

Clocks

Stylistically, the earliest clocks in Britain were the small bracket clocks which were designed to be hung from the wall. The first of these had a single hand and was operated by a system of weights. After about 1610 the pendulum was used increasingly and in an effort to keep this mechanism dust free the long case or "Grandfather" clock gradually evolved. Those with narrow cases are in great demand since the earliest long case clocks offered protection only to the weights and not to the pendulum which swung free. Later, when the pendulum was also enclosed, the case had to be widened to allow for the swing of the pendulum.

Long case clocks vary greatly in style and value, from the handsome products of such famous makers as Brequet, Knibb and Tompion to "country" clocks made by obscure, local clock makers, often a decade or more behind London in the fashionability of their appearance. Less elegant than the clocks of the famous makers, perhaps, but desirable none the less and still available at prices from £35 upwards. If space is at a premium then mantel clocks may be the answer. Here again the range is infinite, from French Ormolu (q.v.) to Victorian marble eight-day clocks, complete with quarter chimes. Prices range from a pound or two upwards, but few classes of antiques may be said to be so undervalued as clocks.

"Act of Parliament" clock,
English, 1750

READING

The Book of Old Clocks and Watches, E von Basserman-Jordan (Allen & Unwin)
The Plain Man's Guide to Antique Clocks, W J Bentley (Joseph)
The True Book about Clocks, E Bruton (Muller)
Clocks and Watches, E Bruton (Arthur Barker)
Investing in Clocks and Watches, P W Cumhail (Barrie & Rockcliffe)
The Grandfather Clock, E L Edwards (Sherratt)
Clocks, Simon Fleet (Weidenfeld & Nicholson)

French china and gilt
bracket clock, 1750

English Clocks, M Goaman (Connoisseur and Michael Joseph)
Chats on Old Clocks, Arthur Hayden (Benn)
The Country Life Book of Clocks, E T Joy (Country Life)
The Knibb Family—Clockmakers, R A Lee (Manor)
The Collectors Dictionary of Clocks, H A Lloyd (Country Life)
Thomas Tompion, R W Symonds (Batsford)
In Quest of Clocks, K Ullyet (Barrie & Rockcliffe)
Old Clocks, Edward Wenham (Spring Books)

TO VIEW

Guildhall Museum of the Clockmakers Company, London. London Museum, London. Science Museum, London. Victoria and Albert Museum, London. Wallace Collection, London. Waddesdon Manor, Aylesbury. City Museum and Art Gallery, Birmingham. Art Gallery and Museum, Brighton. Royal Pavilion, Brighton. The Gershom-Parkington Memorial Collection of Clocks and Watches, Bury St Edmunds. National Museum of Wales, Cardiff. Minories Art Gallery, Colchester. Corporation Museum, Dover. National Museum of Antiquities of Scotland, Edinburgh. Royal Scottish Museum, Edinburgh. City Museum, Hereford. Temple Newsam House, Leeds. Newark House Museum, Leicester. The Wernher Collection, Luton Hoo. Central Museum and Art Gallery, Northampton. Museum of the History of Science, Oxford. Scone Palace, Perth. Salisbury and South Wiltshire Museum, Salisbury. City Museum, Sheffield. County Museum, Stafford. City Museum and Art Gallery, Stoke-on-Trent. Elizabethan House, Totnes. Windsor Castle, Windsor. City Museum and Art Gallery, Worcester. Snowshill Manor, Broadway, Worcester.

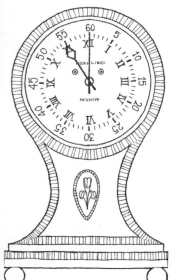

Satinwood and tulipwood
English bracket clock, 1790

DEALERS

D Boulstridge Limited, 47 Lower Belgrave Street, London SW1. Aubrey Brocklehurst, 124 Cromwell Road, London SW7. The Chiltern Hundreds, 11 Chiltern Street, London W1. Daniel Desbois and Sons, 51 Carey Street, London WC2. Philip and Bernard Dombey, 174 Kensington Church Street, London w8. Charles Frodsham and Co Limited, 173 Brompton Road, London sw3. Keith Harding Antiques, 93 Hornsey Road, London n7. E Hollander, 80 Fulham Road, London sw3. Ronald Lee, 1–9 Bruton Place, London w1. C & J Bryce Morris, 26 St Christopher's Place, London w1. Quality Chase, 17a St Christopher's Place, London w1. Brian R Verrall, 48 Maddox Street, London w1. John Walker, 1 South Molton Street, London w1. John Bell, Bridge Street, Aberdeen. Willow Tree Antiques, Amersham, Bucks. Antiques and Crafts, Tandaragee, County Armagh, N Ireland. Beryl Birch Antiques, 89 Elmfield Road, Castle Bromwich, Birmingham. E White, G Hume, 45 Upper North Street, Brighton. Yellow Lantern Antiques Limited, 34 and 65b Holland Road, Hove. Ronald A Lee, The Manor House, Byfleet, Surrey. Old Thatch Antiques, Cerne Abbas, Dorset. W & J Turner, 22 Montpellier Walk, Cheltenham, Glos. John McIntosh, 60 Grassmarket, Edinburgh. S L Chislett, Bradstone House, Alvington, Lydney, Glos. Morley's Antiques, Mildenhall, Suffolk. P W Gottschals, 107 Sneinton Boulevard, Nottingham. John E Davis, 14 Wokingham Road, Reading, Berks. Quinney's Antiques, Walnut Tree Corner, Sawbridgeworth, Herts. Malcolm Gardner, Bradbourne Farmhouse, Bradbourne Vale Road, Sevenoaks, Kent. Robinson and Co Limited, 9–10 The Square, Shrewsbury, Shrops. Riverside Chimes, Stratford-St-Mary, Essex. Avon House, Market Place, Tetbury, Glos. C H Thorpe, High Street, Uppingham, Rutland. G H Bell, 32a The Square, Winchester, Hants. Richard J Piner Limited, 51 High Street, Windsor, Berks.

Carved ebonised wood English clock, 1880

Coalport

This pottery was established about 1796 by John Rose who had previously been connected with the Caughley Pottery (q.v.). Later he took over Caughley and had the biscuit wares previously manufactured there sent to Coalport for decoration and glazing. The Caughley part of the enterprise was closed down in 1814. The factory has undergone several changes of ownership and location in the past 150 years and is now known as Coalport China Limited at Stoke-on-Trent.

Early Coalport is indistinguishable from Caughley, but from about 1820 onwards Coalport was renowned for its vivid floral decorations, particularly of roses. Coalport also specialised in clever imitations of Sèvres and Meissen wares (q.v.).

READING
Caughley and Coalport Porcelain, F A Barrett (F. Lewis)

TO VIEW
British Museum, London. Victoria and Albert Museum, London. Art Gallery and Museum, Brighton. National Museum of Wales, Cardiff. Royal Scottish Museum, Edinburgh. City Museum, Hereford. Museum and Art Gallery, Leicester. Central Museum and Art Gallery, Northampton. City Museum and Art Gallery, Stoke-on-Trent. City Museum and Art Gallery, Worcester.

CLUB
The English Ceramic Circle, 8 Church Row, London NW3.

DEALERS
Those specialising in pottery and porcelain.

NOTE—See china marks on page xx.

Commodes

It is perhaps unfortunate that this word should conjure up, for most people, the receptacle for a chamber pot or "night stool" when, in fact, it is the cabinet makers' term for a small chest of drawers, usually fitted with twin doors. With its fine decorative inlays and veneered surfaces this elegant piece of furniture was a useful addition to the drawing room and *not* the bedroom as many people erroneously imagine.

READING
Georgian Cabinet Makers, R Edwards & M Jourdain (Country Life)

TO VIEW
London Museum, London. Victoria and Albert Museum, London. Wallace Collection, London. Waddesdon Manor, Aylesbury. Art Gallery and Museum, Brighton. Royal Pavilion, Brighton. Royal Scottish Museum, Edinburgh. Temple Newsam House, Leeds. Museum and Art Gallery, Leicester. Windsor Castle, Windsor.

DEALERS
Dealers in antique furniture.

Copper ware

Beaten copper has been turned to many uses – from kettles and frying pans, to warming pans and urns. Brightly polished copper ware has a very special charm of its own and most utensils and domestic implements have been produced in it at some time or another from the very earliest times, and particularly in the East. In many respects it is allied to brass-ware and items in these metals are to be found side by side in those antique or junk shops which specialise in non-ferrous metals.

READING
Chats on Old Copper and Brass, F W Burgess (Benn)
Collecting Copper and Brass, G Wills (Arco)

TO VIEW
London Museum, London. City Museum and Art Gallery, Birmingham. Art Gallery and Museum, Brighton. Royal Pavilion, Brighton. Blaise Castle Folk Museum, Bristol. Central Museum and Art Gallery, Northampton. City Museum, Sheffield. City Museum and Art Gallery, Worcester.

DEALERS
Felix Hilton, 45 St John's Wood High Street, London NW8. Jans Antiques, 69 Portobello Road, London W11. The Treasure House, 138 Waterloo Road, Burslem, Stoke-on-Trent. Millhouse Antiques, The Old Mill, Clophill, Beds. Desmond Antiques, Welford Road, Leicester. C H & D Burrows, 15b St Thomas Street, Scarborough, Yorks. Leonard Metcalfe, 5 Lord Street, Southport, Lancs. Woburn Antique Galleries, Woburn, Bucks.

Cornucopias

These small decorative containers for flowers were fashionable from about 1750 to 1870 and were either flat-backed for hanging on walls, or mounted on a small base (usually of marble) to serve as ornaments for desks or mantelpieces. They may be found in a wide variety of materials, the commonest being porcelain, pottery or coloured glass.

TO VIEW
Victoria and Albert Museum, London. Central Museum and Art Gallery, Northampton. City Museum, Sheffield. City Museum and Art Gallery, Stoke-on-Trent. Wedgwood Museum, Stoke-on-Trent.

DEALERS
Most general antique dealers and junk shops.

Late 18th century cornucopia

Cow creamers

These delightful creatures originated in the Netherlands about the middle of the 18th century. Basically
they consist of a hollow cow, her tail looped to form
a handle and her mouth open to form a spout. Milk
or cream was poured into the jug through an aperture in the back of the cow, a stopper being inserted
to keep out the dust. Cow creamers or milk jugs must
have been rather unhygienic in practice, on account
of the difficulty of keeping them clean. They vary
considerably in material, from black glazed earthen
ware, Jackfield ware, Leeds cream ware and Staffordshire ware to agate ware. The style also varies: some
include a calf or a seated milkmaid, while others have
a large daisy beneath the cow. Most cow creamers
are mounted on a solid base, but modern imitations
may be found standing unsupported on their feet.
They have been extensively imitated in comparatively
recent times and expert knowledge and experience is
required to distinguish genuine antique creamers
from the modern imitations. Beware of repaired
horns or jugs with their stoppers missing.

Silver gilt cow creamer, 1767

READING
More Small Decorative Antiques, Therle Hughes (Lutterworth)

TO VIEW
London Museum, London. Victoria and Albert Museum, London. National Museum of Wales, Cardiff. Littlecote House, Hungerford. City Museum, Sheffield. City Museum and Art Gallery, Stoke-on-Trent.

DEALERS
De Havilland (Antiques) Limited, 14 Grafton Street, Bond Street, London w1.

Cream ware

This attractive type of earthen ware, with its distinctive creamy glaze, is usually associated with the town of Leeds where many of the finest examples were produced. A mark inscribed LEEDS POTTERY between two asterisks was applied, but unfortunately its presence is no guarantee to authenticity since it was extensively pirated by other potteries, both contemporary (mid-18th century) and down to recent times. Conversely, much genuine Leeds cream ware was never marked at all.

Cream ware actually originated c. 1720 across the county border in Staffordshire and was extremely popular throughout the 18th century. Articles vary considerably in style, from the popular 'basket weave' patterns used on dishes, to the ornate pierced decoration favoured by the potters of Leeds and the surrounding neighbourhood.

Prices in cream ware range immensely in value Particularly prized are the large statues of horses modelled on Chinese porcelain statues. Two exceptionally fine examples of Leeds cream ware horses fetched £1,050 and 1,700 guineas respectively at Christies in 1967. At the other end of the scale, however, plates and dishes can still be picked up for a pound or two each, while cups, saucers, jugs and bowls are obtainable in the price range £2–£20.

READING

English Cream Coloured Earthenware, D C Towner (Faber)
Leeds Pottery, D C Towner (Cory)

TO VIEW

London Museum, London. Victoria and Albert Museum, London. Curtis Museum, Alton. Art Gallery and Museum, Brighton. National Museum of Wales, Cardiff. Astley Hall, Chorley. Royal Scottish Museum, Edinburgh. City Art Gallery, Leeds. Temple Newsam House, Leeds. Museum and Art Gallery, Leicester. Central Museum and Art Gallery, Northampton. Salisbury and South Wiltshire Museum, Salisbury. City Museum, Sheffield. City Museum and Art Gallery, Stoke-on-Trent. Spode-Copeland Museum and Art Gallery, Stoke-on-Trent. Wedgwood Museum, Stoke-on-Trent.

DEALERS

Beauchamp Galleries, 8 Beauchamp Place, London sw3. D M and P Manheim, 69 Upper Berkeley Street, Portman Square, London w1. David Newbon, 56 Beauchamp Place, London sw3. Spink and Son Limited, King Street, London sw1. J and E D Vandekar, 138 Brompton Road, London sw3. Victor Needham Limited, 119 Old Christchurch Road, Bournemouth. Margaret Cadman, 26 Ship Street, Brighton, Sussex. Gerald C Dimery, 154 Shadwell Lane, Moortown, Leeds. Smiths Antiques, 17 St Michael's Lane, Headingly, Leeds.

Davenport

This word has two meanings, pertaining either to furniture or ceramics. It can be applied to the earthen ware and bone china manufactured by John Davenport and his descendants at Longpost in Staffordshire between 1793 and 1882. Specialities of this pottery included fine lustre ware and children's plates decorated with zoo animals.

Davenport in the furniture sense is the name given to a type of small writing desk invented by a Captain Davenport. Fine examples range in price from £40 to about £100.

TO VIEW
Victoria and Albert Museum, London. Art Gallery and Museum, Brighton. National Museum of Wales, Cardiff. Royal Scottish Museum, Edinburgh. Central Museum and Art Gallery, Northampton. City Museum, Sheffield. City Museum and Art Gallery, Stoke-on-Trent. City Museum and Art Gallery, Worcester.

CLUB
The English Ceramic Circle, 8 Church Row, London NW3, or Furniture History Society, Victoria and Albert Museum, London SW3.

DEALERS
Most general antique furniture dealers.

Decanters

The origin of the decanter can be traced back to the carafe used for table wines in the 17th century. The increasing use of Portuguese wines in Britain from 1704 onwards led to the need for a more elegant vessel in which to serve it. The earlier decanters were slim and light, on account of the Glass Excise Act of 1745 which taxed glassware by weight. An interesting feature of early decanters was the relative absence of ornament on the sides, though the name of the wine would often be engraved. By the end of the 18th century however the necks of decanters were heavily girt with knops and the sides extravagantly covered with cutwork decoration. The advent of the wine label (q.v.) removed the necessity for the name of the wine to appear on the decanter itself. The latter style, with variations, has remained in favour to this day. The value of antique decanters depends largely on the quality of the glass, the period in which it was manufactured and the style of decoration. Rarities such as early magnums and broad-based ship's decanters would today fetch over £100, though early Victorian art glass decanters are still available for less than £30 in perfect condition, and less if the base is scratched or slightly chipped.

READING

How to Identify English Drinking Glasses and Decanters, D Ash (Bell)

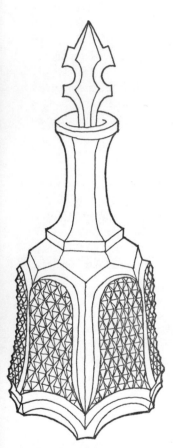

Cut glass decanter, 1845 to 1850

TO VIEW

British Museum, London. London Museum, London. Victoria and Albert Museum, London. Royal Pavilion, Brighton. Art Gallery and Museum, Brighton. Royal Scottish Museum, Edinburgh. City Museum, Hereford. Pilkington Glass Museum, St Helens, Lancs. City Museum, Sheffield. City Museum and Art Gallery, Stoke-on-Trent. Windsor Castle, Windsor. City Museum and Art Gallery, Worcester.

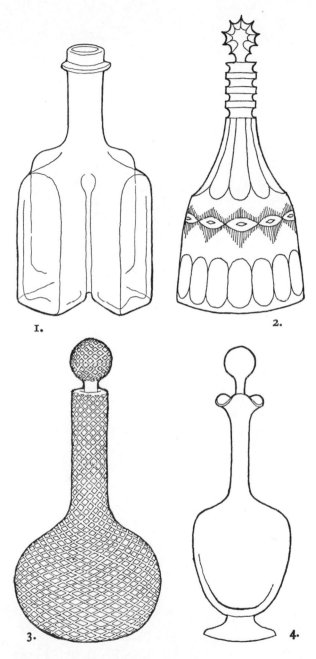

I.

2.

3.

4.

(1) Early 18th century clear glass decanter.   (2) Late 18th century wheel engraved decanter.   (3) 19th century cut glass decanter, ruby glass with white.   (4) 1870/80 Stourbridge decanter

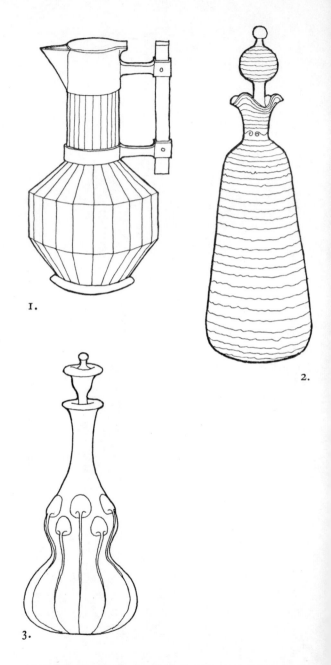

(1) English clear glass decanter with silver mounts and ivory handle, 1881. (2) Clear glass decanter with slipped on design, 1880. (3) American decanter, 1902

Cecil Davis Limited, 3 Grosvenor Street, New Bond Street, London, w1. Dolphin Antiques, 2b Englands Lane, London nw3. Spink and Son Limited, King Street, St James', London sw1. Hilton Gallery, 3 St Mary's Passage, Cambridge. L Rapstone, 11 Savile Street, Hull, Yorks. John Maggs, 114 Bold Street, Liverpool, Lancs.

Delft ware

Although this coarse earthen ware bears the name of a Dutch town it in fact originated in the Near East and its development may be traced in the wares known as maiolica and faience (q.v.). Long before Delft established its international reputation in the 17th century as a centre for delft ware, this type of pottery was being made in England. The Flemish potters, Jaspar Audries and Jacob Janson, began manufacturing delft ware at Norwich in the reign of King Henry VIII. Janson, or Johnson, subsequently moved to London where several other Flemish potters worked in the 17th century.

Early English delft ware of established provenance is excessively rare, but in the 17th century it was produced not only in London but in Liverpool, Bristol, Wincanton (Somerset), at Limerick and Dublin in Ireland and at the appropriately named Delftfield near Glasgow. Delft ware had passed out of fashion by 1780 and little tin-glazed pottery was manufactured after that date. True Delft ware may easily be recognised by its opaque glaze, usually decorated in a vigorous manner of short, sharp strokes, necessitated by the painters having to work on a porous surface which quickly absorbed the pigment. London delft is characterised by its tendency to chip or flake readily, while the enamel is a good white with an occasional pinkish tinge. Bristol delft is usually more bluish white, with a more rough and ready treatment in decoration.

Delft ware takes many forms, varying greatly in scarcity and value. Still reasonably priced, at anything from a pound or two upwards, are blue and white tiles (though beware of later Continental imitations). Dishes come in a variety of shapes, from saucers to basins and bleeding bowls. Mugs and beakers with commemorative inscriptions and rather crude portraits of royalty are in great demand.

READING
Delftware, John Bedford (Cassell)
English Delftware, F G Gainer (Faber)
Collecting Delft, Diana Imber (Arco)
English Delftware Pottery, A Ray (Faber)

TO VIEW
British Museum, London. Guildhall Museum, London. London Museum, London. Pharmaceutical Society's Museum, London. Victoria and Albert Museum, London. Victoria Art Gallery, Bath. Art Gallery and Museum, Brighton. City Museum and Art Gallery, Bristol. National Museum of Wales, Cardiff. Royal Scottish Museum, Edinburgh. Central Museum and Art Gallery, Northampton. Scone Palace, Perth. Museum and Art Gallery, Reading. Salisbury and South Wiltshire Museum, Salisbury. City Museum, Sheffield. City Museum and Art Gallery, Stoke-on-Trent. Windsor Castle, Windsor. City Museum and Art Gallery, Worcester. The Yorkshire Museum, York.

CLUB
The English Ceramic Circle, 8 Church Row, London NW3.

DEALERS
Balcombe Galleries, 7 Stanley Studios, Park Walk, SW10. A S Embden, Hector Court, Cambalt Road, London SW15. Gordon Hand and Co, 18 Chepstow

Mansions, Westbourne Grove, London w2. Mercury
Antiques, 1 & 1b, Ladbroke Road, London w11.
Spink and Son Limited, King Street, London sw1.
Patrick Oliver, 4 Tivoli Street, Cheltenham Spa,
Glos. The Antique Shop, High Street, Dedham,
Essex. S. Montagu-Puckle, The Oaks, Coopers
Hill, Eversley, Hants. Commander England Limited,
26 Causewayhead and 57 Adelaide Street, Penzance,
Cornwall.

Derby

The manufacture of porcelain in Derby was certainly
being carried on by 1751 if not before. By 1756
William Duesbury and John Heath had formed a
partnership which lasted till Heath's bankruptcy in
1779. Duesbury took over a number of other potteries
including Chelsea (q.v.) and built up a flourishing
concern specialising in Chinese figure groups as well
as a rather heavy, creamy porcelain used for dishes,
jugs, etc.

Duesbury closely imitated the styles of Meissen
and concentrated on decorative rather than useful
wares towards the end of the century. Later wares are
known as the "Patch Family" on account of the
marks on the base caused by the wads of clay on
which they lay during firing.

After Duesbury's death the pottery eventually
came into the hands of Robert Bloor who re-issued
figures from earlier moulds but also had a strong
predilection for florid ornamentation and extravagant gilding.

The original pottery closed down in 1848 though
it was resurrected in 1876 in the form of the Royal
Crown Derby Porcelain Company and noted for its
ornamental wares and dinner services.

READING

Derby Porcelain, F B Gilhespy (MacGibbon & Kee)
Royal Crown Derby China, F B Gilhespy (C Skilton)

TO VIEW

British Museum, London. Fenton House, London. London Museum, London. Victoria and Albert Museum, London. Art Gallery and Museum, Brighton. National Museum of Wales, Cardiff. Museum and Art Gallery, Derby. Royal Scottish Museum, Edinburgh. City Museum, Hereford. The Wernher Collection, Luton Hoo. Central Museum and Art Gallery, Northampton. Scone Palace, Perth. Salisbury and South Wiltshire Museum, Salisbury. City Museum, Sheffield. City Museum and Art Gallery, Stoke-on-Trent. Windsor Castle, Windsor. City Museum and Art Gallery, Worcester.

CLUB

The English Ceramic Circle, 8 Church Row, London NW3.

DEALERS

Albert Amor Limited, 37 Bury Street, St James', London SW1. The Antique Porcelain Co Limited, 149 New Bond Street, London W1. Delomosne and Son Limited, 4 Campden Hill Road, London W8. Spink & Son Limited, King Street, London SW1. J & E D Vandekar, 138 Brompton Road, London SW3. Andrew Dando, 4 Wood Street, Queen Square, Bath. Buckingham Antiques, The Old Vicarage, Chetwode, Bucks. (Buckingham Antiques is run by John Twitchett who is the foremost specialist dealer in Derby Porcelain in this country).

NOTE—See china marks on page xx.

Dolls

Tiny images of the human figure are almost as old as mankind itself. Examples have been found in Egyptian tombs dating back to 2,000 B.C. and are thought to be a humane substitute for the slaves who were previously killed and interred with their dead master. It is a far cry from these *ushabti* figures of Egypt to the present day child's plaything. Not until the 18th century, when childhood came to be recognised as a distinct phase between babyhood and adulthood, did dolls begin to be manufactured in appreciable quantities.

The first commercially produced dolls were the aptly named pegwoodens, originating in Germany in the 1820s. Poured wax dolls, known as slit-heads on account of the slits in the scalp through which the hair was attached, appeared about 1830. Heads in glazed porcelain or bisque "Parian" ware date from the middle of the 19th century. The best-known English dolls of the late 19th century were the wax dolls produced by Montanari, Perotti or Marsh. Dolls bearing the names or marks of these firms are now highly prized by collectors, though many genuine examples are known without markings.

The most famous of the French dolls were the beautifully dressed Parisians manufactured by Huret, Jumeau, Martin and Rohmer. Comparatively late are the *bébé* (baby) dolls in which Juneau and Bru excelled. The German dollmakers, however, led the world until 1914; the best makers in this period are Gebruder Heubach, Armand Marseille, Kammer Reinhardt, and Simon & Halbig. Many fine examples of dolls being produced today will become the collectors' pieces of the future.

READING

Dolls, Antonia Fraser (Weidenfeld & Nicholson)
Dolls and Dollmakers, Mary Hillier (Weidenfeld & Nicholson)

Small Decorative Antiques, Therle Hughes (Lutterworth)
Queen Victoria's Dolls, F H Low (Newnes)
European and American Dolls, Gwen White (Batsford)

TO VIEW
Bethnal Green Museum, London. British Museum, London. London Museum (Queen Victoria's Dolls), London. Pollock's Toy Museum, London. Victoria and Albert Museum, London. City Museum and Art Gallery, Birmingham. Art Gallery and Museum, Brighton. The Grange, Rottingdean, Brighton. Blaise Castle Folk Museum, Bristol. Royal Scottish Museum, Edinburgh. City Museum, Hereford. Museum and Art Gallery, Leicester. Central Museum and Art Gallery, Northampton. Salisbury and South Wiltshire Museum, Salisbury. City Museum, Sheffield. County Museum, Stafford. City Museum and Art Gallery, Stoke-on-Trent. Elizabethan House, Totnes. Royal Tunbridge Wells Museum and Art Gallery, Tunbridge Wells. The Doll Museum, Warwick. Windsor Castle, Windsor. City Museum and Art Gallery, Worcester. Snowshill Manor, Broadway, Worcester.

CLUB
United Federation of Dolls Clubs Inc., 4035 Kessler Boulevard Drive, Indianapolis, Indiana 46220, USA

DEALERS
Kay Desmonde Antiques Limited, The Antique Hypermarket, 24–26 Kensington High Street, London w8. Gordon Hand and Co, 18 Chepstow Mansions, Westbourne Grove, London w2. Jill Lewis, 27 Stanhope Gardens, London sw7 (by appt.). Whytes, 22 Park Road, Regents Park, London nw1. The Victorian Cottage, High Street, Attleborough, Norfolk. Roger Warner, High Street, Burford, Oxford. W & J Turner, 22 Montpellier Walk, Cheltenham. "55 Antiques", Spring Bank, Hull, Yorks. Robinson Limited, 9 Church Street, Warwick.

Dolls' Houses and Furniture

Dolls' houses, like dolls themselves, are relatively modern creations dating for the most part from the latter half of the 18th century. Basically most of them consist of small cupboards with a door hinged to reveal "shelves" divided into rooms, each decorated in miniature according to contemporary fashion. More elaborate examples, however, have staircases, chimney breasts, windows that open and close and some form of interior lighting. They range from the simple, mass-produced houses of the present day to the magnificent Titania's Palace which was sold at Christie's in London in 1968 for 30,000 guineas.

Dolls' furniture is even more varied and almost every conceivable object has been miniaturised at some time or other for inclusion in dolls' houses. Exquisite porcelain dinner services and king silver cutlery vie with miniature beds, tables and chairs. Many so-called items of dolls' furniture were in fact apprentice pieces produced by trainee cabinet makers. Others were used by Victorian salesmen to demonstrate their company's wares. But whatever their origin these delightful miniature items are eagerly sought after, not so much by children but by the many adults who recapture something of their childhood by collecting dolls' houses and furniture.

READING
Dolls' Houses in the Victoria and Albert Museum, (H.M.S.O.)
The Dolls' House, J Grant (Studio Vista)
English Dolls' Houses, V Greene (Batsford)
A History of Dolls' Houses, F G Jacobs (Cassell)

TO VIEW
Bethnal Green Museum, London. London Museum, London. Art Gallery and Museum, Brighton.

Blaise Castle Folk Museum, Bristol. Tolsey Museum, Burford. Willmer House Museum, Farnham. City Museum, Hereford. Museum and Art Gallery, Leicester. Central Museum and Art Gallery, Northampton. The Rotunda, Grove House, Oxford. Blithfield, Rugeley, Staffs. City Museum, Sheffield. City Museum and Art Gallery, Stoke-on-Trent. Elizabethan House, Totnes. Windsor Castle, Windsor. Snowshill Manor, Broadway, Worcester.

DEALERS

Kay Desmonde Antiques Limited, The Antique Hypermarket. 26–40 Kensington High Street, London w8. Stephen Long, 348 Fulham Road, London sw10. Whytes, 22 Park Road, Regents Park, London nw1.

Door knockers

Cast iron door knocker,
late 16th century

Prior to the late 16th century people rapped on doors with sticks or their knuckles, but about that time the fashion for heavy iron or brass knockers began to develop. The early examples had a spur-shaped rapper attached but this could easily be wrenched off at the pivot and was unpopular as a result. By the middle of the 18th century the now familiar knocker in massive wrought iron had emerged. They were made in all shapes and sizes, ranging from simple, utilitarian designs to ornate knockers embellished with ducal coats of arms. Corrosion was prevented by black lacquer but in 1812 Hubball of Clerkenwell invented a process using bronze powder mixed with turpentine varnish. Knockers incorporating slots for letters are comparatively late, having to await the introduction of pre-paid penny postage in 1840 before coming into fashion.

READING

English Decorative Ironwork, J Harris (Tiranti)
More Small Decorative Antiques, Therle Hughes
(Lutterworth).

TO VIEW

London Museum, London. Victoria and Albert
Museum, London. Wallace Collection, London.
Royal Scottish Museum, Edinburgh. Museum and
Art Gallery, Leicester. Central Museum and Art
Gallery, Northampton. City Museum, Sheffield.
City Museum and Art Gallery, Stoke-on-Trent.

DEALERS

J D Beardmore and Company Limited, 3–5 Percy
Street, London w1. Jack Casimir Limited, The Brass
Shop, 23 Pembridge Road, London w11. The Old
Metalcraft Shop, 194 Brompton Road, London sw3.
J H Blakey and Sons Limited, 5 Colne Road, Brier-
field, Lancs. Crowther of Syon Lodge, Syon Lodge,
Bush Corner, Isleworth, Middlesex. Dunnings
Antiques, 58–62 Holywell Hill, St Albans, Herts.
G R Wimsett, Old House, 30 Hastings Road, Pem-
bury, Tunbridge Wells. Wyatt of Worcester, The
Barn, Hawford, Worcester.

Doulton

John Doulton (1793–1873) formed a partnership in
1815 with John Watts and manufactured pottery in
Lambeth. They specialised in bottles, mugs and jugs
in saltglazed stone ware with relief decoration. The
Lambeth School of Art had a strong influence on the
firm in the 1870s, decorative stone ware being produced in great quantities from that date onward.
Bone china was manufactured at Doulton's subsidiary

in Burslem from 1884 and it is for this that the company is best known today.

TO VIEW
London Museum, London. Victoria and Albert Museum, London. Art Gallery and Museum, Brighton. National Museum of Wales, Cardiff. Royal Scottish Museum, Edinburgh. City Museum, Hereford. Central Museum and Art Gallery, Northampton. City Museum, Sheffield. City Museum and Art Gallery, Stoke-on-Trent. City Museum and Art Gallery, Worcester.

CLUB
English Ceramic Circle, 8 Church Row, Hampstead, London NW3.

DEALERS
Antique Porcelain Co Limited, 149 New Bond Street, London W1. D M & P Manheim, 69 Upper Berkeley Street, Portman Square, London W1. Andrew Dando, 4 Wood Street, Queen Square, Bath. Silver Cottage Antiques, The Green, Datchet, Bucks.

NOTE—See china marks on page xx.

Duelling pistols

The practice of duelling with pistols rather than with swords was at first regarded as un-English, but once gentlemen became reconciled to the idea the English gunsmiths swiftly achieved an international reputation for the accuracy and precision of their duelling pistols. The best-known names in this field were Wogdon, Nock and Manton, all gunsmiths in 18th century London. Incidentally, the pistols used in the famous duel between Aaron Burr and Alexander Hamilton were made by Wogdon. Cased pairs of duelling pistols by these gunmakers, together with the accessories and cleaning equipment, fetch four figures nowadays. Many of the so-called duelling pistols on the market, however, are ordinary target pistols. The true duelling pistol is characterised by a long, heavy barrel, often octagonal in shape, and by a gently curved "saw-handle" butt. Many duelling pistols incorporate a hair trigger, a combination of levers which required only a very slight pressure to fire the pistol.

READING
Duelling Pistols, J A Atkinson (Cassell)

TO VIEW
London Museum, London. Victoria and Albert Museum, London. Wallace Collection, London. Waddesdon Manor, Aylesbury. Art Gallery and Museum, Brighton. Royal Scottish Musuem, Edinburgh. City Museum, Hereford. Museum and Art Gallery, Leicester. Central Museum and Art Gallery, Northampton. Salisbury and South Wiltshire Museum, Salisbury. City Museum, Sheffield. City Museum and Art Gallery, Stoke-on-Trent. Windsor Castle, Windsor.

CLUB
Arms and Armour Society, 40 Great James Street, Holborn, London wc1.

DEALERS
Peter Dale Limited, 11 & 12 Royal Opera Arcade, Pall Mall, London sw1. E Fairclough Limited, 25 Conduit Street, London w1. Armoury Antiques, 47 Market Street, Brighton. Staddles Antiques, Church Street, Lavenham, Suffolk. J A Morrison Limited, 153 Scraptoff Lane, Leicester.

Dummy board figures

Boards cut to the outline of human figures and painted in contemporary fashions were used to decorate the empty fireplaces of inns and public houses during the summer months. They were mounted on solid wooden bases so that they stood upright. The idea seems to have originated in the Netherlands and been introduced to Britain during the reign of William and Mary (1688–1702) if not earlier. On account of the considerable wear and tear to which they were subject not many have survived in reasonable condition. As a result they tend to be rather expensive; a pair of figures representing a boy and girl in the dress of about 1690 were sold at Christie's in 1968 for 190 guineas, while a similar pair of about 1720 made 130 guineas.

READING
Small Antique Furniture, Bernard and Therle Hughes (Lutterworth)
Dummy Board Figures, Amoret and Christopher Scott (Golden Head Press)

TO VIEW
National Army Museum, Camberley. Wilberforce House, Hull.

Electro-plate

Strictly any metal deposited on another by means of electric current is electro-plate, although, from the collector's viewpoint, this usually means a deposit of silver or gold on base metal. It was in 1840 that Elkington's patented their process for electro-plating and thereby put an end to the popularity of Sheffield plate as a cheap substitute for silver. Electro-plate was used extensively for flatware (cutlery), tea pots, coffee pots and dishes and vessels of all kinds. Nowadays an alloy of copper and nickel is thus treated with a deposit of silver, hence the mark EPNS (electro-plated nickel silver) stamped on it. Beware of imitation hallmarks on such pieces.

READING
Electro-plating, Field & Weill (Pitman)
Modern Electro-plating, W Hughes (Lutterworth)

TO VIEW
Victoria and Albert Museum, London. City Museum, Hereford. City Museum, Sheffield. Windsor Castle, Windsor. City Museum and Art Gallery, Worcester.

DEALERS
N Bloom and Son Limited, 15 Norton Folgate, Bishopsgate, London E1. Bond Street Silver Galleries, 111–112 New Bond Street, London W1. William Walter Antiques Limited, Chancery House, Chancery Lane, London WC2. L A Kaitcer Limited, 89 Dublin Road, Belfast. Kingsbury Antiques, 59 Ship Street, Brighton, Sussex. Fyfe's Antiques, 6 Ballantyne Road, Edinburgh. J Freeman, 83 Herent Drive, Ilford, Essex. M Kemp, 89–91 Derby Road, Canning Circus, Nottingham. J Feather, 120 Gledhow Valley Road, Leeds 17. Cottage Antiques, 52 Northam Road, Southampton. Jefferies Antiques, The Ivy House, 36 High Street, Stevenage, Herts. Nell Gwynn's House, 5 Church Street, Windsor.

Embroidery

Fine needlework patterns on fabric have been recorded since the dawn of history. Unfortunately few examples in fine condition have survived from periods earlier than the 17th century and for all practical purposes the bulk of the embroidery seen today was produced during the 19th and early 20th centuries. Hand embroidered articles worth looking for include samplers, cushion covers, firescreens, tidies (mats placed on table tops and dressers) and antimacassars. Once neglected but now much in demand are examples of Berlin work, named not for the city from which they emanated but from the Berlin print-seller who introduced the designs to the United Kingdom. Berlin work was an early form of mechanical weaving which simulated the embroidery formerly done so painstakingly by hand.

READING
Linen Embroideries, C Campbell (Pitman)
Byzantine Tradition in Church Embroidery, P Johnstone (Tiranti)
Greek Island Embroidery, P Johnstone (Tiranti)
History of English Embroidery, B Morris (H.M.S.O.)
Victorian Embroidery, B Morris (Jenkins)

TO VIEW
London Museum, London. Victoria and Albert Museum, London. Waddesdon Manor, Aylesbury. City Museum and Art Gallery, Bristol. Gawthorpe Hall, Burnley. National Museum of Wales, Cardiff. Royal Scottish Museum, Edinburgh. Museum and Muniment Room, Guildford.

DEALERS
A Arditti, 12b Berkeley Street, London W1. Corner Cupboard, 14 Pierrepoint Arcade, London N1. S Franses, 71–3 Knightsbridge, London SW1. Mayorcas Limited, 38 Jermyn Street, London SW1. Perez Limited, 112 Brompton Road, London SW3. Chas

Woollett and Son, The Stratford Gallery, 59–61
Wigmore Street, London w1. John Bell, 56–58
Bridge Street, Aberdeen. Joyce Cherrington Anti-
ques, Malmesbury, Wilts. Quality Wood, Cropley
Grove, Ousden, Newmarket, Suffolk. Katherine
Christophers, Kings Mill, Painswick, Glos. Peter
Westbury, Ripon, Yorks.

Etagère

The French term for a whatnot or tier of open shelves
supported by posts. They vary from simple tiers in
walnut or mahogany, to those richly decorated with
ormolu.

TO VIEW
Windsor Castle, Windsor.

CLUB
Furniture History Society, Victoria and Albert
Museum, London sw1.

DEALERS
Spink and Sons Limited, King Street, St James,
London sw1. Halls Antiques, Ash Priors, Nr Taunton,
Somerset. Leslie Davey Antiques, Bangor, North
Wales. Trevor Antiques, 14–15 Ship Street, Brighton.
Hill Mayo Antiques, The Malt House, 59 Market
Place, Henley-on-Thames.

Etuis

These small cases containing scissors, needles, and other accessories for the sewing table or reticule were fashionable in the 18th and early 19th centuries. They vary considerably from plain leather ones to elaborately chased and ornamented silver cases, and they were a favourite subject with the enamelled box-makers of Battersea and Bilston. The best of them were produced before 1780. Thereafter they were mass produced in great quantities and sold as souvenirs as well as for purely utilitarian purposes. Prices vary from about £10 for a 19th century étui to several hundreds for a Battersea enamel.

READING
Battersea Enamels, E Mew (Medici)
All Kinds of Small Boxes, John Bedford (Cassell)
Silver Boxes, Eric Delieb (Jenkins)

TO VIEW
London Museum, London. Victoria and Albert Museum, London. Art Gallery and Museum, Brighton. National Museum of Wales, Cardiff. Royal Scottish Museum, Edinburgh. City Museum, Sheffield. City Museum and Art Gallery, Stoke-on-Trent. Windsor Castle, Windsor.

DEALERS
Antiques Corner Limited, 104 Mount Street, London W1. N Bloom and Son Limited, 39 Albemarle Street, London W1. Jill Lewis, 27 Stanhope Gardens, London SW7 (by appt. only). Tessiers Limited, 26 New Bond Street, London W1. Staplegrove Lodge Antiques, Taunton, Somerset. Richard H Everard, Woodhouse Eaves, Nr Loughborough, Leicester.

Façon de Venise

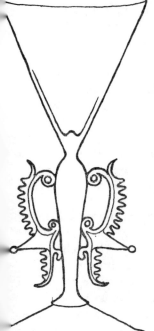

Literally "style of Venice", this term describes a type of glass-making which the Venetians introduced to France and the Low Countries in the 16th century. Vases and jugs were popular objects for this Venetian treatment, characterised by decorative exrescences known as raspberry or strawberry prunts. It was extensively copied down to the late 19th century and is now much in demand with collectors again. It was also produced in this country under the self-explanatory name of "Stourbridge Venetian".

READING
English Table Glass, P Bate (Newnes)
Glass Through the Ages, E B Haynes (Penguin)
Glass: A World History, F Kampfer and K G Beyer (Studio Vista)
Glass, G. Savage (Weidenfeld and Nicholson)

TO VIEW
Guildhall Museum, London. Victoria and Albert Museum, London. Royal Scottish Museum, Edinburgh.

CLUB
The Glass Circle, 50a Fulham Road, London sw3.

DEALERS
W G T Burne Limited, 11 Elystan Street, London sw3. Arthur Churchill Limited, Marjorie Parr Gallery, 285 King's Road, London sw3. Spink and Son Limited, 5–7 King Street, London sw1.

Façon de Venise, mid
17th century

Famille rose, verte, noire and jaune

The rose, green, black and yellow families are the somewhat misleading terms used to denote groups of Chinese porcelain, distinguishable by their transparent enamel glaze. The earliest of these was famille rose, produced during the Ming period and recognisable by its rosy tinge and slight "orange-peel" texture. Genuine pieces of famille rose ware are now exceedingly rare and highly priced.

Almost 40 years elapsed after the Ming dynasty was overthrown by the Manchus before Chinese ceramics made a come-back. During the reign of K'ang Hsi (1662–1722) the Imperial porcelain factory at Ching-te Chen began producing famille verte ware. The green family includes two shades of green, a coral pink, a bright yellow and a distinctive shade of purple known as aubergine. The glaze itself has a rather bluish tinge.

When the enamel was applied to black-outlined designs painted direct on the unglazed porcelain the result was known as famille noire. This technique in green, yellow or aubergine enamels gave a startling result and led the way to the gorgeous deep greens and greenish blacks which distinguish this "family".

Ornaments such as birds (usually parrots), human figures, lions, pagodas and horses were produced during the reigns of K'ang Hsi and his successors. Small sweetmeat dishes with attractively enamelled animals and flowers are still fairly plentiful, though prices for famille verte, noire and jaune have increased five-fold since the Second World War.

READING

Chinese Porcelain, Antony de Boulay (Weidenfeld & Nicholson)
Later Chinese Porcelain, Soame Jenyns (Faber)

TO VIEW
British Museum, London. Percival David Founda-
tion of Chinese Art, London. Victoria and Albert
Museum, London. Royal Pavilion, Brighton. City
Museum and Art Gallery, Bristol (Rose, Verte &
Noir). National Museum of Wales, Cardiff (Rose &
Verte). Royal Scottish Museum, Edinburgh. Central
Museum and Art Gallery, Northampton (Rose &
Verte). County Museum, Stafford (Rose & Verte).
City Museum and Art Gallery, Stoke-on-Trent
(Rose & Verte). Windsor Castle, Windsor.

CLUB
The Oriental Ceramic Society, 31b Torrington
Square, London WC1.

DEALERS
Bluett and Son, 48 Davies Street, London W1.
John Day Limited, 53 Buckingham Court, Kensing-
ton Park Road, London W11. Gordon Hand and Co,
18 Chepstow Mansions, Westbourne Grove, Lon-
don W2. David Newbon, 56 Beauchamp Place,
London SW3. Sydney Moss Limited, 51 Brook
Street, London W1. John Sparks Limited, 104 Mount
Street, London W1. Jacob Stodel Antiques, 172
Brompton Road, London SW3. J Vandekar, 138
Brompton Road, London SW3. Andrew Dando,
4 Wood Street, Queen Square, Bath, Somerset.
Denys Cowell, 60 Middle Street, Brighton. Collins
& Clark, 81 Regent Street, Cambridge. F C Dixon,
54 Bridgegate, Retford, Notts. Michael Brett, Picton
House, Broadway, Worcester.

Fans

Although it has been deduced, from paintings in particular, that fans were in use in European society from the Middle Ages at least, only a handful have survived which can be attributed to the period before 1700. The earliest fans were rigid pieces, not unlike table tennis bats in shape and composed of feathers sewn on to net stretched over a fine wire frame with a wooden or ivory handle. The more compact folding fan, thought to have been introduced from the Far East at the beginning of the 16th century by Portugese traders, rapidly ousted the rigid type and had completely superseded it by the time of the Restoration.

The earliest folding fans seem to have been decorated fairly simply, with geometric designs and formal patterns. By the beginning of the 18th century fan leaves were being covered with realistic pictures, court scenes and landscapes. The materials used varied from fine parchment, to silk or thick paper. The sticks, blades, "outers" and handles may be found in all kinds of wood, while ivory, mother-of-pearl and tortoise shell were not uncommon. Although the best fans were hand-painted, printed fan leaves were invented in England by 1720. Most of these were badly executed and rather cursorily painted, but, on account of the fact that they were never meant to last, they are comparatively rare and priced accordingly. Though poor artistically, they have an immense appeal for the social historian, with their prints of contemporary places, events and personalities. Fan leaves depicting balloons in flight appeared in the 1790s and are particularly sought after. The Italians produced fans decorated with post-Renaissance frescoes and relics of Pompeii, as souvenirs of the Grand Tour. 19th century fans are generally poorer in workmanship, but even they are becoming harder to find as the demand increases.

READING
The Fan Book, M Percival (Allen & Unwin)
The History of the Fan, W Rhead (Kegan Paul)

TO VIEW
London Museum, London. Victoria and Albert Museum, London. Waddesdon Manor, Aylesbury. Royal Scottish Museum, Edinburgh. City Museum, Hereford. Temple Newsam House, Leeds. Central Museum and Art Gallery, Northampton. Museum and Art Gallery, Reading. Blithfield, Rugeley, Staffs. Salisbury and South Wiltshire Museum, Salisbury. City Museum and Art Gallery, Stoke-on-Trent. Elizabethan House, Totnes. Royal Tunbridge Wells Museum and Art Gallery, Tunbridge Wells. City Museum and Art Gallery, Worcester.

CLUB
The Costume Society, Department of Textiles, Victoria and Albert Museum, London sw7.

DEALERS
Cross Street Antiques, Leiston, Suffolk.

Firearms curiosa

This term is used to embrace combinations of firearms with other objects. The best-known examples of firearms curiosa consist of rapiers, daggers, swords or staves which have a pistol cunningly incorporated in them. Howard Ricketts, in *Firearms*, illustrates a Bible with a pair of Italian flintlock pistols set into its covers in the early 19th century. Pistols built into pipes, statuettes and even fountain pens have not been unknown.

Such firearms were seldom efficient as such, the difficulty in sighting and aiming being obvious. But what they lacked in accuracy they no doubt made up with their element of surprise.

READING
Firearms, Howard Ricketts (Weidenfeld and Nicholson)
Firearms Curiosa, L Winant (H Jenkins)

TO VIEW
London Museum, London. Victoria and Albert Museum, London. Windsor Castle, Windsor.

CLUB
Arms and Armour Society, 40 Great James Street, Holborn, London WC1.

DEALERS
E Fairclough Limited, 25 Conduit Street, London W1. Geoffrey Kenyon-May, Green Acre, Broad Oak, Newnham-on-Severn, Glos. Leonard Metcalfe, 5 Lord Street, Southport, Lancs.

Fire backs

Cast iron fire backs served a dual role: to protect the brickwork from cracking in excessive heat and to reflect as much of that heat as possible back into the room. Many of these fire backs, since they graced the fire places of the nobility and the landed gentry, are embellished with coats of arms or heraldic emblems. The *nouveau riche* of the time, who had not yet acquired a grant of arms, had to make do with biblical or allegorical subjects. Fire backs were popular from Tudor times right down to the end of the 19th century when more modern and more efficient forms of room heating were introduced.

Late 18th century fireback, with firedogs in position

READING
The English Fireplace, L A Shuffrey (Batsford)

TO VIEW
Hampton Court, London. Victoria and Albert Museum, London. Waddesdon Manor, Aylesbury. Art Gallery and Museum, Brighton. Royal Scottish Museum, Edinburgh. City Museum, Hereford. The Museum, Horsham. Museum and Art Gallery, Leicester. Anne of Cleves House, Lewes. Central Museum and Art Gallery, Northampton. Salisbury and South Wiltshire Museum, Salisbury. City Museum, Sheffield. City Museum and Art Gallery, Stoke-on-Trent. Royal Tunbridge Wells Museum and Art Gallery, Tunbridge Wells. City Museum and Art Gallery, Worcester. Snowshill Manor, Broadway, Worcester. Windsor Castle, Windsor.

DEALERS
J Crotty and Son Limited, 157 Greyhound Road, London w6. The Old Metalcraft Shop, 194 Brompton Road, London sw3. Period Metals, 25–27 Chalk Farm Road, London nw1. H W Poultner, 158 Fulham Road, London sw10. Eversley Galleries, Dorchester-on-Thames, Oxon. George Wright Limited, Rotherham, Yorks. Dunnings Antiques, St Albans, Herts.

Fireplaces

In this age of builders' redevelopments when old country houses are being pulled down to make way for new housing estates, fireplaces of the past are becoming more and more plentiful, though at a price. At one time they could be picked up at give-away prices from builders' yards or demolition sites, but nowadays the demand for them is such that quite high prices are asked and paid. A good example of a Regency marble fireplace now costs over £100, while fine fireplaces in the Adams style of a generation earlier are rather more expensive. At the same time the various accessories which go with the fireplace are also in great demand. Fire dogs (intended to support the huge logs formerly burned in country fireplaces) in cast or wrought iron, often highly ornamented, are worth looking out for in pairs. Andirons, found in wrought iron with copper, brass or even silver mounts, stood at the fire side and supported the pokers, tongs, brushes and ash pans which are, of course, collectable items in themselves. Grates, trivets and fenders are all worth seeking out.

READING

English Fireplaces, Alison Kelly (Country Life)
Iron and Brass Implements of the English House, J S Lindsay (Tiranti)
The English Fireplace, L A Shuffrey (Batsford)

TO VIEW

Geffrye Museum, London. London Museum, London. Victoria and Albert Museum, London. Wallace Collection, London. Waddesdon Manor, Aylesbury. Museum and Art Gallery, Brighton. Royal Pavilion, Brighton. Royal Scottish Museum, Edinburgh. City Museum, Hereford. Temple Newsam House, Leeds. Museum and Art Gallery, Leicester. Central Museum and Art Gallery, Northampton. County Museum,

Stafford. City Museum and Art Gallery, Stoke-on-Trent. Elizabethan House, Totnes. Windsor Castle, Windsor.

Firescreens

These objects were once an indispensable feature of the drawing room, in the days of roaring log fires which gave out a fierce heat. Firescreens, as their name implies, were placed in front of the fire to screen the occupants of the room from scorching or the effects of exposure to the intense heat.

They vary considerably in size, from the large cheval glasses to the diminutive but elegant pole screens, in materials used, from wood, glass and papier maché to metals of different kinds. Glass firescreens were often embellished with pictures painted on them or laid on in embroidery, while, at one time, Victorian young ladies used to cover glass screens with the new-fangled postage stamps. Many a Penny Black or Twopence Blue was irremediably damaged in this way!

READING
Nineteenth Century English Furniture, E Aslin (Faber)

Early Victorian Furniture, A Bird (Hamish Hamilton)
Victorian Furniture, F Roe (HMSO)
Victorian Furniture, R B Symonds and B B Whinnery
(Country Life)

TO VIEW
Victoria and Albert Museum, London. Wallace
Collection, London. Waddesdon Manor, Aylesbury.
The Royal Pavilion, Brighton. City Museum and Art
Gallery, Birmingham. City Museum, Hereford.
Museum and Art Gallery, Leicester. Temple Newsam
House, Leeds. Central Museum and Art Gallery,
Northampton. City Museum, Sheffield. City Museum
and Art Gallery, Stoke-on-Trent. Elizabethan House,
Totnes, Devon. Windsor Castle, Windsor.

DEALERS
Most antique furniture dealers.

Food warmers

Sotheby's sale at Gleneagles in the summer of 1968
contained an unusual item described as a whiskey
still. Closer inspection of this tall contraption in
Wedgwood cream ware, however, revealed it to be a
veilleuse, a contrivance used for heating the gruel fed
to invalids a century or more ago. It consisted of a tall
two-handled stand containing a bowl and cover, with
an aperture beneath for a lamp to provide the heat.
These food warmers were manufactured in the 18th
and 19th centuries in many different materials, from
procelain and cream ware to enamelled metal. Similar
vessels, but with a bottle superimposed instead of a
gruel bowl, were produced by Wedgwood as tea-
warmers, in the days when people appreciated strong,
stewed tea.

More modern food warmers come in a wide variety of shapes depending on their function, from patent egg warmers to portable hot plates and spoon-warmers. They are delightful relics of the days when it was a long walk from the kitchen to the dining room. Many of them, of course, are still perfectly serviceable.

TO VIEW
British Museum, London. Geffrye Museum, London. Wallace Collection, London. Art Gallery and Museum, Brighton. Royal Pavilion, Brighton. Royal Scottish Museum, Edinburgh. Temple Newsam House, Leeds. Museum and Art Gallery, Leicester. Central Museum and Art Gallery, Northampton. Salisbury and South Wiltshire Museum, Salisbury. City Museum, Sheffield. County Museum, Stafford. City Museum and Art Gallery, Stoke-on-Trent. Wedgwood Museum, Stoke-on-Trent. City Museum and Art Gallery, Worcester.

Garden furniture

This category covers a wide range of subjects, from wrought iron chairs, tables and benches to stone urns, sundials and balusters. Old wheelbarrows and even butter-churns have been converted into containers for flowers and plants. Nearer the present time I have seen the steel helmets of two World Wars painted and converted into hanging baskets for flowers!

Among the heavy items are statuary, stone mounting blocks and granite corner posts. Corn stones, used for hand-grinding corn, also make attractive ornaments.

(See also Implements)

READING
Decorative Wrought Iron Work in Great Britain,
R Lister (Bell)

TO VIEW
Victoria and Albert Museum, London. Blithfield,
Rugeley, Staffs. Also most stately homes.

DEALERS
Angel Antiques, 116–118 Islington High Street, London N1. T Crowther and Son Limited, 282 North End Road, Fulham, London SW6. W R Harvey and Co Limited, 69 Chalk Farm Road, London NW1. Mallett at Bourdon House Limited, 2 Davies Street, London W1. The Old Clock House, High Street, Ascot, Berks. Elizabeth White – George Hume, 45 Upper North Street, Brighton. Michael Brett, Picton House, Broadway, Worcs. Stanley Blanchard, Greatham House, Brookley Road, Brockenhurst, Hants. Victor Mahy Limited, The Close, Broughton, Hants. G Oliver and Sons, St Catherine's House, Portsmouth Road, Guildford, Surrey. H and C M T Cotton, Ellerslie House, Hawkhurst, Kent. Crowther of Syon Lodge, Isleworth, Middlesex. Armstrong Antiques, Long Melford, Suffolk. Dunning's Antiques, 58–62 Holywell Hill, St Albans, Herts. Manor Antiques, 43 Hoddesdon Road, St Margarets, Herts. Old Curiosity Shop, South Walsham, Norfolk. Wyatt of Worcester, The Barn, Hawford, Worcester, Worcs.

Glass

As one of mankind's most versatile creations, found in every part of the world from the dawn of history onwards, it would be impossible to give even a brief survey in a book of this nature. Listed below are a number of books, both general and specialised, which treat the subject in some detail.

READING
General
Glass, E Dillon (Methuen)
The Collector's Dictionary of Glass, E M Elville (Spring Books)
Glass Through the Ages, E B Haynes (Penguin)
Glass: A World History, F Kampfer and K G Boyer (Studio Vista)
Old Glass and How to Collect it, J S Lewis (Laurie)
Glass, G Savage (Weidenfeld & Nicolson)
Collecting Old Glass, J H Yoxall (Heinemann)

British Glass
British Table and Ornamental Glass, L M Angus (Butterworth)
How to Identify English Drinking Glasses and Decanters, D Ash (Bell)
English Table Glass, P Bate (Newnes)
English Crystal Glass, John Bedford (Cassell)
History of Old English Glass, F Buckley (Benn)
English Glass, S Crompton (Ward, Lock)
The Country Life Book of Glass, Frank Davis (Country Life)
English and Irish Glass, F Davis (A Barker)
English Table Glass, E M Elville (Country Life)
Old English Glasses, A Hartshorne (E Arnold)
English, Scottish and Irish Table Glass from the 16th Century, G B Hughes (Batsford)
Old Irish Glass, G Stannus (Connoisseur)
A History of English and Irish Glass, W A Thorpe (R Hale)

Art Nouveau Glass
Louis C Tiffany; Rebel in Glass, R Koch (Crown Pubs, USA)

TO VIEW
Bethnal Green Museum, London. British Museum, London. Guildhall Museum, London. London Museum, London. Victoria and Albert Museum, London. Wallace Collection, London. Haworth Art Gallery, Accrington (Tiffany Glass). Victoria Art

Gallery, Bath (Bohemian Glass). Ulster Museum, Belfast (Irish Glass). Art Gallery and Museum, Brighton. Royal Pavilion, Brighton. National Museum of Wales, Cardiff. National Museum of Ireland, Dublin (Irish Glass). National Museum of the Antiquities of Scotland, Edinburgh. Royal Scottish Museum, Edinburgh. City Museum, Hereford. Museum and Art Gallery, Leicester. Central Museum and Art Gallery, Northampton. Salisbury and South Wiltshire Museum, Salisbury. City Museum, Sheffield. County Museum, Stafford. City Museum and Art Gallery, Stoke-on-Trent. Windsor Castle, Windsor. City Museum and Art Gallery, Worcester. Snowshill Manor, Broadway, Worcester.

CLUB

The Glass Circle, 50a Fulham Road, London sw3.

DEALERS

W G T Burne Limited, 11 Elystan Street, London sw3. Arthur Churchill Limited, Marjorie Parr Gallery, 285 Kings Road, London sw3. Cecil Davis Limited, 3 Grosvenor Street, New Bond Street, London w1. Delomosne and Son Limited, 4 Campden Hill Road, London w8. Richard Dennis, 144 Kensington Church Street, London w8. Thomas Goode and Co, 19 South Audley Street, London w1. A Henning, 61 George Street, Portman Square, London w1. H W Newby, 130c Brompton Road, London sw3. Marjorie Parr Galleries, 285 Kings Road, London sw3. Leslie S Scott, Halkin Arcade, London sw1. Spink and Son Limited, King Street, St James, London w1. Alan Tillman Antiques, 6 Halkin Arcade, Motcomb Street, London sw1. J Vandekar, 138 Brompton Road, London sw3. R Wilkinson and Son, 11 High Street, Wimbledon Common, London sw19. Vyse Millard, The Mill Stream, Old Amersham, Bucks. Charles Angell, 34 Milsom Street, Bath. Hazel James' Antiques, Bodmin, Cornwall. Grace Doyle, 9–10 Union Street, Brighton, Sussex.

Glass paperweights

Although credit for inventing glass paperweights must go to the Venetians, who revived the Egyptian art of glass mosaics known as millefiori, the French undoubtedly raised it to a fine art. These enchanting glass globes, with their delicate and intricate patterns, have been made in Britain also and indeed their manufacture is continued to this day by Ysart of Perth in Scotland and Powells of Wealdstone, Essex.

From the collector's viewpoint the most desirable paperweights are those which were produced at three French factories in the middle of the 19th century. The esteem in which the glass weights of St Louis, Baccarat and Clichy are held is justified on account of their superlative workmanship, vivid colouring and intricate designes. The millefiori (literally 'thousand flowers') patterns were built up of short lengths of bundles of glass canes laid on a bed plate. Each bundle might contain anything from six to fifty canes and up to one hundred bundles would comprise the 'set-up' of a paperweight with an average diameter of three inches. Various motifs other than florets were often incorporated – featuring animals, insects or dancing figures.

Although scattered patterns were the most popular, other types of millefiori were used. Comparatively rare are the mushrooms on which the central tufts of millefiori are surrounded by concentric bands entwined in a latticed pattern. Other types are known as sulphides or incrustations, in which a cameo portrait of some celebrity was incrusted in the glass. Millefiori may also be found arranged in a serpentine pattern; these "snakes" were a speciality of the St Louis factory and are exceedingly rare. Other types include bouquets and overlays, the latter having windows ground and polished into the sides and top of the globe. Few French weights bear an identifying mark and they have also been extensively imitated in more recent years, so a great deal of skill and

(b) 17th century green glass paperweight

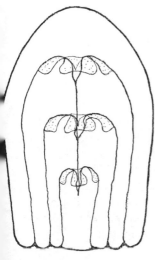

(a) Millefiori glass paperweight, Italian, 17th century

experience is required in the collecting of glass paper-weights.

READING

Paperweights, John Bedford (Cassell)
Old Glass Paperweights, E H Bergstrom (Faber)
Paperweights and Other Glass Curiosities, E M Elville (Spring Books)
French Crystal Paperweights, Imbert and Arnic
Antique French Paperweights, P Jokelson

TO VIEW

Victoria and Albert Museum, London. Art Gallery and Museum, Brighton. City Museum and Art Gallery, Bristol. Royal Scottish Museum, Edinburgh. Willmer House Museum, Farnham, Surrey. Littlecote House, Hungerford. Museum and Art Gallery, Leicester. Scone Palace, Perth. Pilkington Glass Museum, St Helens, Lancs. City Museum, Sheffield. City Museum and Art Gallery, Worcester.

CLUBS

The Glass Circle, 50a Fulham Road, London sw3. Paperweight Collector's Association, 47 Windsor Road, Scarsdale, New York, U.S.A.

DEALERS

Richard Dennis, 144 Kensington Church Street, London w8. Lories Limited, 89b Wigmore Street, London w1. Marjorie Parr Galleries, 285 Kings Road, London sw3. Alan Tillman, 6 Halkin Arcade, Motcomb Street, London sw1. J & E D Vandekar, 138 Brompton Road, London sw3. R E Porter, 2–4 Post Office Road, Bournemouth. John Fileman, Ravenscroft, 4 Powis Villas, Brighton.

Glass paste cameos

These exquisite gems owe their origin to James Tassie, a Scotsman who was employed in 1763–6 by Dr Henry Quinn of Dublin in research into vitreous substances. Quinn and Tassie perfected a white enamel composition which the latter afterwards used to cast wax portraits modelled from the life. In 1766 Tassie moved to London where he speedily won a reputation for his glass plaste cameos. Many of his earlier items were sold by Wedgwood though subsequently Wedgwood employed his own artists and, in fact, this firm specialise in glass paste cameos to this day.

In the earliest examples only the heads and busts were executed in vitreous paste, being afterwards mounted on backgrounds of glass which were tinted by placing coloured papers beneath them. Later, however, Tassie succeeded in perfecting the technique of casting the portrait and background in one piece. Sometimes a porcelain-like colour and surface were obtained; other cameos show the yellow tone and peculiar markings of time-mellowed ivory; yet others reproduce the delicate veining of marble.

Although the finest glass paste cameos were produced by Tassie, he had his imitators, both in his lifetime and afterwards. Few of them have ever matched the quality and excellence of his medallions. Genuine Tassie cameos range in price from about £20 to over £1,000, depending on quality and the subject portrayed. Glass paste cameos by other artists are generally available for smaller sums, while many comparatively modern items can be picked up for a pound or two.

TO VIEW

British Museum, London. Victoria and Albert Museum, London. Pilkington Glass Museum, St Helens, Lancs.

DEALERS
Asprey and Co Limited, 165/169 New Bond Street, London W1. Cameo Corner, 26 Museum Street, London WC1. Mayflower Antiques, 5 St Christopher's Place, London W1. S J Phillips Limited, 139 New Bond Street, London W1.

Glass pictures

There are several categories of glass picture. The most expensive kind consisted of a form of transfer printing on glass. Mezzotints were stuck on the glass and the paper subsequently removed. The remaining outline was then coloured and varnished over and the glass mounted and framed with the image on the reverse side. This was painstaking work and the resultant pictures were expensive to produce and consequently rather costly today.

Less ambitious were those glass pictures in which a design was painted by hand on to the reverse side and then framed. Examples of this type have been produced from the 17th century onwards only, and were popular in the Far East as well as Europe right down to the present time.

A third type of glass picture consists of a montage of coloured tinsel and silver paper which is pressed on to the glass and then framed, usually with a black surround and passe partout edging.

TO VIEW
Victoria and Albert Museum, London. Royal Pavilion, Brighton. City Museum and Art Gallery, Bristol. Royal Scottish Museum, Edinburgh. Museum and Art Gallery, Leicester. Central Museum and Art Gallery, Northampton. Pilkington Glass Museum, St Helens, Lancs. City Museum and Art Gallery, Stoke-on-Trent.

Glass toys

Tiny figures, novelties and ornaments made of clear or opaline glass come under the heading of glass toys. Originally they were produced as a side line by glass blowers to earn their beer money and were sold as trinkets and souvenirs. Latterly, however, their manufacture has been carried on as a full time occupation and at the present day they form no inconsiderable part of the glass industry. Nowadays the majority of glass toys consist of animals and birds – deer, swans, rabbits, dogs and ducks – and very attractive they look when set on a sheet of mirror on a shelf.

At one time, however, a much wider range of glass toys was produced. Miniatures of Cinderella's famous slipper were a prime favourite, but tobacco pipes, hats, miniature walking sticks and bells were also turned out in great profusion. This latter category, popular in Victorian times, is greatly sought after today and becoming increasingly hard to find.

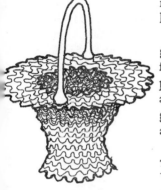

TO VIEW
Victoria and Albert Museum, London. Pilkington Glass Museum, St Helens, Lancs. City Museum, Sheffield.

Glass toy - glass basket of the mid 19th century

Goss china

William Henry Goss founded the Falcon Pottery at Stoke-on-Trent some time between 1858 and 1862. Although he manufactured the usual pieces in porcelain and also produced parian ware figures he is best remembered for his small china novelties embellished with the coats of arms of cities and boroughs of Britain. The firm was renamed the Goss China Company in 1934 when it was taken over by Cauldron Potteries, but ceased production ten years later.

Goss armourial china was very popular before the Second World War as souvenirs of holidays and visits to places of interest. Many a home boasted a china cabinet filled with these small ornaments. After a couple of decades in oblivion they are now coming back into favour with collectors, filled, perhaps, with nostalgic memories of prewar seaside holidays which these mementoes so often represented.

Many other potteries, of course, imitated Goss but to him goes the honour of having bestowed his name on this peculiar type of ornament. As yet, however, only items bearing the marks of the Goss factory are regarded with interest by collectors. They are quite plentiful and can be found in almost any antique or junk shop at prices from a shilling or two upwards.

TO VIEW
Art Gallery and Museum, Brighton. Museum and Art Gallery, Derby. Salisbury and South Wiltshire Museum, Salisbury. City Museum and Art Gallery, Stoke-on-Trent. Royal Tunbridge Wells Museum and Art Gallery, Tunbridge Wells.

DEALERS
Almost any antique or junk shop.

Horse brasses

These popular brass ornaments originated in the amulets or charms worn by horses to ward off the "evil eye". Although ornaments of this sort were known in Classical times they did not become fashionable in

Britain till the end of the 18th century when several hundred distinctive designs were evolved. Agricultural symbols such as the plough and wheatsheaf, were very popular. Many of these incorporate emblems derived from armourial bearings; others allude to contemporary personalities. Royal events, such as coronations and jubilees were also commemorated. Among the more recent brasses are those portraying Sir Winston Churchill and Field Marshal Montgomery.

Early brasses were hand-beaten from latten and can be identified by the tell-tale hammer marks on the reverse. Cast brasses were introduced in the 1830s. Many of the earliest of these were produced in calamine brass, recognisable by its pitted surface. Cast brasses can be identified by the marks of the small studs on the back by which they were held in the vice for finishing and polishing. During the last century brasses were die stamped from rolled spelter brass and should not be confused with modern reproductions which are comparatively thin, machine-made pieces of little value to the collector.

READING

Horse Brasses, G Hartfield (Abelard Shumann)
Horse Brasses and Other Small Items for the Collector, G Bernard Hughes (Country Life)

Horse brass

TO VIEW

London Museum, London. Victoria and Albert Museum, London. Blaise Castle Folk Museum, Bristol. National Army Museum, Camberley. City Museum, Hereford. Transport Museum, Hull. Central Museum and Art Gallery, Northampton. Pitt Rivers Museum, Oxford. City Museum, Sheffield. Somerset County Museum, Taunton. Castle Museum, York.

DEALERS

The Curio Shop, 21 Shepherd Market, London W1. Josephine Grahame-Bellin, St Albans, Herts. The Lion Galleries, Rye, Sussex. Temeside Antiques, 55/57 Teme Street, Tenbury Wells, Worcs. The Quarter Jack Antiques Limited, 6 Cook Row, Wimborne Minster, Dorset.

Icons

The word "icon" is derived from the Greek *eikon* meaning an image, and is applied to small pictures which were intended either to be hung in churches separating the nave from the sanctuary, or borne in procession on religious festivals and holidays. To the believer the icon was no mere adornment but came to be invested with something of the divinity or sancitity of the personage depicted on it.

Icons are peculiar to the Greek Orthodox Church and may be found in churches, chapels and even private houses, wherever the Church or its branches held sway. Experts classify icons according to whether they are Greek, Russian, Bulgar or Asiatic Byzantine. They may be found all over the Orthodox world from the Balkans to the Caucasus, from Cyprus to the Baltic.

Icons vary considerably in style, appearance and material used. They were often painted on small wood panels and portrayed individual saints or allegorical scenes of a religious nature. Others were extravagantly decorated with inlays of precious metals, ivory and jewels.

An outbreak of iconoclasm in Russia in the 1650's was followed by the need for replacements in large numbers and from this period date the purely metal icons, usually in bronze or brass, which were mass-produced from moulds. Such icons are difficult to date since the moulds were often used till fairly recent times.

Collectors should beware of reproductions consisting of coloured lithographs which have been varnished over and mounted on wood to give the appearance of the real thing. Icons of this sort did serve a genuine need, for the poor who could not afford anything better, but they are of little value to the collector.

1. A very fine George II gold teapot; made in 1736 by James Ker of Edinburgh as a royal race prize. It was sold at Christie's in London in 1967 for £40,000; 120 years previously it was bought from a London silversmith by the Rothschild family for £70.

2. Florentine bronze
stallion of early 16th
century, mounted on a
marble base.

3. A Charles II plain
silver porringer, London
1683. Maker's mark, E.G.

4.   Louis XV gold snuff box, 1736; $2\frac{3}{4}$ inches wide.

5.   Miniature portrait in engraved gold frame, painted by John Smart in 1794, of Major-General Sir Barry Close, Bt.

6. Louis XV ormolu mount bearing Chinese porcelain figure of a Li-t'ieh-po. 9¼ inches high.

7. Louis XV ormolu and Meissen porcelain (by J. J. Kandler) candelabra.

8. 18th century Chinese export porcelain bowl, finely painted with English sailing ships, with a pair of 18th century Chinese porcelain horses, rare and unrecorded.

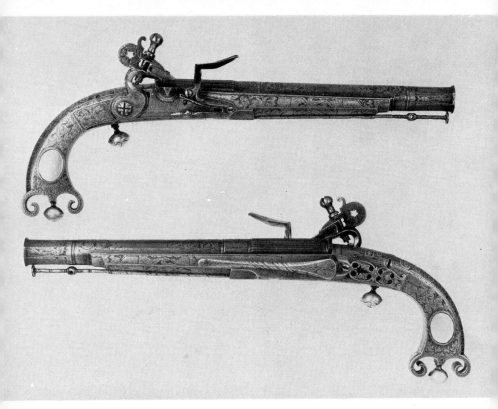

9. Mid 18th century
pair of Scottish flintlock
pistols, made by Thomas
Cadell.

10. A Baccarat magnum
flat bouquet paperweight.

11. A rare astronomical
compendium of diptych
form, made in 1575 by
Ulrich Schniep.

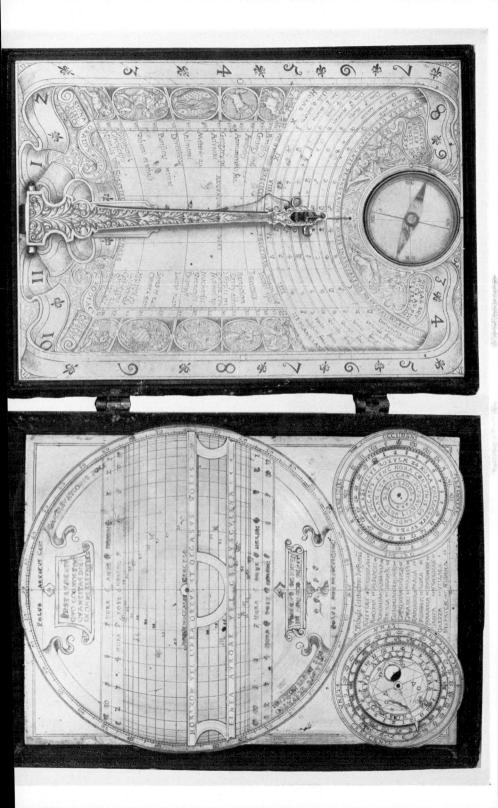

12.   Fine pair of Giles–decorated blue glass decanters.
11 inches high.

13.   Fine 18th century sapphire and diamond spray brooch.

14. Sung Dynasty pale
celadon jade carving of a
Mongolian pony.

15. Painted fan with
tortoiseshell sticks;
circa 1665–1675.

16.   Louis XV ormolu
mounted Chantilly
porcelain Chinoiserie
Cartel clock, made by
Estienne Le Noir,
dated 1740.

17.   One of a pair of early Meissen blue and white double
gourd vases. 20½ inches high.

18.   A very fine pair of Paris porcelain vases in the manner
of Jacob Petite, *circa* 1850.

19. Mid 18th century
carved and painted
wooden doll.

20. *Left to right:* Heavy
baluster wine glass;
Large engraved baluster
wine glass; Fine engraved
opaque twist goblet and
cover; Fine baluster
wine glass.

21. 17th century
Flemish crucifix group
in ivory and
tortoiseshell.

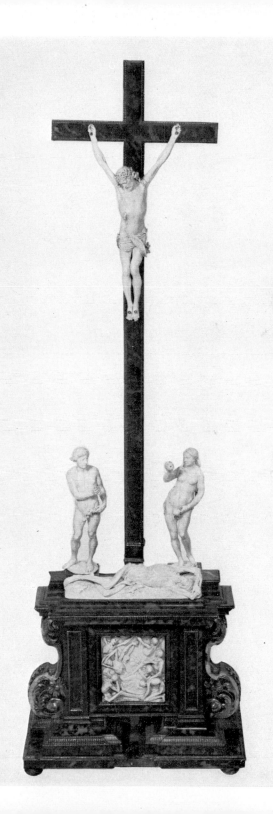

22. Louis XV ormolu and Chinese (K'ang Hsi) celadon
potpourri bowl and cover; 16½ inches high.

READING
Byzantine Icons, T Talbot Rice (Faber)
Icons, Tamara Talbot Rice (Hamlyn)
Icons, H Skrobuche (Oliver)
Russian Icons, Tamara Talbot Rice (Spring Books)

TO VIEW
Victoria and Albert Museum, London. Art Gallery
and Museum, Brighton. City Museum, Sheffield.

DEALERS
Bowater Gallery Limited, 63a Kensington Church
Street, London w8. Temple Gallery, 4 Yeoman's
Row, London sw3.

Implements

With more and more of England's green acres disappearing under the bulldozer of the property
developer – it seems paradoxical that greater interest
should be shown in the past ways of agriculture. In a
bid to save some record of past agricultural methods
many counties and districts have been establishing
museums devoted to obsolete farm implements and
this, in turn, has stimulated interest in collecting such
mundane objects. Sickles and scythes, pitch-forks and
rakes are increasingly things of the past as farming
becomes more highly mechanical. There is something
oddly appealing about the harness and saddlery of the
Shire horses who have now been superseded by the
ubiquitous tractor. Further afield you may light upon
a *cas chrom* or foot plough, such as was used till
recently (and may still be in use in some remote
areas) in the Hebrides. Granite quern-stones, used for
hand-grinding corn may occasionally be seen propped

up against the doorways of cottages – making a most
effective rustic decoration. It is surprising to note the
wide divergence in styles of implements from one
county to another and you may prefer to collect the
regional variants of one type of implement, or
alternatively, collect all the different kinds of implements found in a particular county or district. Auction sales of farms and farm equipment often bring to
light some surprising relics – even such grim items as
gin-traps and man-traps from the bad old days of the
Game Laws. Most country antique shops have a few
oddments in the way of agricultural implements in
stock.

TO VIEW
London Museum, London. Museum of Welsh
Antiquities, Bangor. Art Gallery and Museum,
Brighton. Blaise Castle Folk Museum, Bristol.
National Museum of Antiquities of Scotland,
Edinburgh. Royal Scottish Museum, Edinburgh.
Almony Museum, Evesham. City Museum, Hereford.
Museum, Keighley. Museum and Art Gallery,
Leicester. Central Museum and Art Gallery, North-
ampton. Pitt Rivers Museum, Oxford. English Rural
Life Museum, Reading. Salisbury and South Wilt-
shire Museum, Salisbury. City Museum, Sheffield.
County Museum, Stafford. Elizabethan House,
Totnes. Royal Tunbridge Wells Museum, Tunbridge
Wells. City Museum and Art Gallery, Worcester.

Inro

This Japanese word signifies a small flat box which
was used as a receptacle for medicines, writing
materials or tobacco, and which was suspended by
cords from the sash of the kimono worn by both

sexes. It was often composed of two, three or more compartments neatly fitted together. Inro are found in wood, lacquer-ware, ivory or bone, either relatively plain and devoid of decoration, or beautifully inlaid with precious metals and exquisitely engraved and carved. Prices for inro vary from about £20 upwards, depending on the quality and complexity of the ornamentation.

READING

ABC of Japanese Art, J F Blacker (S Paul)
Japanese Handicrafts, Yuzuro Okada (Probsthain)
Handbook of Japanese Art, Noritako Tsuba (Allen & Unwin)

TO VIEW

British Museum, London. Victoria and Albert Museum, London. City Museum and Art Gallery, Bristol (comprehenseive collection). Royal Scottish Museum, Edinburgh. City Museum and Art Gallery, Stoke-on-Trent.

DEALERS

J Harounoff Limited, 180 Kensington Church Street, London w8. Gordon Lawrence, 38 Conduit Street, London w1. S Marchant and Son, 120 Kensington Church Street, London w8. Tortoishell and Ivory House Limited, 24 Chiltern Street, London w1. William Williams, The Dolls House, 27a Kensington Church Street, London w8. Douglas J K Wright, 11 Piccadilly Arcade, London w1.

Ivory

This attractive material, from the tusks of elephants, has been widely used in the carving of ornaments and for inlaid work all over Asia and Africa and, in more recent years, in Europe. Much so-called ivory is, however, made from the tusks of seals and narwhals, while bone is frequently carved and polished to resemble ivory. In the latter category come the interesting pieces such as chess-sets and model ships which were carved by French prisoners of the Napoleonic Wars.

READING

Ivory, O Beigberger (Weidenfeld & Nicholson)
English Ivories, M H Longhurst (Putnam)
Early Christian Ivories, J. Nathansan (Tiranti)
Chinese Ivories, Sassoon (Country Life)
The Book of Ivory, C. G. Williamson (Muller)
Ivory, G Wills (Arco)

TO VIEW

British Museum, London, Courtauld Institute Galleries, London. Victoria and Albert Museum, London. Wallace Collection, London. Art Gallery and Museum, Brighton. City Museum and Art Gallery, Bristol. National Museum of Wales, Cardiff. Royal Scottish Museum, Edinburgh. The Wernher Collection, Luton Hoo. Pitt Rivers Museum, Oxford. Scone Palace, Perth. City Museum, Sheffield. Graves Art Gallery, Sheffield. City Museum and Art Gallery, Stoke-on-Trent. Windsor Castle, Windsor. Bantock House, Bantock Park, Wolverhampton.

DEALERS

E Fairclough, 25 Conduit Street, London W1. J Harounoff Limited, 180 Kensington Church Street, London W8. Gerald Kerin Limited, 9 Mount Street, Berkeley Square, London W1. Gordon Lawrence, 38 Conduit Street, London W1. S Marchant and Son,

120 Kensington Church Street, London w8. Tortoishell and Ivory House Limited, 24 Chiltern Street,
London w1. William Williams, The Dolls House,
27a Kensington Church Street, London w8.

Jackfield ware

A black glazed earthen ware which takes its name
from the village of Jackfield in Shropshire. It seems
to have been first produced about the middle of the
18th century, though pottery of this type may well
have been produced elsewhere at an earlier date.
Jackfield ware was also manufactured at other
potteries in the north Midlands in the latter half of
the 18th century and it is still fairly plentiful in the
form of crockery and decorative items.

TO VIEW
Victoria and Albert Museum, London. Royal
Scottish Museum, Edinburgh. Central Museum and
Art Gallery, Northampton. Salisbury and South
Wiltshire Museum, Salisbury. City Museum and Art
Gallery, Stoke-on-Trent.

CLUB
The English Ceramic Circle, 8 Church Row, London
NW3.

DEALERS
Antique shops with a general stock of pottery.

Jacobite glasses

Designed for toasting the health of "the king over the water" – ie: the Stuart monarch in exile after the Bloodless Revolution of 1688 – the so-called Jacobite glasses are now in tremendous demand by collectors.

They were produced in the 18th century both before and after the great rebellion of 1745–6. Most highly prized are those with a portrait of the Young Pretender, Bonnie Prince Charlie, engraved on the bowl. Others have verses of the Jacobite Anthem; those concluding with the word "Amen" are known as Amen Glasses and are particularly sought after. The commonest types merely show the Jacobite emblem of a rose with two buds. Prices for genuine Jacobite glasses range from about £50 for the rose glasses to over £1,000 for the more ornate portrait and Amen glasses.

On account of their popularity, however, these glasses have been extensively forged in recent years. Points to watch for are the pontil work on the underside of the base where the glass was held during blowing. Genuine glasses show a small jagged lump where the pontil rod was broken off. For this reason also the base of the genuine glasses should be slightly raised. Flat bases without a pontil mark indicate modern reproductions. The glass should also exhibit the clear lustrous quality of early English flint glass while the bowl, being hand blown, should exhibit slight irregularities.

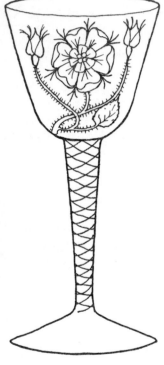

Jacobite cordial glass of the mid 18th century

READING

Scottish and Jacobite Glass, J A Fleming (Jackson)

TO VIEW

London Museum, London. Victoria and Albert Museum, London. City Museum and Art Gallery, Bristol. Royal Scottish Museum, Edinburgh. Glynde Place, Lewes. Pilkington Glass Museum, St Helens, Lancs. Salisbury and South Wiltshire Museum,

Salisbury. City Museum, Sheffield. Snowshill Manor, Broadway, Worcester. The Yorkshire Museum, York.

CLUB
The Glass Circle, 50a Fulham Road, London sw3.

DEALERS
W G T Burne Limited, 11 Elystan Street, London sw3. Arthur Churchill Limited, 285 Kings Road, London sw3. Howard Phillips, 11a Henrietta Place, London w1. John Fileman, Ravenscroft, 4 Powis Villas, Brighton. J Hutton, 108 High Street, Berkhamsted, Herts.

Japanned furniture

Lacquered furniture was introduced to Western Europe from the Far East in the second half of the 16th century. The dark glossy appearance of such pieces was a refreshing contrast to the dull, massy furniture of the period and it was not long before lacquer ware was being imitated in the Low Countries and England.

The art of lacquering, practised in Japan, was a fine art calling for a great deal of skill and patience. The basis for oriental lacquer consisted of ground-varnishes of various colours derived from the sap of the *rhus vermicifera*. Each coat was allowed to dry for several weeks and anything up to three years might be spent on lacquering a single piece of furniture.

Western imitators were hampered by lack of the proper materials, though shellac provided a reasonable substitute. The drying processes were enormously speeded up, no more than a day being allowed for the drying out of each coat. Inevitably, "japanning" as this process was known, failed to achieve the brilliant lustre and durability which characterised the oriental lacquer.

After the publication in 1688 of *A Treatise on Japanning and Varnishing* by John Stalker and George Parker, the practice of japanning furniture became a popular pastime in England. Japanned furniture decorated with gilt chinoiserie was all the rage from 1690 till 1720. It revived briefly from 1790 till 1820. Furniture from the later period is not so good technically or artistically, the decoration being often stencilled mechanically. European lacquer work is easy to distinguish from the oriental, by the fine lines of engraving which cover the former. Small chests in European japanning can still be found for £30–£50 but larger pieces such as sideboards and cabinets can run into thousands of pounds.

READING
Chinese and Japanese Lacquer, John Bedford (Cassell)
Pontypool and Usk Japanned Wares, W D John (Ceramic)
A Treatise on Japanning and Varnishing, J A Stalker (Tiranti)

TO VIEW
Geffrye Museum, London. Victoria and Albert Museum, London. Wallace Collection, London. Royal Pavilion, Brighton. Temple Newsam House, Leeds. Newport Museum and Art Gallery, Monmouth. Windsor Castle, Windsor.

CLUB
The Furniture History Society, Victoria and Albert Museum, London.

DEALERS
Most specialists in antique furniture.

Jasper ware

Josiah Wedgwood conducted a series of experiments in the early 1770's and eventually evolved what he, somewhat loosely, described as 'a white porcelain *bisque* of exquisite beauty and delicacy'. It is in fact a fine, close-grained stoneware, dense and hard enough to withstand polishing and capable of being stained throughout with metallic oxides in delicate shades ranging from yellow, green and olive to lavender and blue. Jasper ware has been a speciality of the Wedgwood factory from 1774 to the present day.

READING
Wedgwood Jasper Wares, John Bedford (Cassell)
Wedgwood, Wolf Mankowitz (Spring Books)

TO VIEW
Victoria and Albert Museum, London. Museum and Art Gallery, Birmingham. National Museum of Wales, Cardiff. Royal Scottish Museum, Edinburgh. Central Museum and Art Gallery, Northampton. City Museum and Art Gallery, Nottingham. Lady Lever Art Gallery, Port Sunlight. City Museum, Sheffield. City Museum and Art Gallery, Stoke-on-Trent. Spode-Copeland Museum and Art Gallery, Stoke-on-Trent. Wedgwood Museum, Stoke-on-Trent. Windsor Castle, Windsor.

DEALERS
Peerage Antiques, 29 Thayer Street, London W1. Alfred Spero, 4 Park Mansions Arcade, London SW1. Tunnicliffe's Antiques, 17 Broad Street, Hanley, Stoke-on-Trent. Joseph Clough, Cleckheaton, Yorks. Also most dealers in antique pottery and porcelain.

Jet

This fine black stone, capable of taking a high polish, was once in great demand by the sombre Victorians for use as mourning jewellery – the sole concession to ornament allowed following a bereavement. The singer Adeline Patti, however, had a penchant for jet jewellery and her frequent use of it at all times helped to popularise it for ordinary wear. Necklaces, bracelets and brooches in jet were despised and neglected till fairly recently, but current fashions for white lace blouses and black skirts have brought it back into vogue again.

READING
English Victorian Jewellery, E Bradford (Spring Books)
Victorian Jewellery, M Flower (Cassell).

TO VIEW
British Museum, London. London Museum, London. Victoria and Albert Museum, London. Royal Scottish Museum, Edinburgh. City Museum, Hereford. Museum and Art Gallery, Leicester. City Museum, Sheffield. City Museum and Art Gallery, Stoke-on-Trent. City Museum and Art Gallery, Worcester.

DEALERS
Cameo Corner Limited, 26 Museum Street, London WC1. Carrington and Co Limited, 130 Regent Street, London W1. J S Phillips Limited, 139 New Bond Street, London W1.

Jewellery

Of all the tangible expressions of wealth jewellery is probably the oldest as well as the most widespread. It has a twofold purpose, both for ornament and as a convenient means of carrying one's worldly goods in compact form. Rings and brooches from tombs and graves have survived in remarkably good condition though thousands of years old, but for all practical purposes we can only consider jewellery from the late 17th century onwards, when designs and styles appeared which would be deemed wearable today. Scarcity, coupled with wearability, is at its height when 18th century pieces are considered – yet this is the period which seems to be the most underpriced today.

The best of Victorian jewellery is already very expensive, although there is a vast amount of second-rate material available which the discriminating collector would do well to avoid.

Also highly regarded, especially on the Continent, are examples of iron jewellery produced in Germany from about 1813 to 1850. They originated during the war of liberation when patriotic citizens traded in their jewellery of gold and silver and wore iron trinkets instead.

READING

Jewellery, John Bedford (Cassell).
English Victorian Jewellery, E Bradfield (Spring Books).
Four Centuries of European Jewellery (Country Life).
Investing in Antique Jewellery, Richard Falkiner (Barrie and Rockliffe).
Victorian Jewellery, Margaret Flower (Cassell).

TO VIEW

British Museum, London. London Museum, London. Victoria and Albert Museum, London. Wallace Collection, London. Waddesdon Manor, Aylesbury. Bowes Museum, Barnard Castle. Art Gallery and

Museum, Brighton. National Army Museum, Camberley. National Museum of the Antiquities of Scotland, Edinburgh. Royal Scottish Museum, Edinburgh. City Museum, Hereford. Museum and Art Gallery, Leicester. Wernher Collection, Luton Hoo (15th and 16th century). Central Museum and Art Gallery, Northampton. Museum and Art Gallery, Rotherham. City Museum, Sheffield. City Museum and Art Gallery, Stoke-on-Trent. City Museum and Art Gallery, Worcester. Museum and Art Gallery, Worthing.

DEALERS

Cameo Corner Limited, 26 Museum Street, London WC1. Carrington and Co Limited, 130 Regent Street, London W1. P G Dodd and Son Limited, 42 Cornhill, London EC3. Garrard and Co Limited, 112 Regent Street, London W1. Harris Limited, 5 Hatton Gardens, London EC1. Levy Antiques, 10 Hatton Gardens, London EC1. The London Silver Vaults, Chancery Lane, London WC2. Mayflower Antiques, St Christopher's Place, London W1. S J Phillips Limited, 139 New Bond Street, London W1. The Treasure House, Holburn Street, Aberdeen. Willow Tree Antiques, Amersham, Bucks. Antiques and Crafts, Tanderagee, County Armagh, N. Ireland. The Snuff Box, Newtown Road, Bishop's Stortford, Herts. Bernard Walsh Limited, 11 St Michael's Row, Chester. F R Cooper and Son, Culver Street, Colchester, Essex. P D & S Solden, 65 Mabgate, Leeds 9, Yorks. The Antique Shop, 12 Exchange Street East, Liverpool. Raymond Warren, 54 Ramshill Road, Scarborough, Yorks. Robinson and Co Limited, 9–10 The Square, Shrewsbury, Shrops. Wolseley Bridge Antiques, Wolseley Bridge, Staffs. Bernard Edinburgh, 4 St Mary's Street, Stamford, Lincs. Temeside Antiques, Tenbury Wells, Worcs. C H Thorpe, Uppingham, Rutland. Bowes Antiques, Utley, Yorks. J Shepherdson, 33 Flowergate, Whitby, Yorks.

Jig-saws

Originally known as dissected puzzles, jig-saws were invented in the second half of the 18th century. Far from being mere playthings they were intended as educational aids, primarily for the teaching of history and geography. Maps and tables of kings and queens were among the most popular subjects. They were comparatively expensive when new, half a guinea being the average price for jig-saws sold by John Wallis in the 1780s and, as a result, few of them are in existence today. Bearing in mind the wear and tear from youthful fingers and the unfortunate tendency for pieces to go astray it is, in fact, amazing that any 18th century jig-saws have survived intact. These interesting relics of the nursery and schoolroom of yesteryear now fetch very high prices when they make their infrequent appearance in the sale-room.

In the 19th century biblical and moral subjects of an "improving" nature were prime favourites for jig-saws. The true jig-saw in the modern sense did not appear till the end of the 19th century when improved techniques in the manufacture of plywood, together with better machinery for cutting the wood, led to the adoption of the familiar interlocking pattern. Earlier puzzles had pieces cut in undulating lines rather than in the irregular tongue and groove pattern used today.

While the antique puzzles, carefully mounted on cedar or mahogany, are definitely worth having as collectors' pieces it is doubtful whether the same will ever be said about the cheap, mass-produced puzzles of today.

READING

London Museum Catalogue of the Exhibition "200 Years of Jig-Saw Puzzles", with a Historical Introduction by Linda Hannas.

TO VIEW

London Museum, London. Victoria and Albert Museum, London. Museum and Art Gallery,

Leicester. Central Museum and Art Gallery, North-
ampton. City Museum, Sheffield. Royal Tunbridge
Wells Museum and Art Gallery, Tunbridge Wells.
City Museum and Art Gallery, Worcester.

DEALERS
Petersfield Bookshop, Petersfield, Hants. Also
country salerooms and antique shops specialising in
Victoriana.

Kakiemon

The introduction of an indigenous porcelain industry
to Japan was due to Korean immigrants working in
the Kutani area in the early 17th century, but the best
known porcelains developed somewhat later, at the
other end of the country, in the island of Kyusha
where suitable clays for porcelain were discovered
about 1616, a date which coincided with the arrival
of a potter named Kakiemon (1596–1666) in the
village of Arita. He is thought to have discovered the
distinctive red overglaze in 1640, though some
experts maintain that this was more likely to have
happened during the time of his son (circa 1660–90).

Kakiemon ware can be recognised by the delicate
application of overglaze decoration in green, blue or
black as well as red, on that flawless milky white
porcelain known as *nigoshide*. Favourite motifs were
the rose, cherry-blossom, prunus, phoenix and deer,
but it is in the vigorous use of the enamel overglaze
that the style is seen at its most distinctive, while blue
and white underglaze was also a feature of Kakiemon
porcelain.

Much of the Kakiemon pieces which are to be
found consist of tableware – cups, bowls, platters and
sweet-meat dishes. Relatively scarce are such items

as candle-sticks and figures. Prices vary from over
£1,000 for early Kakiemon figures to £20–£30 for
small sweet-meat dishes of early 19th century vintage.

TO VIEW
British Museum, London. Victoria and Albert
Museum, London. City Museum and Art Gallery,
Bristol. National Museum of Wales, Cardiff. Royal
Scottish Museum, Edinburgh. City Museum and Art
Gallery, Stoke-on-Trent. Blenheim Palace, Wood-
stock.

CLUB
Oriental Ceramic Society, 31b Torrington Square,
London WC1.

DEALERS
Gordon Hand and Co, 18 Chepstow Mansions,
Westbourne Grove, London W2. David B Newbon,
56 Beauchamp Place, London SW3. Rodney W Lytle,
222 Old Christchurch Road, Bournemouth. Denys
Cowell, 60 Middle Street, Brighton. Collins &
Clark, 81 Regent Street, Cambridge. W R Cam-
bridge and Sons, 145 Bath Road, Cheltenham Spa,
Glos. Duncombe House, Bilsborrow, Preston, Lancs.

Knife boxes

These curiously shaped boxes, containing apertures
into which knives could be slotted, are a reminder of
the days when cutlery was expensive and jealously
guarded. Knife boxes were fitted with strong lids
which could be locked when not in use, as a precau-
tion against theft of the contents. Knife boxes vary
in style, decoration and materials employed in their

Mahogany knife box with silver mounts, 1785

construction. Some are made in plain polished walnut or mahogany; others are richly inlaid with marquetry. Others were produced in japanned tinware with intricate designs painted on them. Boxes in original condition are now scarce, since many of them had their linings removed to convert them into writing cases.

READING
Small Antique Furniture, Bernard and Therle Hughes (Lutterworth).
Pontypool and Usk Japanned Wares, W D John (Ceramic).

TO VIEW
London Museum, London. Victoria and Albert Museum, London. Royal Pavilion, Brighton. Royal Scottish Museum, Edinburgh. Temple Newsam House, Leeds. Museum and Art Gallery, Leicester. Central Museum and Art Gallery, Northampton. Salisbury and South Wiltshire Museum, Salisbury. City Museum, Sheffield. City Museum and Art Gallery, Stoke-on-Trent.

Lace

Although primitive cut and drawn work has been found in the tombs of the Pharaohs at Thebes, lace as we know it today was a medieval European invention. At some date in the 15th century Continental seamstresses evolved a system of working with the needle-point "in the air" (hence the term *punta in aria* which described the working over and connecting of patterns of thread in a geometric fashion on a parchment base which could then be cut away when the work was completed).

The earliest form of point lace was Reticella, produced in the convents of Italy. From this developed Needlepoint which became very popular all over Europe in the 17th century. A parallel development was Pillow Lace which is thought to have originated in Flanders. The Venetians brought lace-making to France in the 1580s and the Huguenot refugees took the art to England at the beginning of the 17th century. Many of these lace workers settled in Devon, and Honiton lace is still regarded as the finest produced in Britain. Lace-making spread to Ireland in the mid-19th century, being introduced as a cottage industry to alleviate unemployment. Carrickmacross became renowned as a centre for fine *appliqué* lace.

The production of lace was long and tedious and so it was very expensive. By the beginning of the 20th century most lace was being made by machine while the austerity measures of the First World War killed the fashion for lace. Interest in old lace has been maintained by a dedicated few, but there are signs that the general market is reviving, with a corresponding upward trend in prices.

READING

An Introduction to Lace, Gabrielle Pond (Garnstone Press).
The Romance of Wool, Lace and Pottery Trades in Honiton, Coxhead (Coxhead).
A History of Handmade Lace, F N Jackson (Upcott Gill).

TO VIEW

London Museum, London. Victoria and Albert Museum, London. Waddesdon Manor, Aylesbury. City Museum and Art Gallery, Bristol. Royal Scottish Museum, Edinburgh. City Museum, Hereford. Public Museum, Honiton. Museum and Art Gallery, Leicester. Central Museum and Art Gallery, Northampton. City Museum and Art Gallery, Nottingham. Pitt Rivers Museum, Oxford. Salisbury and South Wiltshire Museum, Salisbury. City Museum and Art Gallery, Stoke-on-Trent. Elizabethan House, Totnes. City Museum and Art

Gallery, Worcester. Art Gallery and Museum, High Wycombe.

DEALERS
A Arditti, 12b Berkeley Street, London w1. Royal School of Needlework, 25 Princes Gate, London sw7. Vigo Art Galleries, 6a Vigo Street, London w1.

Lace bobbins

Lace bobbins were used to hold the threads in lace-making at the right tension. Anything from a dozen to several hundred bobbins were required, depending on the size and intricacy of the lace being worked. They were used from the middle of the 18th century onwards. The earliest examples, known as dumps and bobtails, were fairly small and thick, with a pear-shaped shank and a thin neck to hold the thread. Later specimens were longer and slimmer and had a number of small beads attached to the foot of the shank. These spangles of beads varied very considerably, since it was necessary that the lacemaker could differentiate between the bobbins on the piece of lace.

Lace bobbins were usually made of bone or close-grained wood, boxwood, holly, beech, or fruit wood. Occasionally they are found in ivory or metal such as brass or even silver or gold.

The names given to different styles of bobbins were often quaint: those with spots on the shank were called leopards, while butterflies were bobbins with splayed wings. Plain bobbins were known as old maids and a cow-in-calf was a large bobbin with a small one inside. Many bobbins have commemorative inscriptions relating to births, marriages and deaths carved on them. Others bear interesting slogans of a political nature. Most antique and junk shops carry a stock of bobbins at prices from a few shillings to several pounds depending on the material used, the amount of decoration, and the inscription, if any.

READING
An Introduction to Lace, Gabrielle Pond (Garnstone Press).
Romance of Wool, Lace and Pottery Trades in Honiton, Coxhead (Coxhead).

TO VIEW
London Museum, London. Victoria and Albert Museum, London. Art Gallery and Museum, Brighton. Blaise Castle Folk Museum, Bristol. Royal Scottish Museum, Edinburgh. City Museum, Hereford. Museum and Art Gallery, Leicester. Central Museum and Art Gallery, Northampton. Pitt Rivers Museum, Oxford. Salisbury and South Wiltshire Museum, Salisbury. City Museum, Sheffield. City Museum and Art Gallery, Stoke-on-Trent. Elizabethan House, Totnes. Royal Tunbridge Wells Museum and Art Gallery, Tunbridge Wells.

Lamps

The collector will find a vast array of lamps and lanterns in antique and junk shops; many of them still have a functional purpose while others can be converted to electricity or are nice decorative items in themselves. Ornamental oil lamps, with painted glass shades and brass bowls are still to be picked up for £10–£50 depending on quality and age as well as condition. At the other end of the scale miners' safety lamps, in brass and steel, seem to be popular at the moment and change hands for about £3–£5. In between there are a host of different sizes, types and styles of lamps – night lights, coaching lanterns (ideal for illuminating your porch), table lamps and cut glass candelabra. Very much in demand today are the Burmese glass lamps manufactured by Thomas Webb a century ago. Rather later – and strictly outside the scope of this book since they are not antique – are the lamps produced by Louis Tiffany in America, and by Daum, Gallie and Lalique in France in that curious style known as Art Nouveau. Some very high prices have recently been paid at auctions for Art Nouveau glass table lamps moulded in the form of the dancer Loie Fuller whose version of the dance of the seven veils was a sensation at the time. These lamps contained an electric bulb which, when lit, heightened the diaphanous effect of her costume and gave the figure an ethereal quality.

READING
Small Antique Furniture, Bernard & Therle Hughes (Lutterworth).

TO VIEW
British Museum, London. London Museum, London. Art Gallery and Museum, Brighton. National Museum of Antiquities of Scotland, Edinburgh. Royal Scottish Museum, Edinburgh. City Museum, Hereford. Museum and Art Gallery, Leicester. Central Museum and Art Gallery, Northampton. Blithfield, Rugeley, Staffs. City Museum, Sheffield. City Museum and Art Gallery, Stoke-on-Trent. Windsor Castle, Windsor. City Museum and Art Gallery, Worcester.

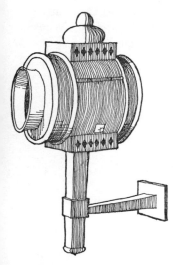
Copper lamp–1840

DEALERS
Adanac Antiques, 19 Uxbridge Street, London w8. The Chiltern Hundreds, 11 Chiltern Street, London w1. Philip Duncan, Lowndes Lodge, 28 Lowndes Street, London sw1. Robert Eldridge, 238 Brompton Road, London sw3. Michael Inchbald Limited, 10 Milner Street, Cadogan Square, London sw3. The Lacquer Chest, 75 Kensington Church Street, London w8. Mallett and Son (Antiques) Limited,

40 New Bond Street, London w1. Edward Marno, 162 Kings Road, London sw3. Owain Glyndwr Antiques, Druid House, Bala, Merionethshire. Mrs H G James, 3 Higher Bore Street, Bodmin, Cornwall. D H Llewellen, Earsham Street, Bungay, Suffolk. Causeway Antiques, 11 Market Square, Horsham, Sussex. Peter Bromley, 72 King Richards Road, Leicester. Desmond Antiques, Welford Road, Leicester. E M Cheshire, Mansfield Road, Nottingham. Leonard Metcalfe, 5 Lord Street, Southport, Lancs. The Barn, School Lane, Sprowston, Norwich.

Letter balances

Before the introduction of Penny Postage in 1840 the postage on letters was computed according to the number of sheets and the distance travelled. No account was taken of the weight of the letter till 1840 when flat rates of 1d per half ounce, irrespective of sheets and distance, were introduced. It thus became necessary to weigh letters in order to fix on the correct rate of postage. As a result a number of devices were introduced in order to weigh letters. One ingenious device consisted of a circular weight about the size of a penny attached to an arm which could be clamped to the edge of the table. At the other end the letter was held in a clip and the weight ascertained by means of a sliding scale.

More conventional balances, however, were very popular throughout the second half of the 19th century. They can often be dated according to the tables of postal rates engraved on the tray on which the letters were placed. It is essential when purchasing such letter balances to ensure that the sets of weights (usually from ¼ oz to 8 ozs) are complete.

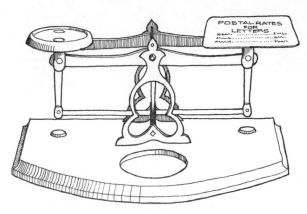

Early 20th century letter balance

TO VIEW
London Museum, London. Museum and Art
Gallery, Leicester. Central Museum and Art Gallery,
Northampton. Blithfield, Rugeley, Staffs. City
Museum, Sheffield. Elizabethan House, Totnes. City
Museum and Art Gallery, Worcester.

Locks and keys

It seems odd to think that, 150 years ago, the need for
security in the form of locks and keys was very small
– in keeping with the fact that few people had any
material possessions which were worth locking up.
The lock on a strong-box or cupboard was thus, in
itself, something of a status symbol and this explains
the workmanship and lavish decoration which was
often lavished on it. The art of the locksmith was an
exacting and intricate one, calling for great skill and
patience. Thus early locks were very costly to produce and consequently have a high antique value,
depending on the intricacy of the mechanism, and

the amount of decoration embellishing it. Mediaeval locks, and the keys that went with them, were often beautifully carved and adorned with filigree work, inlays of brass in blued steel or precious metals. Few of these are available to the collector nowadays. On the other hand early examples of the work of lock-smiths such as Hobbs and Yale in America or Jeremiah Chubb (first of a long line of this family who are still engaged in the manufacture of locks.) Combination locks are known to have existed since the early 16th century. Though mass-production has now put the lock within reach of everyone, there are still precision locks which have to be constructed by hand. Apart from metal locks there are primitive wooden locks, found all over the world from the Faeroe Islands to Egypt, which are of interest to the ethnographical collector.

READING
Locks and Keys Throughout the Ages, V M Evans (Bailey and Swinfen)

TO VIEW
British Museum, London. Guildhall Museum, London. London Museum, London. Victoria and Albert Museum, London. Wallace Collection,

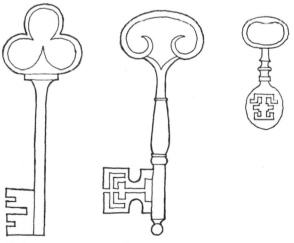

15th century, 18th century and 19th century keys

London. Blaise Castle Folk Museum, Bristol. National Museum of Antiquities of Scotland, Edinburgh. Royal Scottish Museum, Edinburgh. Gloucester City Museums. City Museum, Hereford. Museum and Art Gallery, Leicester. Salisbury and South Wiltshire Museum, Salisbury. City Museum, Sheffield. County Museum, Stafford. Windsor Castle. Snowshill Manor, Broadway, Worcester. City Museum and Art Gallery, Worcester.

DEALERS
J D Beardmore & Company Limited, 3–5 Percy Street, London W1. J H Blakey & Sons Limited, 5 Colne Road, Brierfield, Lancashire.

French 18th century cast iron lock

Longton Hall

The earliest porcelain factory in Staffordshire was established at Longton Hall in 1750 but it barely lasted a decade. Very little is known of the brief history of this factory though its wares are quite distinctive. The commoner form of porcelain manufactured at Longton Hall was somewhat crude in appearance though characterised by a comparatively translucent nature. Less usual was a fine porcelain consciously emulating Meissen in subject as well as texture. As well as useful wares Longton Hall specialised in the production of figures, the famous "snow man" figures being attributed to this factory. Though generally inferior to the products of Chelsea, Longton Hall pieces are now highly regarded by collectors.

READING
Longton Hall Porcelain, B Watney (Faber)

TO VIEW
British Museum, London. Fenton House, London. Victoria and Albert Museum, London. Art Gallery and Museum, Brighton. National Museum of Wales, Cardiff. Royal Scottish Museum, Edinburgh. Museum and Art Gallery, Leicester. Central Museum and Art Gallery, Northampton. Salisbury and South Wiltshire Museum, Salisbury. City Museum, Sheffield. City Museum and Art Gallery, Stoke-on-Trent.

NOTE—See china marks on page xx.

Loving cups

Two handled cups, usually of generous proportions, were produced as loving cups. The situation was that lovers, or just friends, drank from the same cup, each grasping the vessel by one of the handles. They are often found inscribed with sentimental mottoes and verses, or the emblem of a Masonic society. Needless to say they were produced in a wide variety of earthen ware, porcelain and even silver. For a comprehensive account of these interesting mementoes of past friendship see *Horse Brasses and Other Small Antiques* by G B Hughes which contains a chapter based on the late Clifford Chubb's collection of loving cups.

READING
Horse Brasses and Other Small Antiques for the Collector, G B Hughes (Country Life)
Small Antiques for the Collector, Therle Hughes (Lutterworth)

TO VIEW
British Museum, London. London Museum, London. Victoria and Albert Museum, London. Art Gallery and Museum, Brighton. City Museum and Art Gallery, Bristol. National Museum of Wales, Cardiff. Royal Scottish Museum, Edinburgh. Temple Newsam House, Leeds. Central Museum and Art Gallery, Northampton. City Museum, Sheffield. City Museum and Art Gallery, Stoke-on-Trent. City Museum and Art Gallery, Worcester.

Lowestoft

Soft paste porcelain was first produced in Lowestoft in 1757, simple blue-and-white ware being a speciality of the firm. Small trinkets and trifles – tea caddies, inkstands, etc., are found in this ware which, though unpretentious, has a certain attraction about it. The factory closed down in 1802. Despite claims to the contrary, the Lowestoft factory never produced hard-paste porcelain. Its wares were never highly regarded during its life time, but today its trifles and souvenirs have quite a large following among collectors, while its distinctive Oriental pieces are now in great demand.

READING
The Illustrated Guide to Lowestoft Porcelain, G A Godden (Jenkins)
Oriental Lowestoft, J A L Hyde (Ceramic)
Lowestoft China, W W R Spelman (Jarrold)

TO VIEW
British Museum, London. Victoria and Albert Museum, London, Art Gallery and Museum, Brighton. National Museum of Wales, Cardiff. Royal Scottish Museum, Edinburgh. Central Museum and Art Gallery, Northampton. Salisbury and South Wiltshire Museum, Salisbury. City Museum, Sheffield. City Museum and Art Gallery, Stoke-on-Trent.

CLUB
The English Ceramic Circle, 8 Church Row, London NW3.

DEALERS
General dealers in antique china.

NOTE—See china marks on page xx.

Lustre ware

An attempt to simulate, in earthen ware, bone china or porcelain, the sumptuous appearance of gold or silver plate, led to the production of lustre ware. Decoration was applied to the object in the form of a brilliant metallic glaze. It is interesting to note that the powdered metal used for silver lustre was in fact platinum – a metal which was disregarded until industrial uses were found for it in the mid-19th century. Copper lustre was effected by using a solution containing gold powder. Apart from articles wholly covered in plain lustre there are attractive items decorated in silver or copper "resist". This term is derived from the process of covering the article with decoration outlined in a substance which was lustre-resistant, so that when the object was subsequently immersed in the lustre solution the "resist" portions were left clear.

READING
Early Wedgwood Lustre Wares, W D John & J Simcox (Ceramic)
More Small Decorative Antiques, Therle Hughes (Lutterworth)
Old English Lustreware, J Bedford (Cassell)
Old English Lustre Pottery, W D John and W Baker (Ceramic)

TO VIEW
British Museum, London. Geffrye Museum, London. Victoria and Albert Museum, London. Haworth Art Gallery, Accrington. Art Gallery and Museum, Brighton. City Museum and Art Gallery, Bristol. Royal Scottish Museum, Edinburgh. City Museum, Hereford. Central Museum and Art Gallery, Northampton. City Museum, Sheffield. Salisbury and South Wiltshire Museum. Wedgwood Museum, Stoke-on-Trent. City Museum and Art Gallery, Stoke-on-Trent. Royal Tunbridge Wells Museum and Art Gallery.

Antiques Unlimited, Canton, Cardiff. Bown's Antique Stores, 10 Sardis Road, Pontypridd, Glamorgan.

Maiolica

Derived from Maiorca, one of the Balearic islands, this term was used to describe the vigorously coloured tin glazed earthenware introduced to Western Europe via the Hispano-Moresque wares of Spain. Maiolica is simply the name under which a popular type of pottery was known in Italy, where it was produced in the Faienza district (hence the name "faience" by which it is known in France). Maiolica was the forerunner, if not a parallel development of, the Delft ware (q.v.) popular in England and the Low Countries. It differs from Delft ware principally in its brilliant colouring, and in subject matter which favoured religious, historical or mythological scenes.

READING
Italian Maiolica, Bernard Rackham (Faber)

TO VIEW
British Museum, London. Courtauld Institute Galleries, London. London Museum, London. Victoria and Albert Museum, London. Wallace Collection, London. Waddesdon Manor, Aylesbury. Holbourne of Menstrie Museum, Bath. City Museum and Art Gallery, Birmingham. Polesdon Lacey, Dorking. Royal Scottish Museum, Edinburgh. Temple Newsam House, Leeds. Wernher Collection, Luton Hoo. Central Museum and Art Gallery, Northampton. City Museum and Art Gallery, Stoke-on-Trent.

DEALERS
Fisher Gallery Limited, 18a Duchess Mews, Mansfield Street, London W1. Newman and Newman Limited, 156 Brompton Road, London SW3.

Majolica

Great confusion is often caused in the minds of collectors over the distinction between Maiolica and Majolica. The latter was, in fact, a name devised by early 19th century English potters to describe a type of earthen ware with a thick coloured glaze which was very popular in Victorian times. The flower pots which held innumerable aspidistras in Victorian houses were usually majolica. Majolica tiling was fashionable in the latter half of the 19th century and it is surprising how much of this has survived. I have even seen some of it in the London Underground, not, like the Moscow Metro, noted for its aesthetic qualities. Majolica wares are rather neglected at the moment but, with the passage of time, they may come into fashion once more.

TO VIEW
Victoria and Albert Museum, London. Central Museum and Art Gallery, Northampton. City Museum and Art Gallery, Stoke-on-Trent. Wedgwood Museum, Stoke-on-Trent. Dyson Perrins Museum of Porcelain, Worcester.

DEALERS
Newman and Newman Limited, 156 Brompton Road, London SW3.

Maps

Cartography, the science of maps, map-making and map-collecting, is a very large collecting field, literally covering every part of the globe. Maps are of interest both for the detail they provide of places past and present, and for their aesthetic appeal which may be considerable if they are attractively coloured with ornamental detail. Map-making was practised by the Greeks, Romans and Chinese, but did not begin to emerge as an exact science till the 16th century. At a time when Continental map-makers were gradually filling in the gaps on the outline of the continents at least, English cartographers were concentrating on producing quite accurate maps of the country, county by county.

Earliest in this field was Christopher Saxton whose late 16th century maps of the English counties are now extremely scarce. A complete set is held by the British Museum which publishes facsimiles of them at low cost. The maps of Norden and Speed produced in the early 17th century and those of Robert Morden a century later are also in great demand nowadays. In the 18th century came the county maps of Bowens while the early 19th century saw the county atlas of Wood. Complete atlases are excessively rare but individual maps of counties, boroughs and towns are still fairly plentiful.

Maps of a more specialised nature include military maps, maps of railways and canal systems, postal maps showing the routing of letters and, of course, the vast fields of naval charts and surveyors' plans. Early examples of Ordnance Survey maps, introduced in 1791, are also highly desirable.

READING

Decorative Printed Maps of the 15th to 18th Centuries, R A Skelton
How to Identify Old Maps and Globes, R Lister (Bell)
Maps and Their Makers, G R Crone (Hutchinson)

Marine Cartography in Britain, A H W Robinson
(Leicester University Press)

TO VIEW
British Museum, London. Geological Museum,
London. London Museum, London. National Mari-
time Museum, Greenwich, London. Victoria and
Albert Museum, London. Museum of Welsh
Antiquities, Bangor. Borough Museum, Dartmouth.
City Museum, Hereford. Central Museum and Art
Gallery, Northampton. City Museum, Sheffield.
Salisbury and South Wiltshire Museum, Salisbury.
Central Museum and Art Gallery, Stoke-on-Trent.
Elizabethan House, Totnes. City Museum and Art
Gallery, Worcester.

CLUB
Map Collector's Circle, Durrant House, Chiswell
Street, London EC1.

DEALERS
Baynton-Williams, 70 Old Brompton Road,
London SW7. Arthur Reader, 71 Charing Cross
Road, London WC2. The Parker Gallery, 2 Albemarle
Street, London W1. Walter T Spencer, 47 Upper
Berkeley Street, London W1. Weinreb & Dowma
Limited, 39 Great Russell Street, London WC1. Woburn
Antique Galleries, 19 Market Place, Woburn, Beds.
Richard A Nicholson, 17 Chester Road, Shotton,
Cheshire. Laurence Oxley, 17 Broad Street, Alresford,
Hants. P J Radford, Furzeley Corner, Denmead,
Hants. Mrs Mary Walshaw, 4 Leopold Avenue,
Farnborough, Hants. F E Norwood Limited, 23
Holywell Hill, St Albans, Herts. Hall's Bookshop,
Tunbridge Wells, Kent. Charles Lowe & Sons,
37–40 Church Gate, Loughborough. Ian H R Cowley,
233 Mansfield Road, Nottingham. Starboard Light
Antiques, Cob Lane, Tenby, Pembrokeshire. Reigate
Galleries, 45 Bell Street, Reigate, Surrey. University
Prints, 65 High Street, Uxbridge, Middlesex. Collec-
tor's Treasures Limited, 8–9 Church Street, Windsor.

Martin ware

This distinctive type of pottery takes its name from Robert Wallace Martin who established a factory in Fulham in 1873. He and his three brothers originally concentrated on ceramic decoration, but after the firm moved to Southall in 1877 they started producing unusual stone ware figures and vases. They are primarily remembered for the grotesqueries, in the form of birds and beasts with curiously human expressions. Other bizarre items included jugs with gargoyle faces. In addition, however, many more orthodox vases and bowls were produced, all readily identifiable by the marks of R W Martin & Bros. The Martins ceased production in 1914 and their unusual wares have now come back into fashion. Prices for typical Martin ware objects are in the range from £5 to £30.

Martinware grotesque of the 1880's

READING
Catalogue of the Nettleford Collection, C R Beard (Quaritch)

TO VIEW
London Museum, London. Victoria and Albert Museum, London. Art Gallery and Museum, Brighton. Royal Scottish Museum, Edinburgh. Museum and Art Gallery, Leicester. Public Library,

Southall, Middlesex (most important collection). City Museum and Art Gallery, Stoke-on-Trent.

DEALERS
General antique shops dealing in pottery.

Match boxes

The earliest commercially produced matches of the mid-19th century were sold in nondescript tins so it is hardly surprising that ingenuity and artistry should be applied to the manufacture of ornamental containers for them. The hey-day of the decorative match box was at the end of the century though they survived as late as the First World War. These ornamental boxes were originally known as fusee or vesta boxes, such being alternative names for matches in the early days.

Match boxes came in all shapes and materials. Many of them were fashioned like birds and animals, others were round, or bottle-shaped, but the majority were produced in the more orthodox flat rectangle, not unlike modern commercial match boxes. Some of them had pictures of holiday resorts on the lids, while others served to advertise cigarettes, household commodities and consumer goods; in this respect they foreshadowed the book-matches of today.

Novelty boxes sometimes contained secret compartments to house pencils and tooth picks. Others were shaped like, and incorporated, whistles. Silver boxes seem to have survived in comparatively large quantities on account of their intrinsic value and most antique shops can produce a reasonable stock among the general bric-a-brac. The cheap novelty and advertisement boxes, which were never meant to last, are comparatively scarce, though they are just the sort of unconsidered trifle which you might be lucky enough to pick up for a song.

Match boxes were made in tin plate, brass and gun metal as well as silver, but very seldom in gold. They also exist in ivory, wood, vulcanite and even leather.

TO VIEW

London Museum, London. Art Gallery and Museum, Brighton. City Museum, Hereford. Museum and Art Gallery, Leicester. Central Museum and Art Gallery, Northampton. Salisbury and South Wiltshire Museum, Salisbury. City Museum, Sheffield. Royal Tunbridge Wells Museum and Art Gallery, Tunbridge Wells. City Museum and Art Gallery, Worcester.

Mazers

Originally these shallow vessels were small wooden bowls used throughout Europe as drinking cups in the Middle Ages. The early mazers were quite flat, without a stem, but by the mid-16th century they were being raised on stems, often elaborately ornamented in silver or even gold. Decoration was also applied lavishly to the rim and the inner side of the bowl. Wealthy families would commission the production of such mazers for special occasions and they are often found with coats of arms or commemorative inscriptions engraved on them.

The bowls of these mazers were fashioned from birds' eye maple, a wood which is spotted with tiny knots. The word "mazer" is thought to be derived from the German word *masa* meaning a spot (compare this with "measles".)

Victoria and Albert Museum, London. National Museum of Wales, Cardiff. National Museum of the Antiquities of Scotland, Edinburgh. Royal Scottish Museum, Edinburgh. City Museum, Sheffield.

Meissen

The name given to the first true European porcelain comes from the town of Meissen in Saxony where the Elector Augustus the Strong established a ceramics factory in 1710. The substitute for the costly Oriental porcelain which Augustus admired so much was discovered almost accidentally by Johann Friedrich Bottger, an alchemist employed by the Elector in the search for the philospher's stone which would transmute base metal into gold. Bottger succeeded in manufacturing porcelain of a sort in 1709 but eleven years elapsed before it was perfected to resemble the hard, translucent material invented by the Chinese. The best period of Meissen was from 1720 till 1750, when J J Kändler produced his delightful harlequinade figures based on the Commedia dell'Arte which was so popular in Western Europe at the time. Kändler's figures of Harlequin, Columbine and their companions now rank among the most expensive articles in porcelain, prices approaching £10,000 having been paid for the finest and rarest examples. The Meissen factory also specialised in the production of porcelain flowers, each leaf and petal being exquisitely moulded. The 'bread and butter work' – if it can be called that – consisted of plates and dishes, but a complete 18th century Meissen dinner service would be worth a king's ransom today. Occasional pieces, old cups and saucers etc., do turn up fairly frequently and range in price from £5 to £50, depending on condition, quality and period. Meissen ware is still being produced in East Germany and the best examples would undoubtedly have a bright prospect for the collector investing in it today. Note, however, that the crossed swords mark of Meissen has been very widely forged.

READING

Eighteenth Century German Porcelain, G Savage (Barrie & Rockliffe)

TO VIEW

British Museum, London. Victoria and Albert Museum, London. Wallace Collection, London. Waddesdon Manor, Aylesbury. National Museum of Wales, Cardiff. Royal Scottish Museum, Edinburgh. Central Museum and Art Gallery, Northampton. Scone Palace, Perth. City Museum and Art Gallery, Stoke-on-Trent. City Museum and Art Gallery, Worcester.

CLUB

The English Ceramic Circle, 8 Church Row, London NW3.

DEALERS

The Antique Porcelain Co Limited, 149 New Bond Street, London W1. Willy Lissauer, 16 Old Manor Court, 40–42 Abbey Road, London NW8. D M & P Manheim, 69 Upper Berkeley Street, Portman Square, London W1. Spink and Son Limited, King Street, St James's, London SW1. J & E D Vandekar, 138 Brompton Road, London SW3. Andrew Dando, 4 Wood Street, Queen Square, Bath. P W Gottschald, 107 Sneinton Boulevard, Nottingham. Stockman Antiques, 250 Union Street, Torre, Torquay.

Menuki, kodzuka and tsuba

The fittings on Japanese swords were highly ornate and are now regarded as collectable items in themselves. The menuki and other sword furniture were made of iron until the mid-18th century and were usually simple in design. Subsequently gold and silver inlays were occasionally used, but decoration was invariably effected by intricate engraving and etching. Sword furniture of the latter half of the 19th century became increasingly decorative.

The average Japanese sword had decorative fittings as follows: menuki (handle), kodzuka (small knife handle), tsuba (circular guard). Also included are the fuchi-cashira, or top and bottom fitments attached to the sword belt.

Prices vary from about £2 for plain menuki and tsuba to £10 for a fine 19th century tsuba. Decorative pieces, however, can cost up to several hundreds.

READING
Japanese Sword Mounts, H L Joly (Quaritch)
Handbook of Japanese Art, Nositake Tsuba (Allen & Unwin)

TO VIEW
British Museum, London. Victoria and Albert Museum, London. Acton Roundhall, Bridgnorth. Royal Scottish Museum, Edinburgh. City Museum, Sheffield. City Museum and Art Gallery, Stoke-on-Trent.

DEALERS
E Fairclough, 25 Conduit Street, London W1. Sydney L Moss Limited, 51 Brook Street, London W1. Phillips and Page Limited, 50 Kensington Church Street, London W8. Grammar Galleries Limited, Peter Street, Shepton Mallet, Somerset.

Militaria

This term is used to cover a multitude of objects, from the badges and buttons of military formations to larger equipment such as helmets, uniforms, instruments used by military bands, pennons, banners. Anything from a Roman soldier's boot to a modern anti-nuclear combat suit comes within the realms of militaria. Associated objects such as armour, weapons, medals and decorations are usually considered separately.

The field of militaria is so vast that collectors usually specialise in a particular type of object – military badges or helmets, or objects relating to a specific regiment or fighting unit. The latter method has the advantage of providing the collector with a cross-section of material. A collection of militaria relating to the "Death or Glory Boys" – the 17th/21st Lancers – would range from helmets and shakoes, sabretaches and accoutrements of the 19th century to the more prosaic equipment used by tank crews of the Second World War. Books on regimental history, medal and muster rolls, prints and pictures of famous battles, medals awarded to officers and troopers of the regiment, insignia, etc. all form part of the story.

Since the Second World War there has been a curious but strong following for items associated with the ill-starred Third Reich. The Nazis were very conscious of the glamour of smart uniforms and their trappings, and the variety of such items is so immense that Nazi militaria is now a large and important subject in itself. Prices vary from a few shillings for an Iron Cross 2nd Class to several hundred pounds for the full regalia of an SS Ibserstumbarnführer.

READING
Arms and Armour, V Norman (Weidenfeld & Nicholson)

TO VIEW
London Museum, London. H M Tower of London. Victoria and Albert Museum, London. Wellington Museum, London. Art Gallery and Museum, Brighton. National Army Museum, Camberley. Scottish United Services Museum, Edinburgh. City Museum, Hereford. Museum and Art Gallery, Leicester. Central Museum and Art Gallery, Northampton. Pitt Rivers Museum, Oxford. Salisbury and South Wiltshire Museum, Salisbury. City Museum, Sheffield. City Museum and Art Gallery, Stoke-on-Trent. Windsor Castle, Windsor. Artillery Museum, Woolwich Common. City Museum and Art Gallery, Worcester.

CLUBS

Military Historical Society, Duke of York's Headquarters, London SW3. Arms and Armour Society, 40 Great James Street, London WC1.

DEALERS

M & J Appleby, 57 George Street, London W1. Carrington and Co Limited, 27 Throgmorton Street, London EC2. Peter Dale, 12 Royal Opera Arcade, Pall Mall, London SW1. E Fairclough Limited, 25 Conduit Street, London W1. P L German, 125 Edgware Road, London W2. Norman Newton, 44 Dover Street, London W1. David Young, 104 Chepstow Road, London W2. Format Coin and Medal Co Limited, 269 Broad Street, Birmingham 1. Armoury Antiques, 47 Market Street, The Lanes, Brighton. Antiques Unlimited, 78 Cowbridge Road, Canton, Cardiff, Glam. Agincourt House, 27 Lower Street, Dartmouth, Devon. James Masterton, 93 West Bow, Edinburgh 1. Cross Bow House Antiques, High Blantyre, Lanarks. Kenneth H Trotman, 3 Ash Close, Naphill, High Wycombe, Bucks (Books on Militaria only). Highland Antiques, 8 Bridge Street, Inverness. J F Kelly, 32a Church Street, Inverness. J A Morrison (Firearms) Limited, 153 Scraptoft Lane, Leicester. P Bromley, 72 King Richards Road, Leicester. The Old Carpenters Arms, Littlebury, Essex. Kenyon-May, Green Acre, Broad Oak, Newnham on Severn. Langale Limited, 213 Mansfield Road, Nottingham. The Antiquary, 29 London

Road, Reading, Berks. John Wigington, 31 Henley Street, Stratford-on-Avon. Staplegrove Lodge Antiques, Taunton, Somerset. Two Toads Antiques, Long Street, Tetbury, Glos. The Antique Shop, Truro, Cornwall.

Miniature portraits

Miniature painting was introduced to Europe from Persia at the end of the Middle Ages, though its development can also be traced back to the illuminated manuscripts of an earlier period. One of the earliest, and greatest, of the miniaturists was Hans Holbein who produced a number of tiny masterpieces between 1532 and his death in 1543. Among his successors the outstanding artists were Nicholas Hilliard, the Olivers (father and son), John Hoskins and Samuel Cooper, but miniatures painted by them seldom fetch less than £500 nowadays. Only about six pre-1530 English miniatures exist, of which one was bought by the National Portrait Gallery for only £420 in June 1969.

Far more plentiful, however, are the miniatures produced in the 18th century. In this period the rising population, coupled with greater popularity, gave enormous impetus to the miniature "industry". A more specific factor affecting the quantity of miniatures was the custom during the French Revolutionary and Napoleonic Wars of officers having their portraits painted before going overseas. Most of the large garrison towns had at least one miniaturist who would virtually mass-produce portraits for officers. This accounts for the high incidence of uniformed gentlemen, their anonymity as undistinguished as the competence of the portraitist. These examples of hack-work can still be picked up for two or three pounds apiece.

Where the identity of either sitter or artist is known, the value of a miniature would be considerably enhanced. Most of the acknowledged works by the more important artists – Cosway, Crosse, Ingleheart, Meyer and Smart – are now in the £150–£500 range but proven works by lesser artists can be found for £40–£100. In this category come the Bones and Frederick Buck whose relatively undistinguished work is now beginning to fetch quite high prices.

READING

British Portrait Miniatures, D Foskett (Methuen)
History of the British Miniature, R Lister (Pitman)
French Miniatures, J Porcher (Collins)
English Portrait Miniatures, G Reynolds (Black)

TO VIEW

British Museum, London. London Museum, London. National Portrait Gallery, London. Victoria and Albert Museum, London. The Wallace Collection, London. Waddesdon Manor, Aylesbury. Art Gallery and Museum, Brighton. National Army Museum, Camberley. National Museum of Wales, Cardiff. National Gallery of Scotland, Edinburgh. Royal Scottish Museum, Edinburgh. City Museum, Hereford. Museum and Art Gallery, Leicester. Central Museum and Art Gallery, Northampton. Ashmolean Museum, Oxford. City Museum, Sheffield. City Museum and Art Gallery, Stoke-on-Trent. Windsor Castle, Windsor. City Museum and Art Gallery, Worcester.

DEALERS

H Deutsch, 111 Kensington Church Street, London w8. S J Phillips Limited, 139 New Bond Street, London w1. Charles Woollett and Sons, The Stratford Gallery, 59–61 Wigmore Street, London w1. D & H Llewellen, Earsham Street, Bungay, Suffolk. The Hereford Gallery, Kings Caple Court, Kings Caple, Hereford. Hare & Elyard, 48 Market Street, Hove, Sussex. Pillers, 15 Holywell Hill, St Albans, Herts. Reiss Howard, Orwell House, Swaffham, Norfolk. Sarah's Cottage Antiques, 147 Watling Street, Towcester, Northants.

Minton

This famous pottery, still in production, was founded in 1793 by Thomas Minton (1765–1836) at Stoke-on-Trent. The company has produced over the years a great amount of porcelain and pottery, both ornamental and useful wares. Specialities included the wonderful translucent porcelain of the early period (1796–1816) and majolica (q.v.) whose opaque tinglaze won praise for Mintons when it was exhibited at the Great Exhibition of 1851.

The big problem with early Minton wares is identification. Most of the Minton pottery and porcelain before about 1840 bears the mark of the retailer only or no mark at all. There is strong evidence that Thomas and his son Herbert were afraid of the retailers and therefore yielded to them on this question of marks. A great deal of early 19th century porcelain, formerly regarded and prized as Coalport, Derby, Rockingham, Spode or Worcester has hitherto been incorrectly attributed and the publication of recent research by Geoffrey Godden has led to a major re-assessment of the work of this firm. Much anonymous English porcelain of the early Victorian period, which can still be picked up in country antique shops for a song, will now be correctly ascribed – with an inevitable upgrading in the price tag.

READING

Minton Pottery and Porcelain of the First Period, 1793–1850, Geoffrey Godden (Herbert Jenkins).

TO VIEW

British Museum, London. Victoria and Albert Museum, London. Art Gallery and Museum, Brighton. National Museum of Wales, Cardiff. Royal Scottish Museum, Edinburgh. Central Museum and Art Gallery, Northampton. City Museum, Sheffield. City Museum and Art Gallery, Stoke-on-Trent. Windsor Castle.

CLUB

The English Ceramic Circle, 8 Church Row, London NW3.

DEALERS

Albert Amor Limited, 37 Bury Street, St James's, London SW1. Antique Porcelain Company Limited, 149 New Bond Street, London W1. Delomosne & Son Limited, 4 Campden Hill Road, London W8. Spink & Son Limited, King Street, St James's, London W1. Andrew Dando, Bath, Somerset.

NOTE—See china marks on page xx.

Mirrors

Looking glasses came into fashion in England after 1665 when the Duke of Buckingham founded a glass factory at Vauxhall. Previously mirrors had been imported from the Continent and were therefore very expensive. The indigenous mirror industry flourished from the end of the 17th century, though mirrors remained very costly for about a hundred years. Antique mirrors are found in a vast range of shapes, sizes and designs, from small hand mirrors to huge chimney and pier glasses. Between these extremes there are plain cushion mirrors of the early 18th century, the increasingly ornate wall mirrors of Queen Anne's time, the rococo mirrors of Early Georgian decorated with giltwood scrolls, the classic simplicity of Regency mirrors or the heavily gilded oval or circular mirrors of the end of the 18th century.

From the collector's viewpoint the most desirable mirrors are those produced up to about 1820 when the traditional method of mercury and tin-type silvering was abandoned. Old mirrors usually have comparatively thin glass and the silvering, if original,

English carved gilded mirror, 1740

has a dark lustrous quality. When the original silvering has become spotty, almost to the point of no reflection, resilvering is advisable unless the mirror is important on historical grounds. The age of a mirror is not as important as its condition and styling. Prices vary from about £20 for small Regency mirrors to over £1,000 for one by Hepplewhite, though early 18th century mirrors of the cushion type can be found for about £50.

READING
Paperweights and Other Glass Curiosities, E M Eliville (Spring Books)
Mirrors, S Roche (Duckworth)
English Looking Glasses, G Wills (Country Life)

TO VIEW
British Museum, London. Geffrye Museum, London. Victoria and Albert Museum, London. Wallace Collection, London. Waddesdon Manor, Aylesbury. Royal Pavilion, Brighton. Royal Scottish Museum, Edinburgh. Central Museum and Art Gallery, Northampton. Pilkington Glass Collection, St Helens, Lancashire. City Museum and Art Gallery, Stoke-on-Trent. Windsor Castle.

DEALERS
Asprey & Company Limited, 165–9 New Bond Street, London w1. Fernanders & Marche, 80 Islington High Street, London n1. C H Major Limited, 154 Kensington Church Street, London w8. Spink & Son Limited, King Street, St James's, London sw1. Spyer & Son Limited, 237 Earls Court Road, London sw5. Gerald Deacon, Queen Square, Bath, Somerset. Elfreda Rowley Limited, 7 East Stockwell Street, Colchester. Marjorie Quarrington Antiques, East Horsley, Surrey. A T Silvester & Sons, High Street, Warwick.

Mocha ware

This brand of pottery is distinguished by its decoration of coloured bands into which moss or fern-like effects have been introduced by means of a diffusing agent. The decoration was applied while the clay was still wet; the diffusing agent varied in formula but such bizarre ingredients as tobacco juice, printers ink, stale urine, turpentine and water were employed. This gave the decoration its somewhat feathery appearance. Mocha ware was produced from about 1780 till the First World War and was popularly known as moss-ware or tobacco spit-ware. It was particularly popular in East Anglia and was employed for measuring vessels rather than for domestic wares, though jugs and tankards are not unknown.

READING
19th Century English Pottery and Porcelain, G Bemrose (Faber)
Cottage Antiques, Therle Hughes (Lutterworth)

TO VIEW
London Museum, London. Victoria and Albert Museum, London. City Museum and Art Gallery, Bristol. City Museum and Art Gallery, Sheffield. City Museum and Art Gallery, Stoke-on-Trent.

DEALERS
Beauchamp Galleries, 8 Beauchamp Place, London sw3. Miss Fowler, 1a Duke Street, Manchester Square, London w1. Arthur West Antiques, Dawlish, Devon. Runnymede Galleries, Egham, Surrey. S M Collins, 105 Leeds Road, Ilkley, Yorkshire. Evaline Winter, Wolseley Road, Rugeley, Staffs.

Model soldiers

In about 1775 the toy makers of Nuremberg began to produce *zinn-soldaten*. The earliest soldiers were made of pure tin but gradually a greater amount of lead was added to produce a more durable material. Then soldiers were "flats" – two dimensional pieces in low relief mounted on small stands. The earliest soldiers also varied considerably in size and it was not until 1848 (the year of revolutions) that the famous manufacturer, Heinrichsen, adopted the 30 mm Nuremberg scale for his models.

The French introduced the *rond bosse* or "solid" figures about a century ago and many manufacturers, particularly Heyte of Dresden, produced vast quantities of them, mainly for the export market. The model soldier industry was revolutionised 75 years ago when William Britain of London invented a process of hollow cast, three dimensional figures. Britain has dominated the model soldier market ever since, though plastic has replaced the more traditional metal since 1966.

The early Britain soldiers had round bases, whereas the later types had rectangular mounts. Though mass produced they were of very high quality and great attention was paid to detail. Particularly prized nowadays are sets showing gun crews, balloon and winch waggon, ambulance wagon and pontoon engineers, of First World War vintage.

Several craftsmen specialise in finely detailed, hand-made soldiers which vary in price from 70s to £20 (for an infantry man or a cavalry trooper respectively). Look for the 54mm models by artists such as Courtenay, Ping, Greenwood and Ball – these could be the antiques of the future. Model soldiers have increased enormously in price, on account of the popularity of war gaming. In December 1968 the first ever auction sale of model soldiers was held by Knight Frank and Rutley – a sure sign of their acceptance in "antique" circles.

READING
War Games, Donald Featherstone (S Paul)
More War Games, Donald Featherstone (S Paul)
Model Soldiers, Henry Harris (Weidenfeld & Nicholson)

TO VIEW
Imperial War Museum, London. London Museum, London. Blaise Castle Folk Museum, Bristol. National Army Museum, Camberley. Museum and Art Gallery, Leicester. Elizabethan House, Totnes. Royal Tunbridge Wells Museum and Art Gallery, Tunbridge Wells. Blenheim Palace, Woodstock.

DEALERS
Dealers in militaria and medals.

Money boxes

Money boxes come in all shapes and sizes and range from the simple earthen ware piggy bank to the complex mechanical banks devised by the Americans as a political joke. The latter show a prosperous looking gentleman sitting in an easy chair. The inscription "Tammany Bank Halls Patent" is an ironic allusion to the figure in the chair – William Tweed, the Tammany Hall boss who gained control of New York City in the 1860s and embezzled millions of dollars before he was brought to justice in 1871. These American money boxes now fetch £20–£30, though the old fashioned "piggy" can be picked up for shillings.

Staffordshire money box in the form of a cottage, early 19th century

READING
More Small Decorative Antiques, Therle Hughes (Lutterworth)

British Museum, London. London Museum, London. Victoria and Albert Museum, London. Art Gallery and Museum, Brighton. Royal Scottish Museum, Edinburgh. Museum and Art Gallery, Leicester. Central Museum and Art Gallery, Northampton. City Museum, Sheffield. Blithfield, Rugeley, Staffordshire. City Museum and Art Gallery, Stoke-on-Trent.

Musical boxes

Musical boxes were devised by Continental clockmakers and were originally intended for incorporation in clocks and watches. From this it was a simple step to the addition of musical mechanism to other objects such as cane handles, decanters and boxes. The more elaborate boxes had mechanical figures, dancing dolls or singing birds which moved and performed in time to the music. Automata musical boxes are extremely expensive; a monkey musician seated on a musical box made 220 guineas at Christie's in 1968, while a pair of juggling clowns made £420. An ingenious landscape musical box, with a working windmill, a clock and a troop of cavalry on the move, went for the comparatively low figure of 150 guineas in the same sale.

Also classed as musical boxes are those ancestors of today's juke boxes – the nickelodeons and polyphons which rattled out the popular melodies of the time when coins were inserted in them. One occasionally sees them in old-style public houses but they are rarely found in antique shops and sale rooms.

READING

Musical Boxes: A History and Appreciation, J E T Clarke (Allen and Unwin)
Collecting Musical Boxes and How to Repair Them, A W J G Ord-Hume (Allen and Unwin)

TO VIEW

London Museum, London. Waddesdon Manor, Aylesbury. City Museum and Art Gallery (Department of Science), Birmingham. Art Gallery and Museum, Brighton. Elizabethan House, Totnes, Devon. Royal Scottish Museum, Edinburgh. City Museum, Hereford. Museum and Art Gallery, Leicester. Central Museum and Art Gallery, Northampton. City Museum, Sheffield. Blithfield, Rugeley, Staffordshire. Windsor Castle, Windsor.

CLUBS

The Musical Box Society of Great Britain, 11 Devonshire Place, London W1. Musical Box Society International, 1765 East Sudan Circle, Greenville, Mississippi, USA.

DEALERS

Camerer Cuss and Company, 54–56 New Oxford Street, London WC1. Keith Harding Antiques, 93 Hornsey Road, London N7. The Music Box Gallery, 81 George Street, London W1. R S Gordon Antiques, Main Street, Alford, Aberdeen. John E Davis, 14 Wokingham Road, Reading, Berks. W & J Turner, 22 Montpellier Walk, Cheltenham. Old Thatch Antiques, Duck Street, Cerne Abbas, Dorest. Neale Antiques, 21 & 21a Old Cross, Hertford, Herts. "55 Antiques", Spring Bank, Hull, Yorks. P Kirk, 6 and 8 Bond End, Knaresborough, Yorks. Langdale Limited, 213 Mansfield Road, Nottingham.

Musical instruments

Many volumes could be, and have been, written on this subject. The smaller instruments range from the lutes of the late medieval period (now very rare and expensive) to English guitars of the late 18th century (still to be found at around £30 or more). The early stringed instruments had names such as strump, cittern and poliphant – as quaint as the sound they produced. The best of the early 19th century guitars were made by Joseph Panomo of London, whose name may be found by looking through the sound hole at the inside of the guitar. Generally speaking only those guitars made before 1850 are considered desirable as collector's items. Other instruments worth collecting are early 19th century harp-lutes (especially those by Edward Light) and banjos (the important name to look for is Da Silva).

Among wind instruments, flutes and flageolets offer plenty of scope to the collector, ranging from the three-hole flute invented by Jean Hotteterre in the 17th century to the comparatively rare triple flageolet of Regency times. Key bugles such as the Royal Kent or the ophicleide are now in great demand; the fewer the keys the earlier and more desirable they are.

The instruments mentioned here should all be available for less than £100, though, at the other end of the scale, there are exotic items like the viola da gamba (up to £1,000) and early violins by such craftsmen as Stradivarius which can fetch several thousands.

English pedal harp, 1813/31

READING

Musical Instruments Through the Ages, A Buchner (Boosey)
Old English Instruments of Music, F W Galpin (Methuen)
Beautiful Italian Violins, K Jalopec (Hamlyn)
The Harpsichord and Clavichord, R Russell (Faber)

British Piano Museum, London. Fenton House, London. Geffrye Museum, London. Horniman Museum, London. London Museum, London. Royal College of Music, London. Victoria and Albert Museum, London. The Wallace Collection, London. Waddesdon Manor, Aylesbury. Art Gallery and Museum, Brighton. Royal Scottish Museum, Edinburgh. City Museum, Hereford. Museum and Art Gallery, Leicester. Pitt Rivers Museum, Oxford. Central Museum and Art Gallery, Northampton. City Museum, Sheffield. Blithfield, Rugeley, Staffordshire. City Museum and Art Gallery, Stoke-on-Trent. City Museum and Art Gallery, Worcester. Snowshill Manor, Worcester. Windsor Castle, Windsor.

DEALERS
J & A Beare Limited, 179 Wardour Street, London W1. Joanna Booth, 247 Kings Road, London SW3. M Ekstein Limited, 90 Jermyn Street, London SW1. William E Hill and Sons, 140 New Bond Street, London W1. E C Legg and Son, 29 Castle Street, Cirencester, Glos. L P Balmforth and Son, 31–33 Merrion Street, Leeds. A Silvester and Son Limited, Warwick Road, Solihull, Warks. David Kent, 13 Langton Road, Tunbridge Wells, Kent.

Nailsea

Although glass making was carried on at this village near Bristol in the early years of the 19th century, much of the distinctive ware which goes by this name was in fact produced elsewhere, in Bristol, Stourbridge and Birmingham. Nailsea specialised in ornamental wares produced in bottle glass rather than the more elegant clear glass which, on account of the heavy duty on clear glass, made production in this material prohibitive.

Bottles, flasks, vases and rolling pins (q.v.) were produced in this dark bottle glass, flecked or streaked with coloured enamel glass for greater decorative effect.

READING

Bristol and Other Coloured Glass, John Bedford (Cassell)
Paperweights and other Glass Curiosities, E M Elville (Spring Books)
Small Decorative Antiques, Therle Hughes (Lutterworth)

TO VIEW

British Museum, London. Victoria and Albert Museum, London. Art Gallery and Museum, Brighton. Museum and Art Gallery, Bristol. National Museum of Wales, Cardiff. Clevedon Court, Clevedon. Royal Scottish Museum, Edinburgh. City Museum, Hereford. Temple Newsam House, Leeds. Central Museum and Art Gallery, Northampton. Pilkington Glass Museum, St Helens, Lancs. Salisbury and South Wiltshire Museum, Salisbury. City Museum, Sheffield. City Museum and Art Gallery, Worcester.

DEALERS

W G T Burne Limited, 11 Elystan Street, London sw3. Arthur Churchill Limited, Marjorie Parr Gallery, 285 Kings Road, London sw3.

Early 19th century Nailsea, red and white

Nankin

Chinese porcelain, designed specifically for export to Europe in the 18th and 19th centuries, is generally known as Nankin ware, after the city from which a large amount of it was exported. Because it catered for popular demand the quality of workmanship and decoration inevitably suffered. Consequently Nankin ware used to be rejected contemptuously by the cognoscente of fine porcelain.

Nowadays, however, Nankin has a strong following of its own. Complete dinner services are now rated at a premium but individual items can still be purchased from a few shillings (for a sauce boat or cream jug) to £10–£15 for one of those massive oblong tureens for which Nankin was famous.

READING
The Later Ceramic Wares of China, R L Hobson (Benn)

TO VIEW
Victoria and Albert Museum, London. City Museum and Art Gallery, Bristol. Museum and Art Gallery, Birmingham. Gulbenkian Museum of Oriental Art and Archaeology, Durham. Central Museum and Art Gallery, Northampton. City Museum and Art Gallery, Stoke-on-Trent.

CLUBS
The Oriental Ceramic Society, 31b Torrington Square, London WC1.

DEALERS
John Day Limited, 53 Buckingham Court, Kensington Park Road, London W11. Gordon Hand and Company, 18 Chepstow Mansions, Westbourne Grove, London W2. David Newbon, 56 Beauchamp Place, London SW3. John Sparks Limited, 128 Mount Street, London W1. Andrew Dando, Bath, Somerset. Denys Cowell, 60 Middle Street, Brighton, Sussex. Michael Brett, Broadway, Worcestershire. Collins and Clarke, 81 Regent Street, Cambridge. F C Dixon, Retford, Nottinghamshire.

Needlework pictures

Probably the most famous needlework picture ever produced was the Bayeux Tapestry, recording the events surrounding the Norman Conquest. Needlework was a popular pastime with the nobility and upper classes of Europe from early times, but it did not become fashionable with the lower levels of society till the 16th century, when embroidered panels were produced for bibles and prayer books.

In the late 17th century, young ladies began embroidering pictures on cushion covers, pole fire screens and decorative panels for wall adornment. Religious scenes were a very popular subject. "Needle-painting" reached its height in the mid-18th century. Its slow decline marked the emergence of the much less complicated sampler, such as children were made to do to show that they had mastered the alphabet. In the early 19th century samplers bearing pious inscriptions and mottoes, rather than ornate pictorial designs, were produced and framed as wall ornaments. At a slightly later date, woolwork came into vogue. In this medium pictures were worked in brightly coloured yarn on open mesh canvas, but this rough, vigorous treatment cannot be compared to the fine silk on satin pictures of earlier generations.

Early needlework pictures are exceedingly scarce, but 19th century samplers can still be found – at a price.

READING

Art In Needlework, L F Day (Batsford)
English Domestic Needlework, Therle Hughes (Lutterworth)
History of English Embroidery, B. Morris (H.M.S.O.)

TO VIEW

Geffrye Museum, London. London Museum, London. Victoria and Albert Museum, London. Waddesdon Manor, Aylesbury. City Museum and Art Gallery, Bristol. County Museum, Buckinghamshire. Borough Museum, Dartmouth. Royal Scottish Museum, Edinburgh. City Museum, Hereford.

Wilberforce Museum, Hull. Museum and Art Gallery, Leicester. Glynde Place, Lewes. Central Museum and Art Gallery, Northampton. Salisbury and S. Wilts Museum. City Museum, Sheffield. City Museum and Art Gallery, Stoke-on-Trent. Elizabethan House, Totnes.

DEALERS
A Arditti, 12b Berkeley Street, London W1. Corner Cupboard, 14 Pierrepoint Arcade, London N1. S Franses, 71–3 Knightsbridge, London SW1. Mayorcas Limited, 38 Jermyn Street, London SW1. Perez Limited, 112 Brompton Road, London SW3. John Bell, Aberdeen. The Victorian Cottage, Attleborough, Norfolk. The Manor House, Lower Limpley Stoke, Bath.

Nest eggs

No – this is not a reference to one's life savings, but to a quaint type of box made in earthen ware, porcelain or even glass in the middle of the 19th century. These attractive boxes, produced mainly by the Staffordshire potteries, were intended to hold eggs. They were made in the form of a basket or nest, the lid consisting of a brooding fowl. Usually a hen is depicted, though, less commonly, other birds such as ducks, geese and swans were featured. They appear to have been produced mostly in the second half of the 19th century, and are still fairly common.

READING
Antique China and Glass under £5, G Godden (Barker)
TO VIEW
Central Museum and Art Gallery, Northampton. City Museum and Art Gallery, Stoke-on-Trent.

DEALERS
Most general dealers in antique china.

Netsuke

Netsuke (pronounced "nets'ky") is the Japanese word for a toggle (from the verb *tsuke*, to fasten). It is thought to have existed as early as the 15th century when, in the primitive form of pieces of wood or bone, toggles were used to secure a cord to the *obi* (girdle) from which were suspended a variety of objects known collectively as *koshisage* (things hanging from the waist), since pockets in the Western sense were unknown.

The toggle developed as an ornament in itself in the latter part of the 16th century. An edict of Hidetada, the second Tokugawa shogun, in 1617 making the display of Buddhist images compulsory for every household, stimulated the development of the beautiful figure netsuke known as *katabori*. The finest netsuke were carved during the Genroku era (1688–1703) which was characterized by the extravagance and opulence of the court. The final flowering of the art of netsuke came in the Bunsai period (1818–1829) and continued down to the Meiji Restoration of 1863. Increasing Western influence after that date meant a steady decline in indigenous art, though a somewhat artificial revival has taken place in recent years, the commonest being *katabori* (human figures) *jwnishi* (the twelve signs of the zodiac), and the masks derived from characters in the *Noh* drama. Wood and ivory are the materials most frequently found, but coral, amber and jade were occasionally used. Wood netsuke are usually made of boxwood. Japanese cypress was also popular but did not wear well, so cypress netsuke in good condition are hard to find. The finest craftsmen sometimes signed their netsuke and the books on the subject give copious help in identifying them. Prices of netsuke can vary from £2 to several hundreds.

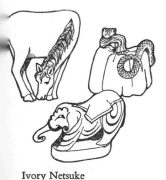

Ivory Netsuke

READING
Japanese Netsuke: Fables in Ivory, Barbanson (Prentice-Hall)

Netsuke, F M Jones (Routledge)
Netsuke: A Guide for Collectors, M L O'Brien
(Tuttle—dist: Prentice-Hall)
The Netsuke Handbook, N Reitchi (Tuttle—dist:
Prentice-Hall)
The Netsuke of Japan, E Ryerson (Yoseloff)

TO VIEW
British Museum, London. Victoria and Albert
Museum, London. City Museum and Art Gallery,
Bristol. Royal Scottish Museum, Edinburgh. Museum
and Art Gallery, Leicester. Museum of the History of
Science, Oxford. City Museum and Art Gallery,
Stoke-on-Trent.

DEALERS
John Crichton, 34 Brook Street, London w1.
J Harounoff Limited, 180 Kensington Church Street,
London w8. S Marchant and Son, 120 Kensington
Church Street, London w8. Sydney L Moss, 51
Brook Street, London w1. Tortoiseshell and Ivory
House Limited, 24 Chiltern Street, London w1.
Antiquity, 266a Charminster Road, Bournemouth.
Grammar Galleries, Peter Street, Shepton Mallet,
Somerset.

New Hall

The New Hall Pottery Company originated at
Tunstall in 1780, producing its first wares the following year. It specialised in the production of hard
paste porcelain, being one of the few potteries in
England to do so. After about 1810, however, it
concentrated on bone china. In addition the New
Hall pottery manufactured earthen ware and lustre
ware. It is particularly noted for its "sprigged muslin"

patterns but intricate painted and gilded wares were also produced. Compared with other types of early English porcelain and bone china the products of New Hall are somewhat undervalued, perhaps on account of their unfashionable appearance.

READING
New Hall Porcelain, G E Stringer (Barrie & Rockcliffe)

TO VIEW
Victoria and Albert Museum, London. Art Gallery and Museum, Brighton. National Museum of Wales, Cardiff. Royal Scottish Museum, Edinburgh. City Museum, Hereford. Central Museum and Art Gallery, Northampton. Salisbury and S. Wiltshire Museum. City Museum, Sheffield. City Museum and Art Gallery, Stoke-on-Trent.

DEALERS
Antique Porcelain Company Limited, 149 New Bond Street, London w1. Beauchamp Galleries, 8 Beauchamp Place, London sw3. Spink and Son Limited, King Street, St James, London sw1. Cothill Antiques, Kincardine O'Neill, Aberdeen. Andrew Dando, 4 Wood Street, Queen Square, Bath. Jan Struther, 13 Randolph Place, Edinburgh.

Niello

An Italian term to describe a delicate form of inlay of base metal alloy on silver, similar to damascening. A design would first be cut into the silver and the resultant grooves then filled in with an alloy of silver, copper, lead and sulphur which was fused and then highly polished. The practice probably arose in Italy during the Renaissance but eventually spread all over Europe as far as Russia. Examples of comparatively modern niello work, in the form of trays, boxes and bowls are still reasonably plentiful, though becoming increasingly expensive. A small box, for example, available a few years ago for about £5 would today cost £20 or more.

TO VIEW
British Museum, London. London Museum, London. Victoria and Albert Museum, London. Wallace Collection, London. Temple Newsam House, Leeds. City Museum, Sheffield.

Nottingham ware

This name was applied to a fine quality of brown stone ware produced in the Nottingham district in the 18th century. It is best remembered for the jugs decorated with small slivers of clay, not unlike the pebble dash rendering on houses in effect. Apart from these "bear jugs", however, Nottingham ware included engraved wine jugs and drinking mugs of various kinds.

TO VIEW
Victoria and Albert Museum, London. Art Gallery and Museum, Brighton. Museum and Art Gallery, Derby. Royal Scottish Museum, Edinburgh. Central Museum and Art Gallery, Northampton. Salisbury and South Wiltshire Museum, Salisbury. City Museum, Sheffield. City Museum and Art Gallery, Stoke-on-Trent.

DEALERS
Those specialising in pottery wares.

Okimono

The use of ivory for ornamental figures in Japan revived in the Kyoho Era (1716–1736) when Yoshimura Shuzan began producing exquisite ivory pieces mainly as netsuke (q.v.). Gradually its use was extended to the larger okimono (literally "place things"), ornaments intended for the alcoves in Japanese houses. The production of ivory okimonos did not become popular until after the Restoration of 1868. The decline in netsuke, due to the adoption of Western dress, led to an increase in the output of okimono and, as tourism developed, more and more of these beautiful little figures carved in wood, bone or ivory, were exported to America and Europe.

The okimono produced in the last quarter of the 19th century have, as a rule, little merit since they were mechanically turned out as tourist souvenirs. The foundation of the Tokyo Fine Art School in 1688 led to a revival of national pride in indigenous art forms and the okimono produced from about the turn of the century onwards is very often of a high quality. Prices vary from about £5 for a tourist souvenir of the 1880s to several hundreds for an authenticated figure by one of the modern masters such as Asahi Meido or Ono Hofu. Okimono are usually signed by the artist, but forgery is not unknown.

READING

Japanese Netsuke: Fables in Ivory, Barbanson (Prentice-Hall)
The Netsuke of Japan, E Ryerson (Yoseloff)
Handbook of Japanese Art, Nositake Tsuba (Allen and Unwin)

TO VIEW

British Museum, London. Victoria and Albert Museum, London. Royal Scottish Museum, Edinburgh.

Antiques Corner Limited, 104 Mount Street, London
W1. Bluett and Sons, 48 Davies Street, London W1.

Ormolu

Chased ormolu bracket,
French, late 18th century

This name was first applied in the 18th century to
gilt-bronze, though the material itself had existed since
medieval times when craftsmen applied gilding to
bronze to imitate the solid gold work of the Byzan-
tines. The method used was to cast the object in
bronze using the *cire-perdue*, or lost wax method. In
this the bronze figures emerge hollow so that little
metal was lost in the casting. An amalgam of mercury
and gold was applied to the bronze and the mercury
vaporized by heat to leave a thin deposit of gold.
This would then be fixed by verdigris. This was
exceedingly dangerous work and it is hardly surprising that the labour costs involved in the production
of ormolu were high. The invention of electro-gilding
in the 1840s reduced the cost of ormolu at first, but
the rising price of bronze forced manufacturers to
devise a cheap form of "gilding" using a clear golden
lacquer which unfortunately did not wear very well.
Ormolu should not be confused with the other substitute materials of the late 19th century using spelter of
brass. Genuine ormolu, found on clock cases and ornaments, is extremely expensive nowadays, though
smaller items, such as boxes, occasionally turn up in
this lustrous material.

TO VIEW
British Museum, London. London Museum, London.
Victoria and Albert Museum, London. Wallace
Collection, London. Waddesdon Manor, Aylesbury.

Royal Pavilion, Brighton. Royal Scottish Museum, Edinburgh. Wernher Collection, Luton Hoo. Central Museum and Art Gallery, Northampton. County Museum, Stafford. Windsor Castle, Windsor. Blenheim Palace, Woodstock.

DEALERS

The Corner Cupboard, 679 Finchley Road, London NW2. Cecil Davis Limited, 3 Grosvenor Street, London W1. Felix Hilton, 45 St John's Wood High Street, London NW8. Howard (Antiques) Limited, 8 Davies Street, 33 New Bond Street and 22 Grosvenor Square, London W1. J Lipitch, 10a, 25 & 26 St. Christopher's Place, Wigmore Street, London W1. Alexander Podd and Son Limited, 57 & 63 High Street, Dunstable, Beds. Norwood Cottage, Killinghall, Harrogate, Yorks. Yellow Lantern Antiques Limited, 34 Holland Road, Hove, Sussex. Patrick Kirk, Bond End, Harrogate Road, Knaresborough, Yorks. Shirley Brown, The Green, Tredington, Warks.

Papier maché

A patent for the manufacture of paper ware was taken out by Henry Clay of Birmingham in 1772. His factory was taken over in 1816 by Messrs. Jennens and Bettridge who developed, stimulated and expanded the papier maché industry and demonstrated the versatility of this unlikely material by making trays, tea caddies, writing cases and even furniture (though it usually had to be reinforced with wood or metal in the case of chairs and tables).

The paper was highly compressed and lacquered in the Oriental manner. The result was a surprisingly durable substance, very light but capable of taking a high gloss. From 1825 onwards Jennens and Bettridge introduced pearly shell decoration in oriental patterns. These "chinoiserie" designs were very popular in the 1820s, though there was a tendency in Victorian times towards a more naturalistic treatment, particularly of flowers. In the later years the decoration became more and more extravagant with florid gilding. The popularity of papier maché declined in the 1860s, being overtaken by the fashion for electroplate.

Papier maché articles have enjoyed a revival in fortune in recent years, even quite small items such as trays and tea-caddies now fetching as many pounds as they did shillings a year or two ago. Several firms were engaged in the manufacture of papier maché ware but collectors put a premium on the work of Jennens and Bettridge whose name was usually (though not always) impressed or painted on their products.

READING
Small Antique Furniture, Bernard & Therle Hughes (Lutterworth)
More Small Decorative Antiques, Therle Hughes (Lutterworth)
Antique Papier Maché in Great Britain and America, J Toller (Bell)

TO VIEW
London Museum, London. Bethnal Green Museum, London. Royal Pavilion, Brighton. Royal Scottish Museum, Edinburgh. City Museum, Hereford. Central Museum and Art Gallery, Northampton. City Museum, Sheffield.

DEALERS
Thomas Goode and Co Limited, 19 South Audley Street, London W1. Tortoiseshell and Ivory House, 24 Chiltern Street, London W1. Marian Craske, 29 Salisbury Road, Hove, Sussex. Causeway Antiques, 11 Market Square, Horsham, Sussex. "55 Antiques", Spring Bank, Hull. Cranford Galleries, 10 King Street, Knutsford, Cheshire. Reiss Howard, Orwell House, Station Street, Swaffham, Norfolk.

Parian ware

White ceramic figures in unglazed (biscuit) porcelain derive their name from a fancied resemblance to the white marble found on the Greek island of Paros. Parian ware was introduced in the 1840s in order to reproduce copies of famous marble statues in miniature at low cost. The best-known examples were manufactured by Minton and Copeland, while Wedgwood produced a similar type which was named Carrara, after the famous Italian marble.

As well as reproductions of well known classical statuary such as the Venus de Milo, the manufacturers produced allegorical figures whose identity may seem obscure today. Parian ware was also used for portrait busts of famous people. Generally speaking the better quality items bear the mark or name of the manufacturer but examples from the lesser firms were unmarked and these are not so highly regarded by collectors. Pieces with the name Benjamin Cheverton impressed on them refer not to the artist or potter, but to the inventor of a reducing machine employed in the manufacture of tiny replicas of large statues. Parian ware was produced mainly between the 1840s and the end of the 19th century. It was also used in the manufacture of dolls' heads.

TO VIEW

Victoria and Albert Museum, London. Art Gallery and Museum, Brighton. Royal Scottish Museum, Edinburgh. Central Museum and Art Gallery, Northampton. City Museum, Sheffield. City Museum and Art Gallery, Stoke-on-Trent. Spode-Copeland Museum and Art Gallery, Stoke-on-Trent. Wedgwood Museum, Stoke-on-Trent. Windsor Castle, Windsor. Dyson Perrins Museum of Porcelain, Worcester.

CLUB

English Ceramic Circle, 8 Church Row, Hampstead, London NW3.

DEALERS
Andrew Dando, 4 Wood Street, Queen Square,
Bath. Reiss Howard, Orwell House, Swaffham,
Norfolk.

Patch-boxes

Small, flat boxes, either circular, rectangular or in fancy shapes, were produced in vast quantities in the 18th century when the wearing of patches was fashionable. These patches were ingenious aids to beauty at a time when the disfiguring marks of small-pox were all too common. The patches themselves were either plain circles in black, brown or other colours, or were intricately cut into patterns in the shape of animals, coaches etc. Patch-boxes, like snuff-boxes (q.v), vary in shape, design and materials used. Consequently their value may range from a pound or two for a wooden patch-box to £100 or more for examples in Battersea enamel (q.v.) or fine pique (q.v.).

READING
All Kinds of Small Boxes, J Bedford (Cassell)
Silver Boxes, Eric Delieb (Herbert Jenkins)

TO VIEW
Victoria and Albert Museum, London. Wallace Collection, London. Royal Scottish Museum, Edinburgh. City Museum, Hereford. Museum and Art Gallery, Leicester. Central Museum and Art Gallery, Northampton. City Museum, Sheffield. City Museum and Art Gallery, Worcester.

DEALERS
Antiques Corner, 104 Mount Street, London W1.
S J Phillips Limited, 139 New Bond Street, London

WI. Tessiers Limited, 26 New Bond Street, London
WI. Joy Chambers Antiques, Sidmouth, Devon.
Thomas Hudson, 4 Dollar Street, Cirencester,
Gloucestershire. Richard H Everard, Mapledene,
Maplewell Road, Woodhouse Eaves, Nr Lough-
borough, Leics. Staplegrove Lodge Antiques, Taun-
ton, Somerset.

Pearl ware

Pearl ware, so called on account of its pearly bluish
glaze, was devised by Wedgwood as an improved
type of cream ware. The bluish tinge was effected by
the addition of cobalt in the composition of the
earthen ware. Wedgwood's competitors in Yorkshire
and Staffordshire increased the cobalt content to
achieve a more bluish appearance which is not un-
attractive. Pearl ware may be found in plates, dishes,
jugs, candle sticks and figures. Apart from Wedgwood, names to look for in pearl ware include
Davenport (q.v.), Neale, Spode (q.v.) and Leeds
pottery.

TO VIEW
Victoria and Albert Museum, London. Royal
Scottish Museum, Edinburgh. Temple Newsam
House, Leeds. City Museum, Sheffield. City Museum
and Art Gallery, Stoke-on-Trent. Spode-Copeland
Museum and Art Gallery, Stoke-on-Trent. Wedg-
wood Museum, Stoke-on-Trent.

Pewter

An alloy of tin and lead which was very popular in times past for utensils of all kinds, inkwells, candlesticks, tankards and pepper-pots, to name but a few objects. Perhaps the dull grey appearance of pewter has put off many people but freshly scoured pewter shines as brightly as silver, though it may be harmful to polish off the patina acquired over the centuries. Modern pewter has a lower lead content and differs quite considerably in appearance from antique pewter. The latter also invariably exhibits pewterers' touch marks which are useful for dating and identifying it.

READING
Pewter, John Bedford (Cassell)
British Pewter, Blair (H.M.S.O.)
Old Pewter: Its Makers and Marks in England, Scotland and Ireland, H H Cotterell (Batsford)
Pewter and the Amateur Collector, E J Gale (Medici Society)
Pewter Marks and Old Pewter Ware, C H Markham (Reeves)
Chats on Old Pewter, H J Massé (Benn)
Antique Pewter of the British Isles, R F Michaelis (Bell)
A Short History of the Worshipful Company of Pewterers of London, R F Michaelis (H.M.S.O.)
Old European Pewter, A J G Verster (Thames and Hudson)
Pewter Collecting for Amateurs, K Ullyett (Muller)

TO VIEW
British Museum, London. Guildhall Museum, London. Geffrye Museum, London. London Museum, London. Victoria and Albert Museum, London. Wallace Collection, London. National Museum of Antiquities of Scotland, Edinburgh. Royal Scottish Museum, Edinburgh. City Museum, Hereford. Museum and Art Gallery, Leicester. Central Museum

and Art Gallery, Northampton. Salisbury and South Wiltshire Museum, Salisbury. City Museum, Sheffield. Somerset County Museum, Taunton. Elizabethan House, Totnes. Windsor Castle, Windsor. City Museum and Art Gallery, Worcester. The Yorkshire Museum, York.

CLUBS

The Pewter Society, The Wold, 12 Stratford Crescent, Cringleford, Norwich. Pewter Collectors' Club of America, 579 Grand Avenue, Lindenhurst, New York 10533, USA

DEALERS

P C L German, 125 Edgware Road, London w2. Gordon Hand and Co., 18 Chepstow Mansions, Westbourne Grove, London w2. Felix Hilton, 45 St John's Wood High Street, London NW8. The Old Pewter Shop, 142 Brompton Road, London sw3. Brian R Verrall, 48 Maddox Street, London w1. P Stebbing Limited, 7 Post Office Road, Bournemouth. Crafts and Curios, 7 Bruntsfield Place, Edinburgh. Charles Toller, 51 High Street, Eton, Bucks. J Feather, 120 Gledhow Valley Road, Leeds 17. Charles Lowe and Sons Limited, 37–8 & 40 Church Gate, Loughborough. Garside Antiques, 38 Back Clough, Northowram, Yorks. C H & D. Burrow, 105 Leeds Road, Scarborough, Yorks. Elizabeth Hughes, Towyn, Merioneth. Woburn Antique Galleries, Woburn, Bucks.

Piecrust ware

Imitation "pies" made in pottery were produced during the Napoleonic Wars when there was a shortage of flour for piecrusts. Meat was placed in these pottery piecases and cooked much in the same way as casseroles are done today. Piecrusts were sometimes produced in cane ware (q.v.) but the ordinary kind were usually ornately decorated with the sort of animals whose meat would be used to make a game pie. Piecrust ware is becoming increasingly difficult to find, about £10–£15 being the average price for good examples.

READING

More Small Decorative Antiques, Therle Hughes (Lutterworth)

TO VIEW

Victoria and Albert Museum, London. Central Museum and Art Gallery, Northampton. City Museum, Sheffield. City Museum and Art Gallery, Stoke-on-Trent. Wedgwood Museum, Stoke-on-Trent.

DEALERS

Arthur West Antiques, 23 The Strand, Dawlish, Devon. Evaline Winter, 1 Wolseley Road, Rugeley, Staffs. Runnymede Galleries, Egham, Surrey. S M Collins Antiques, 105 Leeds Road, Ilkley, Yorks.

Pilgrim bottles

In spite of their name these little bottles were designed more for use as small spirit flasks – and were the ancestors of the more modern hip flask. They have been traced back for more than a thousand years so their original purpose may have been to contain the relic of a saint or water from the River Jordan. They were popular in China and Japan and their squat, flat shape was extensively copied by the European potters of the 18th century. They vary considerably from the coarse brown ware of the Sussex potteries to the elegant bone china of Minton and Worcester.

TO VIEW
British Museum, London. Guildhall Museum, London. Victoria and Albert Museum, London. Art Gallery and Museum, Brighton. Royal Scottish Museum, Edinburgh. Central Museum and Art Gallery, Northampton. Salisbury and South Wiltshire Museum, Salisbury. City Museum and Art Gallery, Stoke on-Trent.

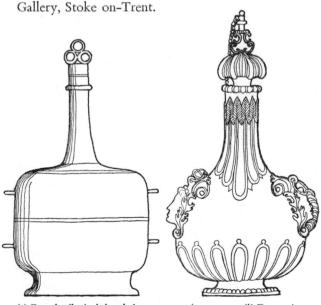

(*a*) French pilgrim's bottle in pewter, 17th century   (*b*) Decorative pilgrim's bottle in silver, 1702/4

Pinchbeck

This word, which has passed into the language as a synonym for cheap or tawdry, is derived from Christopher Pinchbeck (1670–1732), a watchmaker and jeweller who invented an alloy of copper and zinc which was slow to tarnish and simulated gold in appearance. Watches, trinket boxes, seals etc in pinchbeck have a certain appeal and such items are now avidly collected.

TO VIEW
Victoria and Albert Museum, London. City Museum, Sheffield. Windsor Castle, Windsor. City Museum and Art Gallery, Worcester.

Pin cushions

Although it is possible to buy pincushions of recent manufacture, the ones which will appeal most to the collector are those delightful examples of Victoriana, made of stuffed velvet or satin and gaily embroidered. They come in all shapes and sizes; apart from conventional circles and squares, there are hearts and animal shapes. Others, with bases of wood or ivory, are in the form of warming pans, bellows, etc. Many of them bore mottoes and verses or even pictures embroidered on them.

TO VIEW
Victoria and Albert Museum, London. Royal Scottish Museum, Edinburgh. City Museum, Hereford. Museum and Art Gallery, Leicester. City Museum, Sheffield. City Museum and Art Gallery,

Stoke-on-Trent. Elizabethan House, Totnes. City Museum and Art Gallery, Worcester.

DEALERS
A Arditti, 12b Berkeley Street, London w1. The Corner Cupboard, 14 Pierrepoint Arcade, Camden Passage, London n1.

Piqué

This style of decoration was very popular in the 18th century for objects of vertu – etuis, snuff-boxes and bonbonnières in particular. It consisted of inlays of gold or silver on tortoiseshell, ivory or mother of pearl. Experts distinguish these types of piqué: *point*, made up of tiny raised points of metal; *clouté* – similar but with larger points; and *posé* in which the metal is applied in flat, cut-out pieces. The 18th century examples marked the acme of piqué craftsmanship and are prized accordingly. The early Victorian examples, while not so much in demand, are fine pieces of craftsmanship nevertheless, though towards the end of the century die stamping brought a mechanical element to bear.

READING
Piqué: A Beautiful Minor Art, Herbert C Dent (Connoisseur)
More Small Decorative Antiques, Therle Hughes (Lutterworth)

TO VIEW
Victoria and Albert Museum, London. Royal Scottish Museum, Edinburgh.

DEALERS
S J Phillips Limited, 139 New Bond Street, London w1. Spink and Son Ltd, 5–7 King Street, London sw1. Tessiers Limited, 26 New Bond Street, London w1.

Pistols

These hand-guns derive their name from the Italian town of Pistoia where they are thought to have originated in the early 15th century. Other plausible derivations are from *pistole*, an ancient coin to the diameter of which it is said the earliest hand-guns were bored, or *pistallo*, meaning the pommel, where mounted troops were accustomed to keep their weapons.

The chief advantage of the pistol was that it could be fired with one hand only. These weapons range in date from primitive matchlocks of the 16th century, through the snaphaunce (or "pecking fowl" action) of the period 1570–1650, and the wheel-lock (17th century), to the flintlock (1600–1850) and percussion lock (1820 onwards). Metal cartridges detonated by a percussion cap were not invented until the 1860s, but weapons using this type of ammunition are outside the scope of the average collector since they require (in Britain) a firearms certificate. The 1937 Firearms Act states, however, that weapons kept as curios or antiques (in this case weapons over 100 years old) do not require a certificate.

Matchlocks, wheel-locks and snaphaunces are invariably expensive items nowadays and the prospective collector would do well to concentrate on flintlocks and early percussion pistols. This field covers a period of three centuries and within it one can specialise in English, Scottish, German, French, Italian, American, Indian or Far Eastern weapons. Highland all-steel pistols, Birmingham pocket-pistols, the famous miniature pistols known as Deringers or Derringers (the double-r spelling is applied to copies of Henry Deringer's gun), primitive pepper-boxes and Colt six-guns – these are but a few of the types of pistol which each have their own ardent following, as well as a formidable literature.

READING

Antique Pistols, S G B Alexander (Evelyn)
Pistols of the World, C Blair (Batsford)
British Military Firearms, Howard Blackmore (Jenkins)
Antique Pistol Collecting 1400–1860, Firth and Andrews (Holland)
English Pistols and Revolvers, J N George (Holland)
Spanish Guns and Pistols, W K Neal (Bell)
The Book of the Gun, H L Peterson (Hamlyn)
Firearms, Howard Ricketts (Weidenfeld)
Small Arms, Frederick Wilkinson (Ward Lock)

TO VIEW

Tower of London. Victoria and Albert Museum, London. Wallace Collection, London. City Museum and Art Gallery, Birmingham. Art Gallery and Museum, Brighton. National Army Museum, Camberley. National Museum of Antiquities of Scotland, Edinburgh. Royal Scottish Museum, Edinburgh. City Museum, Hereford. Museum and Art Gallery, Leicester. City Museum, Lincoln. Central Museum and Art Gallery, Northampton. Salisbury and South Wiltshire Museum, Salisbury. City Museum, Sheffield. County Museum, Stafford. City Museum and Art Gallery, Stoke-on-Trent. City Museum and Art Gallery, Worcester.

CLUB

Arms and Armour Society, 40 Great James Street, London WC1.

DEALERS

Peter Dale Limited, 11 & 12 Royal Opera Arcade, Pall Mall, London SW1. E Fairclough, 25 Conduit Street, London W1. Geoffrey Kenyon-May, Green Acre, Broad Oak, Newnham-on-Severn, Glos. J F Kelly, Church Street, Inverness. The Treasure Chest, Taunton, Somerset. Two Toad Antiques, Long Street, Tetbury, Glos.

Plaques

These wall decorations are perennially popular, whether they be Italian cinquecento bronze or modern pottery souvenirs of holiday resorts. In between these two extremes is a wealth of material in earthen ware, enamel, brass, copper, pewter and ivory. They range from humble examples of "folk art" to the products of skilled artists. They are found in Wedgwood jasper and basaltes, in Minton china and Worcester porcelain – not to mention Staffordshire earthen ware and brightly tin glazed majolica.

The subjects depicted are equally varied – historic, scenic or just plain sentimental – and they are to be found in almost every country in the world. In diminutive form they are known as plaquettes, usually cast in bronze and very popular in France and Italy in the late Middle Ages and early modern period.

READING
Small Decorative Antiques, Therle Hughes (Lutterworth)

TO VIEW
National Maritime Museum, Greenwich, London. Victoria and Albert Museum, London. Wallace Collection, London. City Museum, Hereford. Central Museum and Art Gallery, Northampton. City Museum, Sheffield. City Museum and Art Gallery, Stoke-on-Trent. Wedgwood Museum, Stoke-on-Trent. Elizabethan House, Totnes. Windsor Castle, Windsor. City Museum and Art Gallery, Worcester.

Poker work

The art of incising wood with a heated point is known as poker work. It varies from the cheap and vulgar boards which form the stock in trade of joke and puzzle shops, to the elegant and ornate wood ware of Victorian times. Boxes and picture frames are the most common media for poker work, but paper knives, writing cases and pipe-racks are also to be found with poker work decoration. The most intricate examples simulated carving in relief, with the wood cut away delicately in layers by the poker.

READING
Treen, James (Pitman)

TO VIEW
Victoria and Albert Museum, London. Also most folk museums.

DEALERS
Coxson Antiques Limited, 63 Cadogan Place, London SW1. W1. Brian R Verrall, 48 Maddox Street, London W1. Trinkets and Treasures, 29 Barns Street, Ayr. J Hutton, 108 High Street, Berkhamsted, Herts. Avon Antiques, 26–27 Market Street, Bradford-on-Avon, Wiltshire. Jan Struther, 13 Randolph Place, Edinburgh. Charles Toller, 51 High Street, Eton, Bucks. Wilkinson's Cottage Antiques, 27/29 Charnham Street, Hungerford, Berks. The Cottage Shop, High Street, Lechlade-on-Thames, Glos. Georgian House, Etnam Street, Leominster. Vincent Wood, Osbournby, Lincs. Elizabeth Hughes, Towyn, Merioneth.

Pomade tops

When wigs went out of fashion at the end of the 18th century and men began to display their own hair, pomatum – the ancestor of today's hair cream – came into use. This substance was manufactured from bear's grease, which explains the fact that the tops of the earthenware jars in which it was sold were decorated with pictures usually showing bears.

These pomade tops had a rather short life being common between 1840 and 1850 only. During this decade there were only four potteries (all in Staffordshire) engaged in the production of these decorated lids and of these F and R Pratt of Fenton are the best-known. Pratt's employed Jerse Austin in the production of pictorial pot-lids by four colour transfer printing and these are now the most highly desired of all, being worth anything up to £100 each.

The decline in the use of bear's grease pomade led to the demise of the pictorial pomade top. Closely allied to these items are the pictorial pot lids used for jars of fish paste and potted shrimps which enjoyed a somewhat longer vogue (from about 1847 till 1880).

READING
Underglaze Colour Picture Prints On Staffordshire Pottery: The Pictorial Pot Lid Book, H G Clarke (Courier Press).

TO VIEW
Pharmaceutical Society's Museum, London.

CLUB
The Pot Lid Circle, "Vines", Hildenborough, Kent.

DEALERS
Alexander Antiques, High Street, Bletchingley, Surrey. Benjamin Sims, Upper North Street, Brighton, Sussex.

Pontypool and Usk wares

Lacquered tinware was a speciality of the Allgood family who flourished in the Welsh towns of Pontypool and Usk in the latter years of the 18th century. Tinware, in the shape of trays, knife-boxes, tea-pots, urns and boxes was japanned in black, green, blue or puce lacquer and gaily decorated in gilt or contrasting colours. The production of japanned wares in South Wales died out early in the 19th century, but similar work known as Pontypool and Usk ware continued to be imitated in Birmingham throughout the century. Genuine 18th century wares are now very scarce and highly sought after, though later copies are still quite plentiful.

READING
Pontypool and Usk Japanned Wares, W D John (Ceramic)

TO VIEW
British Museum, London. Victoria and Albert Museum, London. Royal Pavilion, Brighton. National Museum of Wales, Cardiff. Newport Museum and Art Gallery, Monmouthshire.

Porcelain

No other man-made substance has ever rivalled porcelain in intrinsic value, whether it be a Ch'ien Lung bowl, a Harlequin by J J Kaendler or a bird by Dorothy Doughty. Of course there are many lesser pieces but it is true to say that the best of porcelain can run into five figures in price.

True porcelain (known as "hard paste") was invented by the Chinese and consisted of a fusion of kaolin, or China clay, and a type of felsphatic stone known as petuntse. The kaolin provided the "flesh" and the petuntse the "bones" for the porcelain which, fired at a high temperature, resulted in the hard, strong substance capable of modelling in delicate eggshell thickness. Hard paste porcelain, when broken, shows a uniform consistency since the glaze and the body were fused together in one substance.

Soft-paste porcelain was an English substitute for the hard-paste porcelain rediscovered in the early 18th century by Johann Böttger of Meissen. It was composed of clay, lime and silica compounds. Not only was it expensive to produce and difficult to fire evenly, but it never achieved the delicacy of the Continental or Chinese hard pastes. The chief exponents of this ware were Bow, Chelsea, Caughley, Derby and Worcester. Since the glaze was applied in a separate operation, soft-paste porcelain can easily be identified by minor irregularities and inconsistencies in its texture and also the fact that it breaks with the appearance of hard icing-sugar.

Bone china came into prominence in England towards the end of the 18th century when Spode's produced a passable substitute for hard-paste by adding up to 40% bone ash to the ingredients. The products of some of the more distinctive factories are listed separately in this book.

READING
Continental Porcelain of the Eighteenth Century, Rollo Charles (Benn)
Chinese Porcelain, Antony de Boulay (Weidenfeld & Nicholson)
British Pottery and Porcelain, 1780–1850, G. Godden (A. Barker)
Early Chinese Pottery and Porcelain, Basil Grey (Faber)
Faience, Meissen and Other Continental Porcelain, Hackenbrock (Thames & Hudson)
The Concise Encyclopaedia of Continental Pottery and Porcelain, R Hagger (Deutsch)

A Dictionary of European Ceramic Art, W B Honey (Faber)
English Porcelain and Bone China, Therle Hughes (Lutterworth)
English Porcelain of the Eighteenth Century, Savage (Spring Books)
Digest of Antique Porcelain, J R Scott (Ceramic)

TO VIEW

Bethnal Green Museum, London. British Museum, London. Victoria and Albert Museum, London. Wallace Collection, London. Waddesdon Manor, Aylesbury. Holbourne of Menstrie Museum, Bath. Museum and Art Gallery, Birmingham. Art Gallery and Museum, Brighton. Royal Pavilion, Brighton. City Art Gallery, Bristol. National Museum of Wales, Cardiff. Royal Scottish Museum, Edinburgh. City Museum, Hereford. Temple Newsam House, Leeds. Museum and Art Gallery, Leicester. Wernher Collection, Luton Hoo. Central Museum and Art Gallery, Northampton. Ashmolean Museum of Art and Archaeology, Oxford. Salisbury and South Wiltshire Museum, Salisbury. City Museum, Sheffield. City Museum and Art Gallery, Stoke-on-Trent (one of the largest and finest collections in the world). Spode-Copeland Museum and Art Gallery, Stoke-on-Trent. Windsor Castle, Windsor. City Museum and Art Gallery, Worcester. Dyson Perrins Museum of Porcelain, Worcester

CLUB

The English Ceramic Circle, 8 Church Row, London NW3. The Oriental Ceramic Society, 31b Torrington Square, London WC1.

DEALERS

Albert Amor Limited, 37 Bury Street, St. James', London SW1. Antique Porcelain Limited, 149 New Bond Street, London W1. Beauchamp Galleries, 8 Beauchamp Place, London SW3. Bluett and Sons, 48 Davies Street, London W1. Delomosne and Son Limited, 4 Campden Hill Road, London W8. Philip Duncan, Lowndes Lodge, 28 Lowndes Street,

London sw1. A S Embden, Hector Court, Cambolt Road, London sw15. Filkins and Co, 175 Old Brompton Road, London sw5. Miss Fowler, 1a Duke Street, Manchester Square, London w1. Gordon Hand and Co, 18 Chepstow Mansions, Westbourne Grove, London w2. Keith Harding Antiques, 93 Hornsey Road, London n7. Lories Limited, 89b Wigmore Street, London w1. D M & P Manheim, 69 Upper Berkeley Street, Portman Square, London w1. Mayfair Market, Shepherd's Market, London w1. David Newbon, 56 Beauchamp Place, London sw3. H W Newby, 130c Brompton Road, London sw3. Newman and Newman, 156 Brompton Road, London sw3. Frank Partridge and Sons, 144 New Bond Street, London w1. Quality Chase, 17a St Christopher's Place, London w1. Spink and Son Limited, 5–7 King Street, London sw1. Tilley and Co Limited, 2 Symons Street, Sloane Square, London sw3. Alan Tillman Antiques, 6 Halkin Arcade, Motcomb Street, London sw1. J & E D Vandekar, 138 Brompton Road, London sw3. W W Warner (Antiques) Limited, 226 Brompton Road, London sw3. The Antique Shop, Broadway, Amersham, Bucks. The Old Clock House, High Street, Ascot, Berks. Andrew Dando, 4 Wood Street, Queen Square, Bath. Mrs H. G. James, 3 Higher Bore Street, Bodmin, Cornwall. Victor Needham Limited, 119 Old Christchurch Road, Bournemouth. Studio Antiques Limited, Bourton-on-the-Water, Glos. Margaret Cadman, 25 Ship Street, Brighton. Denys Cowell, 60 Middle Street, Brighton. "Dragonwyck", 42 St Georges Road, Brighton. Michael Brett, Picton House, Broadway, Worcester. The Old Black Horse Antiques, Burnham Market, Norfolk. Collins and Clark, 81 Regent Street, Cambridge. Mowbray House Antiques, High Street, Edinburgh. Janet Lumsden, 51a George Street, Edinburgh. F C Dixon, 54 Bridgegate, Retford, Notts. Thomas Love and Son, Perth. F E Norwood Limited, St Albans, Herts. C H & D Burrows, Scarborough, Yorks. George Newitt, Thame, Oxon. The Ship's Wheel, Thurso, Caithness. Woburn Antique Galleries, Woburn, Bucks.

Porcelain pipes

Appropriately enough, it was the Germans who first graduated from the common clay pipe to the handsome porcelain pipe, and it seems that these items were among the earliest products of the great porcelain factories at Meissen, Nymphenburg, Berlin and Fulda in the middle of the 18th century. By the end of the century porcelain pipes had spread all over the German-speaking part of Europe and were very popular there until the First World War. Only the bowls were actually made of porcelain, the stems being of wood, bone, ivory, amber or metal. While the bowls are usually collected on their own, complete pipes are comparatively rare nowadays and rate a good premium.

Their attraction lies in the infinite variety of their decoration. They may be classified in broad categories according to the subject depicted such as portraits of famous men and women, reproductions of paintings, patriotic scenes, student scenes, sporting subjects, religious subjects, allusions to fairy tales and folklore, and souvenirs of holidays. While the Meissen and Nymphenburg items are now very expensive, there are numerous 19th century examples which can be obtained, particularly on the Continent, for a pound or two.

READING
Tobacco and the Collector, Amoret and Christopher Scott (Golden Head Press)

TO VIEW
Victoria and Albert Museum, London. Art Gallery and Museum, Brighton. Central Museum and Art Gallery, Northampton.

Posset pots

Posset was a form of gruel composed of spiced ale, sugar and milk mixed with pieces of oatcake or bread. It was a popular antidote to the common cold, particularly in the north Midlands, but was supped generally as an evening beverage. In view of its popularity in the Staffordshire area it is hardly surprising that distinctive vessels should be produced for its consumption.

Posset pots as these cups were called may be recognised by their multiple loop handles and slanting or dome shaped lids. They were produced during the 17th and 18th centuries in various types of earthen ware and were usually gaily decorated, often incorporating a motto such as 'The best is not too good for you'. An alternative version was a spout-pot, which had a spout not unlike a tea pot.

TO VIEW

British Museum, London. Victoria and Albert Museum, London. Art Gallery and Museum, Brighton. Royal Scottish Museum, Edinburgh. Temple Newsam House, Leeds. Central Museum and Art Gallery, Northampton. City Museum, Sheffield. City Museum and Art Gallery, Stoke-on-Trent.

Tin glazed earthenware posset pot, 1650

Posters and playbills

In recent years there has been a revival of interest in posters and they are now used as wall decorations irrespective of their original function, which was to advertise. Cheap reproductions of old posters are readily available and, thanks to modern printing processes, these faithfully mirror the style and colour of the originals. At the same time interest in the originals has been greatly stimulated and as a result the price of items by famous artists has risen enormously.

Posters of a strictly functional nature, entirely composed of letterpress, date from the 18th century. Pictorial posters did not become possible till the mid-19th century when lithography was developed as a commercial process. The 1890s witnessed the phenomenal growth of the poster as an advertising medium and most of the examples now extant date from this period. Particularly sought after are posters by acknowledged artists such as Toulouse-Lautrec and Alphonse Mucha. The former is best known for his advertisements for the Moulin Rouge while the latter made his name for his posters portraying Sarah Bernhardt in her great roles such as *Gismonda* and *Lorenzaocio*. Other artists whose posters are in demand include Cheret, Atche and Grasset in France, and Aubrey Beardsley and the Beggerstaff brothers in England. Signed lithographs and posters by these artists now range from £40 to several hundreds.

Of the commercially produced posters those with a historic flavour, or connected with sporting events, theatrical productions, aviation meetings, etc., are the most likely to increase in value.

READING

Original Posters, Mourlot (Zwemmer)
French Posters (Studio Vista)
Posters at the Turn of the Century, Rickards (A & M Evelyn)

TO VIEW

British Museum, London. Museum of British Transport, London. City Museum, Hereford. Museum and Art Gallery, Leicester. Salisbury and South Wiltshire Museum, Salisbury. City Museum, Sheffield. Elizabethan House, Totnes. Royal Tun-

bridge Wells Museum and Art Gallery, Tunbridge
Wells. City Museum and Art Gallery, Worcester.

Posy holders

The solution to the age-old problem of keeping one's
corsage fresh in the heated atmosphere of the ballroom was the posy holder, a small container (the
diminutive form of the cornucopia) which held some
water and kept the flowers moist.

Posy holders pinned to ladies' dresses, both for day
and evening wear, were introduced in the early 18th
century and remained fashionable till the end of the
19th century. The tiny holder, or *porte bouquet*, was
often made of silver, ormolu or gold, often inlaid
with other metals or encrusted with mother-of-
pearl, coral or semi-precious stones.

READING
More Small Decorative Antiques, Therle Hughes
(Lutterworth)

Victorian posy holder

TO VIEW
Royal Scottish Museum, Edinburgh. Central
Museum and Art Gallery, Northampton. City
Museum, Sheffield. City Museum and Art Gallery,
Stoke-on-Trent.

DEALERS
Those specialising in antique jewellery.

Pot lids

An early example of attractive packaging as an aid to merchandising is the pictorial potlid. Those intended for jars of bear's grease are a special case and are dealt with separately under Pomade tops. Apart from pomades and unguents however, decorated jars and pots were used for potted shrimps, a delicacy for which Pegwell Bay, south of Ramsgate in Kent, was renowned. This accounts for the many views of Pegwell Bay and scenes with a nautical flavour found on these potlids. At a somewhat later date the subject matter was expanded, often striking a topical note as, for example, the pot lids depicting the Great Exhibition of 1851, royal occasions and even portraits of contemporary personages.

At the hands of F and R Pratt of Fenton in Staffordshire, the potlid became an established art form in itself, with gay colours and sensitive composition, often reproducing the works of contemporary artists such as Collins, Webster, Wilkie and others. Unfortunately demand for potlids has encouraged the forger to produce passable imitations, sometimes reproduced from the original copper plates, so great skill and experience is required to distinguish the genuine from the false. Pot lids mounted in a circular frame make attractive wall decorations, while the pots themselves are often decorative objects worth collecting for their own sake.

READING

Underglaze Colour Picture Prints on Staffordshire Pottery: The Pictorial Pot Lid Book, H G Clarke (Courier Press)

TO VIEW

Pharmaceutical Society's Museum, London. Royal Scottish Museum, Edinburgh. City Museum, Hereford. City Museum and Art Gallery, Sheffield. City Museum and Art Gallery, Stoke-on-Trent.

Powder flasks

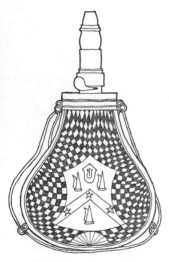

Horn powder flask mounted in brass, mid 18th century

These horns or flasks, receptacles for gunpowder before the invention of cartridges, were in fact used from the 14th century till about 1850 when the use of percussion cap cartridges and breech loading weapons became general. They consisted of a container, made of leather, horn, silver, brass, wood, bone or ivory, surmounted by a stopper which sometimes incorporated a form of dispenser so that the right amount of powder was released. They were often produced in pairs – a large one for the main charge and a small one to contain the priming charge. Not only do they vary immensely in shape and materials used, but in construction and the degree of artistry shown in their design. The best examples were elaborately inlaid with gold and silver or with ivory on wood.

READING
The Powder Flask Book, R Riling (US)

TO VIEW
Victoria and Albert Museum, London. Wallace Collection, London. National Army Museum,

Camberley. Royal Scottish Museum, Edinburgh. City Museum, Gloucester. City Museum, Hereford. Museum and Art Gallery, Leicester. Central Museum and Art Gallery, Northampton. City Museum, Sheffield. County Museum, Stafford. City Museum and Art Gallery, Stoke-on-Trent. Elizabethan House, Totnes. Windsor Castle, Windsor.

East German mid 17th century Powder Flask, wood mounted with mother-of-pearl and brass

CLUB

Arms and Armour Society, 40 Great James Street, London WC1.

DEALERS

M & J Appleby, 57 George Street, London W1. Peter Dale Limited, 11 & 12 Royal Opera Arcade, Pall Mall, London SW1. E Fairclough Limited, 25 Conduit Street, London W1. Geoffrey Kenyon-May, Green Acre, Broad Oak, Newnham-on-Severn, Glos. Two Toads Antiques, 28 Long Street, Tetbury, Glos.

Pratt ware

Felix Pratt, 1780–1859, the founder of F and R Pratt and Co of Fenton, Staffordshire, has given his name to a type of earthen ware distinguished by its colours which were predominantly buff, yellow, blue, pink, red or green. Decorated jugs, tankards and plaques, often reflecting topical interest in the Napoleonic Wars and naval heroes and battles, were the chief stock in trade and they enjoyed considerable popularity in the years before the firm turned to pictorial pot lids in the 1840s. The expensive items include Trafalgar jugs and rather naïve figures (in the £50–£100 range today) though tankards ornamented with pastoral scenes are commoner, of less interest and therefore correspondingly cheaper.

READING
Staffordshire Pots and Potters, G W Rhead (Hutchinson)
Staffordshire Pottery and its History, J C Wedgwood (Sampson Low)

TO VIEW
Bethnal Green Museum, London. British Museum, London. Victoria and Albert Museum, London. Ulster Museum, Belfast. Museum and Art Gallery, Brighton. National Museum of Wales, Cardiff. Royal Scottish Museum, Edinburgh. Central Museum and Art Gallery, Northampton. Salisbury and South Wiltshire Museum, Salisbury. City Museum, Sheffield. City Museum and Art Gallery, Stoke-on-Trent.

DEALERS
Miss Fowler, 1a Duke Street, Manchester Square, London w1. D M and P Manheim, 69 Upper Berkeley Street, Portman Square, London w1. Arthur West Antiques, Dawlish, Devon. Runnymede Galleries, Egham, Surrey. S M Collins, Leeds Road, Ilkley, Yorks. Evaline Winter, Rugeley, Staffordshire. Staplegrove Lodge Antiques, Taunton, Somerset.

Prayer rugs

Wherever the Mohammedan religion is established one will come across prayer mats. Five times a day the faithful are called to prayer and the devout, facing Mecca, unrolls his mat and prostrates himself with arms outstretched till his head touches the ground. Mats designed for use in prayer have a distinctive design known as a *mihrab*, which comes to a point, representing the arch of the mosque. Countless variations on the pattern were used, but the basic *mihrab* motif is common to them all. Occasionally double or treble arch patterns may be found. Various religious symbols, such as the Lamp of Eternal Light, are also incorporated in the design, while some types have the date in Arabic numerals woven into them.

Two types of knot were used in the hand weaving of these rugs – the *ghiordes* (double) and *senna* (single). Rugs vary in fineness from 80 to 700 knots to the square inch. At one time only vegetable dyes were used and these faded very slowly over the years. From the middle of the 19th century onwards, however, synthetic aniline dyes were used with greater frequency and since they do not stand up to strong light they are often found in badly faded condition which should not be confused with the true mellowing of age.

Prayer mats were – and are – woven all over the Islamic world, from Asia Minor to Agra in India and from Arabia to Russian Turkestan. Each village, town and district has its own distinctive styles and predilection for certain colours. Prices vary from £10–£15 for a small modern rug to £500 for an antique Kashan.

READING
Antique Rugs from the Near East, Bode and Künel
Oriental Carpets and Rugs, Hopf (Thames & Hudson)
Turkish Prayer Rugs, M Mostafa
Oriental Rugs and Carpets, Stanley Reed (Weidenfeld and Nicholson)

How to Know Oriental Carpets and Rugs, Heinrich Jacoby (Allen & Unwin).

TO VIEW
Victoria and Albert Museum, London. Royal Scottish Museum, Edinburgh. City Museum and Art Gallery, Worcester.

DEALERS
S Franses, 71–3 Knightsbridge, London sw1. Perez Limited, 112 Brompton Road, London sw3. Philip Stone Limited, 12 Imperial Court, Prince Albert Road, London nw8. The Treasure House, Holburn Street, Aberdeen. Queen Anne House, Church Street, Chesham, Bucks. Thornborough Galleries, Gloucester Street, Cirencester, Glos. David Mann & Son Limited, Cranleigh, Surrey. V Alouf Brothers, 39 Frederick Street, Edinburgh. J Holmes and Co, Cheltenham Spa, Glos.

Railway relics

It has been said, with a great deal of truth, that the British are never as keen on keeping something as when they have lost it. This paradox explains the growing popularity of anything to do with the steam locomotive. The drastic pruning of uneconomic services has led to the mushroom growth of railway preservation societies where members spend much of their time combing the scrap-yards and railway depots for relics of the steam age. British Rail has found this to be a lucrative business; sales of relics at the State depot in 1966, for example, made a profit of £2,390, which included £100 paid by one enthusiast for a nameplate of the "Coronation" class 4-6-2 City of Sheffield.

Name plates and crests form the most expensive class of railway relic, anything from £60 to £150 being paid, depending on the importance of the locomotive: at the other extreme, however, number plates from smoke boxes and cab sides usually change hands at £3 to £5. Builders' or works' plates, destination boards and head boards are also in great demand.

Other collectable items include lamps, engine-whistles, signs of various kinds. In the latter category come such gems as: "Please do not Spit in the Carriage. It is offensive to other Passengers and is stated by the Medical Profession to be a Source of Serious Disease." This interesting commentary on the habits of Victorian commuters made £10 at a sale of railway relics held by Knight Frank and Rutley in London in February 1968.

Railway hats, uniforms, watches and truncheons, station signs and notices, office rubber-stamps and ticket machines – not to mention the tickets themselves – are all within the province of the railway collector.

READING
Railway Enthusiasts' Handbook (David and Charles)

TO VIEW
Museum of British Transport, Clapham, London. City Museum and Art Gallery, Birmingham. Royal Scottish Museum, Edinburgh. Museum and Art Gallery, Leicester. Salisbury and South Wiltshire Museum, Salisbury. City Museum, Sheffield. City Museum and Art Gallery, Stoke-on-Trent. Elizabethan House, Totnes.

CLUBS
There are approximately 40 clubs and preservation societies – see Railway Enthusiasts' Handbook.

DEALERS
Trad, 67 Portobello Road, London w. The Turntable, Wade Street, Leeds. Also – British Railways conduct periodic sales of surplus stock.

Railway passenger's reading lamp with candle inside, 1830

Rockingham

This distinctive pottery and porcelain owes its name to the Marquis of Rockingham, one of the 18th century prime ministers, on whose estate at Swinton in Yorkshire brown-glazed pottery was first produced in the 1760s. Rockingham china, on the other hand, was a product of the early 19th century, produced by the Brameld family of potters. It is noted for its sumptuous, florid decorations and gilding, usually on pale blue or grey grounds. Rockingham ranks among the more desirable (and pricey) of 19th century porcelain, ranging from about £20 for a milk jug with cover to several hundreds for a complete tea and coffee service.

READING

The Rockingham Pottery, Its Fine Porcelain and Earlier Earthenware, A A Eaglestone and T A Lockett (Rotherham Museum)
Rockingham Ornamental Porcelain, D G Rice (Ceramic)

TO VIEW

Victoria and Albert Museum, London. Museum and Art Gallery, Brighton. National Museum of Wales, Cardiff. Royal Scottish Museum, Edinburgh. Museum and Art Gallery, Leicester. Central Museum and Art Gallery, Northampton. Museum and Art Gallery, Rotherham. Salisbury and South Wiltshire Museum, Salisbury. City Museum, Sheffield. City Museum and Art Gallery, Stoke-on-Trent. The Yorkshire Museum, York.

CLUB

The English Ceramic Circle, 8 Church Row, London NW3.

DEALERS

The Antique Porcelain Co Limited, 149 New Bond Street, London W1. Delomosne and Son Limited, 4 Campden Hill Road, London W8. Andrew Dando,

4 Wood Street, Queen Square, Bath. Arthur West Antiques, 23 The Strand, Dawlish, Devon. Bryan Bowden, 22 Chequer Road, Doncaster, Yorks. Runnymede Galleries, Egham, Surrey. S M Collins, 105 Leeds Road, Ilkley, Yorks. Collectors Treasures, Amersham, Bucks. Summertown Antiques, Oxford. Evaline Winter, 1 Wolseley Road, Rugeley, Staffs. Long Farthing Antiques, West Burton, Nr Aysgarth, Leyburn, Yorks.

Rolling pins

Rolling pins made of glass are now considered as collectors' pieces of great interest, and it is a matter of some regret that this has stimulated unscrupulous persons into faking them in large quantities. The originals were either completely solid, in dark (usually blue or green) bottle glass, often flecked with enamel glass and sometimes embellished with gilt scrollwork and inscriptions. Others were hollow, with a stopper at one end. They were filled with sugar, salt, sand or "hundreds and thousands" and, judging by the prevalence of nautical motifs on their decorated sides, were a favourite present from sailors to their wives and sweethearts. Apart from their strictly utilitarian purpose they were kept as good luck charms and keepsakes or exchanged as love tokens.

Early 19th century blue glass rolling pin

TO VIEW
Geffrye Museum, London. Victoria and Albert Museum, London. Royal Scottish Museum, Edinburgh. Museum and Art Gallery, Leicester. Central Museum and Art Gallery, Northampton. Salisbury and South Wiltshire Museum, Salisbury. City Museum, Sheffield. City Museum and Art Gallery, Worcester.

DEALERS
Those specialising in 'bygones'.

Rummers

18th century rummer

Rummers or roemers are wine-glasses constructed on very massive, generous lines and distinguished by their large bowls and solid bases. Although the popular fallacy that they were designed for rum-drinking has now been exploded, experts are still divided on the origin of the name. The word rummer is now accepted as an English corruption of the Germanic word *roemer* and, indeed, this is the term by which such glasses are often described in auction catalogues.

Roemer may be derived from the Dutch word for "romanesque" or from the Rhenish German word meaning to boast. The connection between boasting and wine drinking is fairly obvious. Perhaps there is a somewhat similar analogy with the bumper – a heavy drinking glass of great capacity which was banged on the table with noisy gusto.

The earlier roemers had fairly long stems, though these were usually thick and lavishly decorated. On the later English versions, however, the stem dwindled in size and importance, giving the rummer a rather top-heavy appearance.

READING
Old English Drinking Glasses, G Williams.

TO VIEW
British Museum, London. Victoria and Albert Museum, London. Museum and Art Gallery, Brighton. National Museum of Wales, Cardiff. Royal Scottish Museum, Edinburgh. Central Museum and Art Gallery, Northampton. Salisbury and South Wiltshire Museum, Salisbury. City Museum, Sheffield. City Museum and Art Gallery, Worcester. Snowshill Manor, Worcester.

CLUB
The Glass Circle, 50a Fulham Road, London sw3.

DEALERS
W G T Burne Limited, 11 Elystan Street, London sw3. Arthur Churchill (Glass) Limited, Marjorie Parr Gallery, 285 King's Road, London sw3. Cecil Davis Limited, 3 Grosvenor Street, New Bond Street, London w1. Howard Phillips, 11a Henrietta Place, London w1. J Hutton, 108 High Street, Berkhamsted, Herts. Hilton Gallery, 3 St Mary's Passage, Cambridge. John Maggs, 114 Bold Street, Liverpool. Thomas Love and Son Limited, South Street, Perth.

Satsuma ware

The genuine creamy coloured pottery which emanated from the Japanese province of Satsuma in the 18th century is now quite scarce and highly regarded. It may be recognised by its finely mellowed glaze, covered with tiny cracelure, with delicately gilded and enamelled decoration. Unfortunately, like so much else in Japanese art, Satsuma ware suffered debasement following the Meiji Restoration in 1868, as entrepreneurs pandered to the indiscriminate tastes of European and American tourists. These later wares were extravagantly decorated in a tasteless manner which has not stood the test of time and is therefore unfashionable with collectors at present. Satsuma ware was also extensively copied by English and European potters at the end of the 19th century, but these imitations are quite easy to distinguish from the restrained dignity of the originals.

READING

The Ceramic Art of China and other Countries of the Far East, W B Honey (Faber)

TO VIEW

British Museum, London. Victoria and Albert Museum, London. Museum and Art Gallery, Brighton. Royal Scottish Museum, Edinburgh. City Museum and Art Gallery, Stoke-on-Trent.

CLUB

The Oriental Ceramic Society, 31b Torrington Square, London WC1.

DEALERS

Bluett and Sons, 48 Davies Street, London W1. Gordon Hand and Co Limited, 18 Chepstow Mansions, Westbourne Grove, London W2. David B Newbon, 56 Beauchamp Place, London SW3. J Vandekar, 138 Brompton Road, London SW3. Andrew Dando, Bath, Somerset. Denys Cowell, 60 Middle Street, Brighton, Sussex.

Scent bottles

It is interesting to trace the evolution of the scent bottle from the vinaigrette (q.v.) which was popular till the middle of the 19th century. The first scent bottles, produced in the Victorian era, served two purposes and were thus made in two parts. At one end the stopper would be removed to reveal the smelling salts; at the other a threaded metal cap would be unscrewed to expose the perfume. These double scent bottles may be found in a wide variety of shapes and sizes. The glass ranges from plain clear crystal to opaque and coloured glass, and the stoppers and mounts, usually of silver, were often richly decorated.

The leading French perfumiers such as Chanel, Coty and Lanvin commissioned famous glass manufacturers to produce these exquisite little bottles as a fitting receptacle for the most expensive scents. Bottles by Daum, Galle and Lalique, among others, are eminently collectable and are worth looking out for. Larger scent bottles with a patent vapouriser attached, were produced for ladies' dressing tables and are a distinct, but no less interesting, category.

READING
Scent Bottles, Kate Foster (Michael Joseph)

TO VIEW
British Museum, London. Victoria and Albert Museum, London. Harris Museum and Art Gallery, Preston.

DEALERS
Most general dealers carry a selection of scent bottles.

Scientific instruments

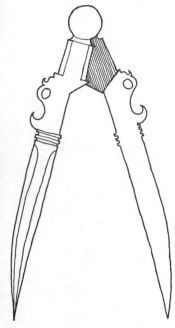

17th century Italian dividers

This is a very wide field ranging from primitive dials and nocturnals used in astronomy and navigation to the precision instruments of the present day. The collector would be well advised to confine his interests to some aspect of scientific instruments, perhaps connected with his profession. Early surgical and dental instruments are already in great demand but there are many aspects as yet relatively unexplored. Surveyor's equipment, early scientific apparatus, weighing and measuring instruments of all kinds and similar devices turn up regularly in junk shops or in auction sales of bygones.

READING
Scientific Instruments in Art and History, Henri Michel (Barrie and Rockliffe)

TO VIEW
British Museum, London. London Museum, London. Science Museum, London (Important collection). City Museum and Art Gallery, Birmingham. City Museum, Bury St Edmunds. National Army Museum, Camberley. Whipple Museum of the History of Science, Cambridge (Important collection). Royal Scottish Museum, Edinburgh. City Museum, Hereford. Museum and Art Gallery, Leicester. Central Museum and Art Gallery, Northampton. Pitt Rivers Museum, Oxford. Museum of the History of Science, Oxford (Important collection). City Museum, Sheffield. Windsor Castle, Windsor. Snowshill Manor, Broadway, Worcester.

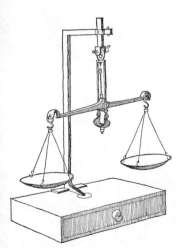

Mid 18th century chemists' scales

DEALERS
Nicholas Gorevic, 97 Jermyn Street, London SW1. Graham Pontet Limited, 102 Mount Street, London W1. Graham Pontet Limited, 78–79 Jermyn Street, London SW1. David Young, 104 Chepstow Road, London W2. Fordham Mote Antiques, Lewes, Sussex. Dunning's Antiques, 58–62 Holywell Hill,

St Albans, Herts. Peter & June Nelson, Digbeth Street, Stow-on-the-Wold, Glos. Christopher Sykes, 11 Market Place, Woburn, Beds.

Seals

Prior to the invention of the wafer (a small circle of adhesive paper) and the envelope with gummed flap, letters had to be sealed with wax. Incidentally, before 1840 the postage on letters in Britain was computed according to the number of sheets used, the envelope counting as an extra sheet. Since this could double the price of the postage, it is hardly surprising that envelopes were slow to catch on!

Instead letters were written on the inner part of a sheet of paper which was then folded over, the address written on the outer side and the two flaps sealed down with wax. To prevent anyone tampering with the wax it was customary for letter writers to use a seal engraved with a device – a monogram coat of arms or emblem being the most usual forms. Small seals were carried by gentlemen on fob or watch chains, or mounted in rings. The seals were cut in semi precious stones such as agate, cornelian, emerald or jasper, and mounted in richly ornamented gold or silver. At a Christie's sale in 1968 an unusual seal of this type, with the handle shaped like a duck composed of a large pearl, with rubies and emeralds, fetched 340 guineas. Small seals intended as a form of jewellery vary in price from £10 upwards, depending on the intrinsic value of the jewels and metals used, as well as the craftsmanship.

Seals with larger handles, either of wood, ivory or metal, semi-precious stones or porcelain were produced for the writing desk. They vary considerably from strictly utilitarian pieces in brass with a criss-cross pattern on the head, to beautifully carved or moulded handles with cornelian dies. Small seals were also produced in sets; these could be screwed on to the handle to suit the occasion. Often they bore mottoes like "Forget me not" or "Thank Rowland Hill for this" – an allusion to cheap postage. Handles were often shaped like statues, horses' hooves or animals' heads; their variety and novelty was infinite.

READING
Seals, W de G Birch (Methuen)
Small Antiques for the Collector, Therle Hughes (Lutterworth)
Romance of Seals and Engraved Gems, Sutherland (Collier-Macmillan)

TO VIEW
British Museum, London. National Maritime Museum, Greenwich, London. Victoria and Albert Museum, London. Royal Pavilion, Brighton. Royal Scottish Museum, Edinburgh. Museum and Art Gallery, Reading. Salisbury and South Wiltshire Museum, Salisbury. City Museum, Sheffield. City Museum and Art Gallery, Stoke-on-Trent. Wedgwood Museum, Stoke-on-Trent. Elizabethan House, Totnes. City Museum and Art Gallery, Worcester.

Sèvres

A factory for the manufacture of porcelain was established at Vincennes in 1738, under the patronage of Orry de Fulvy, by two workmen named Dubois. Although they failed to produce porcelain, a craftsman named Gravant finally succeeded in 1745 and a company was formed, in which King Louis XV had shares. The factory was taken over by the King in 1759, having been transferred to Sèvres, between Paris and Versailles, in 1756. The factory was famous for two types of porcelain (i) a soft paste or frit porcelain (*porcelaine de France*) and (2) a hard paste (*porcelaine Royale*). The latter is distinguished by its compact texture and dead white tone. The earlier soft paste was more suitable for simple vessels and dishes and was most suitable for the brilliant colours then employed. Porcelain flowers, modelled on the productions of Meissen, were among the best-known items made at Vincennes. Figures, modelled in the style of Boucher by Falconet were produced at Vincennes and Sèvres from 1751 onwards. Sèvres porcelain was very popular in Britain between 1763 and the outbreak of the French Revolution but, being very expensive, is seldom seen outside museums and stately houses. The Wallace Collection in London boasts the finest collection of Sèvres porcelain in England. The Sèvres mark consisted of the royal cypher (two cursive L's), but unfortunately it has been faked and copied unscrupulously so that its presence on a piece of porcelain is no guarantee of its origin.

READING

The Soft Paste Porcelain of Sèvres, E Garnier (Nimmo). *French Porcelain of the 18th Century*, W B Honey (Faber) *Sèvres Porcelain of Buckingham Palace and Windsor Castle*, G F Laking (Bradbury) *Seventeenth and Eighteenth Century French Porcelain*, G Savage (Barrie and Rockliffe)

TO VIEW

British Museum, London. Victoria and Albert Museum, London. Wallace Collection, London. Waddesdon Manor, Aylesbury. National Museum of Wales, Cardiff. Royal Scottish Museum, Edinburgh. Harewood House, Leeds. Glynde Place, Lewes. Wernher Collection, Luton Hoo. Scone Palace, Perth. County Museum, Stafford. City Museum and Art Gallery, Stoke-on-Trent. Spode-Copeland Museum and Art Gallery, Stoke-on-Trent. Windsor

Castle, Windsor. City Museum and Art Gallery, Worcester.

DEALERS
Antique Porcelain Co Limited, 149 New Bond Street, London w1. Beauchamp Galleries, 8 Beauchamp Place, London sw3. Spink and Son Limited, 5–7 King Street, London sw1. Andrew Dando, 4 Wood Street, Queen Square, Bath. Margaret Cadman, 25 Ship Street, Brighton.

Shagreen

This word, like the word *chagrin*, is derived from the Turkish *saghri*, meaning a horse's rump. From this unlikely source the word came to mean a kind of rough hide which gave rise to the metaphorical sense of acute disappointment on the one hand, and, in the literal sense, a kind of untanned leather, with an artificially granulated surface. It came from the skins of horses, asses, donkeys or camels and was usually, though not always, dyed green. It was also prepared from shark-skin rough with natural papillae.

This tough yet attractive leather was ideally suited for objects likely to have to stand up to hard wear and tear. Thus it is found in jewel cases, hand bags, travelling boxes of all kinds, cases for matched pairs of scent bottles, étuis (q.v.), etc. Real shagreen has now been largely superseded by artificial leathers made of plastics or paper.

TO VIEW
Bethnal Green Museum, London. Guildhall Museum, London. National Army Museum, Camberley. Royal Scottish Museum, Edinburgh. Temple Newsam House, Leeds. City Museum, Sheffield.

Shaving mugs

The shaving mug is an interesting relic of the period when the open razor had its hey-day. The earliest examples appeared at the end of the 19th century but it was in the hundred years from 1830 till 1930 that the shaving mug enjoyed great popularity. Although mugs were manufactured in Britain and Europe, the United States was the true home of this vessel and no fewer than 94 patents for shaving mugs were granted between 1860 and 1940. This gives some indication of the wide variety of shapes and styles, ranging from the simple, squat, mug to the elaborate device incorporating soap and brush holders and ingenious drainers. They were made in a wide variety of materials, ranging from brass and silver to white opal ware, stone ware, porcelain and lustre ware.

Late 19th century shaving mug.

Peculiar to America was the Barber Shop mug, embellished with the name of a particular customer. These named mugs were kept in special racks in barber's shops and brought out as and when required for the "regulars". Glass covered label mugs were made of white pottery to which was glued a thick, lithographed label covered with a thin coating of glass for protection from moisture. Other designs had floral, bird or scenic motifs, trades emblems or occupational motifs, numerals (used in barber's shops) and, latterly, photographic transfers bearing portraits of prominent citizens, politicians and national celebrities. The best-known manufacturers were Thomas E Hughes of Birmingham, Pennsylvania, Smith Brothers of Boston, Koken Barbers' Supply Co of St Louis and Herold Brothers of Cleveland. Barber's shop mugs went into decline during the First World War when many soldiers learned to shave themselves, but the advent of the safety razor, brushless shaving creams and the electric razor rang their death-knell. Now these quaint relics of the not so distant past are avidly collected, particularly in the United States.

Victoria and Albert Museum, London. Museum and Art Gallery, Leicester. City Museum, Sheffield. City Museum and Art Gallery, Stoke-on-Trent. City Museum and Art Gallery, Worcester.

Sheffield plate

This term, derived from the Yorkshire city of Sheffield, is used to denote a process of coating copper with a thin sheet of silver by fusion. Tradition has it that a Sheffield cutler named Thomas Boulsover, about 1742, was repairing a copper knife haft and while wedging it in the vice with a silver coin during the heating process, discovered by accident that the copper had become fused to the silver. Following tentative experiments Boulsover succeeded in producing small trinkets and buttons of copper with a silver coating fused on but it was left to Joseph Hancock to realise the wider possibilities of the process. He it was who first produced saucepans, candle-sticks, coffee pots and other large articles closely resembling the far more expensive items in solid silver. Hancock was engaged in the manufacture of Sheffield plate from about 1750 until 1765 but the industry received new impetus under the partnership of Tudor and Leader, Thomas Law and Matthew Boulton (the latter operating in Birmingham).

The manufacture of fused silver plate, originally confined to Sheffield and Birmingham, spread to the Continent in the early 19th century but was inferior in quality and craftsmanship to the English plate. The death knell of Sheffield plate was sounded in 1850 when Elkington patented his electro-plating process (q.v.). Genuine examples of Sheffield plate, recognisable often by their tell-tale coppery glow where the silver is wearing thin, are very rare and tend to fetch higher prices than the corresponding articles in silver. Beware, however, of Sheffield plate which has been resilvered by electro-plating.

READING

Old Sheffield Plate, John Bedford (Cassell)
Old Sheffield Plate Makers Marks, 1740–1860, F Bradbury (Northend Pub.)
Old Sheffield Plate, R A Robertson (Benn)
Book of Sheffield Plate, B Wylie (Crown Pub., New York)

TO VIEW

Victoria and Albert Museum, London. City Museum and Art Gallery, Birmingham. National Army Museum, Camberley. Royal Scottish Museum, Edinburgh. City Museum, Hereford. City Museum, Sheffield (Very important collection).

DEALERS

A B Davis, 89–91 Queensway, London w2. P G Dodd and Son Limited, 42 Cornhill, London EC3. I Freeman and Son Limited, 18 Leather Lane, London EC1. Simon Kaye Limited, 1b Albemarle Street, London w1. Prestons Limited, 91 Mount Street, London w1. S J Shrubsole Limited, 43 Museum Street, London wc1. William Walter Limited, Chancery House, Chancery Lane, London wc2. John Bell, Bridge Street, Aberdeen. Charles T Gilmer Limited, 16 Old Bond Street, Bath. Ellis and Co Limited, 16 Constitution Hill, Hockley 19, Birmingham. H A Davis, 10 Duke Street, Brighton. Scott Cooper Limited, 52 The Promenade, Cheltenham, Glos. Thomas Hudson, 4 Dollar Street, Cirencester, Glos. Frank Wine and Son Limited, 71 Barton Arcade, Manchester. The Antiquary, 50 St Giles, Oxford. Thomas Love and Sons Limited, 51, 53 and 62 South Street, Perth. C H Thorpe, High Street, Uppingham, Rutland. Bernfeld Bros Limited, God Begot House, 101 High Street, Winchester, Hants.

Shells

On account of their bright colours and fascinating shapes the shells of molluscs have always held the attention of mankind. In some parts of the world, even to this day, certain shells, especially the small cowrie *Cypraea Moneta*, are used as a form of money. The collecting of shells dates back thousands of years, to pre-Dynastic Egypt and pre-Columbian America. In its present form the hobby is well documented from the Middle Ages onwards. Renaissance princes had their cabinets of rare and beautiful shells and the prices paid for some of these treasures seem fantastic by modern standards. As late as 1750 Kaiser Franz I of Austria is said to have paid 4,000 gulden (£400) for a specimen of the aptly named Precious Wentletrap, only a few of which were known to exist.

Pacific exploration and modern diving techniques seriously affected the rare shell market at the end of the 19th century and today a Precious Wentletrap can be obtained for about £3. Nevertheless shell collecting has revived enormously in the past two decades and in 1968 Sotheby's held an auction of shells – their first sale of this kind for many years.

The revival of the hobby may be traced to the United States. G.I.s serving in the Pacific area were captivated by the beauty and shape of the specimens picked up on the beaches; the development of skin diving as a recreation has greatly popularised shell collecting.

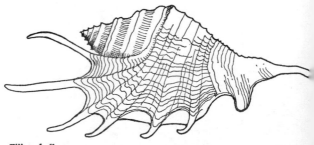

Fijian shell

READING
Collecting Sea Shells, Turk (Foyle)

TO VIEW
Natural History Museum, London. Victoria and Albert Museum, London. Museum and Art Gallery, Brighton. City Museum and Art Gallery, Birmingham. Royal Scottish Museum, Edinburgh. City Museum, Hereford. Central Museum and Art Gallery, Northampton. City Museum, Sheffield. City Museum and Art Gallery, Stoke-on-Trent. City Museum and Art Gallery, Worcester.

DEALERS
Eaton's Shell Shop, Mariotte Street, London W1.

Ships in bottles

These curious relics of Britain's maritime past form a distinctive branch of 19th century folk art. How or when they originated is not known but they were immensely popular in the hey-day of sailing ships. The technique of inserting the hull, with the masts and rigging laid flat and then hoisting them into position by means of thread lines, is well known. Ships in bottles are no longer as plentiful as they once were. At one time they were almost mass-produced as a cottage industry to meet the demands of an embryonic tourist trade. Small simple examples of this sort, containing nondescript three-masters, can still be picked up for a pound or two, but the real "thoroughbreds" – the intricately carved and rigged models of famous ships, perfect in every detail, take some finding and now cost a very great deal.

READING

How to Make a Ship in a Bottle, C Monk (Studio
Publications)

TO VIEW

National Maritime Museum, Greenwich, London.
Victoria and Albert Museum, London. Borough
Museum, Dartmouth. Royal Scottish Museum,
Edinburgh.

Signs

There is a growing fashion for the signs which used
to decorate shop fronts in the days when the general
public was less literate than it is today. Nowadays
even the barber's pole and the pestle and mortar of
the pharmacist are fast disappearing but at one time
every trade had its distinctive emblem – the spec-
tacles of the optician, the shears of the tailor, the
padlock of the ironmonger, the giant shoe of the
cobbler or bootmaker. These quaint items are now
keenly collected. Larger and more ambitious are the
figures of Highlanders which used to decorate the
doorways of tobacconists' shops (cf. the cigar-store
Indian of America) or even ships' figure heads.

Inn signs are also gaining in popularity and it is
surprising how often and in what places they turn
up. At sales of bygones they have been known to
fetch as much as £50 for a particularly fine specimen.
Plain, lettered signs fetch from £8 to £20.

German bracket sign of the
mid 18th century

READING

History of Signboards, Larwood and Hotten (Hotten)
London Signs and Inscriptions, Philip Norman (Stock)

Silhouettes

Etienne de Silhouette (1709–1767), notorious Controller-General of France for a brief period during 1759, antagonised the nobility by proposing a land-tax on their estates and the reduction of their pensions and this led to his speedy downfall. In allusion to the sacrifices which he demanded of the nobles, even the conversion of their table plate into money, *silhouette* became the popular word for a figure reduced to simplest form. Hence it came to be applied to the shadow outline of an object, usually a profile, obtained by projecting the shadow on to a sheet of white paper, tracing in the outline and afterwards filling in with dark colour. In the 1760s it became popular to have profile portraits cut out of black paper with scissors and mounted, though they were in existence for at least a decade before Silhouette unwittingly gave them his name. This form of portraiture went into eclipse a century later with the advent of photography. Framed and mounted silhouettes are highly collectable items, their value

Silhouette showing late 18th century hairstyle

219

depending on their degree of intricacy and elaboration.

READING
The Art of Silhouette, D Coke (Secker & Warburg)
Silhouettes, Peggy Hickman (Cassell)
Profile Art Through the Ages, R J Megroz (Art Trade Press)
British Silhouettes, J Woodiwiss (Country Life)

TO VIEW
Victoria and Albert Museum, London. Fitzwilliam Museum, Cambridge. City Museum, Hereford. Temple Newsam House, Leeds. Museum and Art Gallery, Leicester. Central Museum and Art Gallery, Northampton. Elizabethan House, Totnes.

CLUB
The Silhouette Collectors Club, 15 Shelley Road, Bognor Regis, Sussex.

DEALERS
Most general antique dealers, particularly country dealers.

Slag ware

Despite its unprepossessing name slag ware is a most attractive substance. This ceramic curiosity consists of a blend of glass and stone, produced originally from a mixture of the waste or slag left over at the end of the day at the glass foundry. This was mixed with lead glass to produce a beautiful opaque material in various colours, ranging from greens and blues to purple and white. Slag ware was moulded or pressed into numerous shapes such as sugar basins, jam dishes, vases, bottles and cake baskets.

Under the name of "vitro-porcelain" slag ware was a speciality of Sowerby's of Newcastle-upon-Tyne. Most slag ware seems to have been manufactured in the Tyneside area.

TO VIEW
Victoria and Albert Museum, London. Museum and Art Gallery, Brighton. City Museum, Sheffield.

DEALERS
Those specialising in ceramics.

Slip ware

This is earthen ware which is covered wholly or partly with a "slip" of coloured liquid clay, usually but not always of a different colour from that of the body. The object thus decorated was either wholly immersed in the slip or, more commonly, the liquid was applied rather like the iced decoration on a cake, in a "trail" laid on the earthen ware body while it was still soft, before firing in the kiln.

Slip ware was produced in many countries; in England it was particularly popular with the potters of Staffordshire and Sussex, the latter specialising in an attractive form of inlay using slip of a contrasting colour. The fashion for slip ware died out in the latter part of the 19th century, though a certain amount of "folk-art" pottery produced at the present time uses the same techniques. Early examples of slip ware, dating from the middle of the 17th century onwards, are now extremely rare, having for the most part disappeared into museum collections. Victorian slip ware jugs and dishes, however, are not too difficult to find at prices ranging from a few shillings upwards.

READING

English Slipware Dishes (*1600–1850*), R G Cooper (Tiranti)
Small Antiques for the Collector, Therle Hughes (Lutterworth)
Slipcast Pottery, A T White (Dryad)

TO VIEW

British Museum, London. Guildhall Museum, London. Victoria and Albert Museum, London. Museum and Art Gallery, Brighton. Royal Scottish Museum, Edinburgh. City Museum, Hereford. Temple Newsam House, Leeds. Anne of Cleves House, Lewes. City Museum and Art Gallery, Northampton. City Museum, Sheffield. City Museum and Art Gallery, Stoke-on-Trent. City Museum and Art Gallery, Worcester. The Yorkshire Museum, York.

DEALERS

D M & P Manheim, 69 Upper Berkeley Street, Portman Square, London w1. Arthur West Antiques, The Strand, Dawlish, Devon. Runnymede Galleries, Egham, Surrey. S M Collins, Leeds Road, Ilkley, Yorks. Evaline Winter, Rugeley, Staffs.

Snuff bottles

The Oriental equivalent of the snuff-box was the snuff bottle. These little bottles may be found in a variety of coloured glass, often delicately cut or inlaid or carved in cameo fashion. Semi-precious

Ivory snuff bottle from
Japan

stone, such as jade, amethyst or lapis lazuli, was also
used but bottles carved from such exotic materials
are exceedingly expensive. Bottles made from
coloured glass or Chinese porcelain can still be found
for a pound or two, depending on condition and
degree of ornamentation. They should be complete
with matching stopper, preferably with a tiny spoon
attached, by which the fastidious Mandarin would
measure out the precise quantity of snuff required.

READING
Chinese Snuff Bottles, L S Perry (Prentice Hall)

TO VIEW
British Museum, London. Victoria and Albert
Museum, London. Wallace Collection, London.
Royal Scottish Museum, Edinburgh. City Museum,
Hereford. Central Museum and Art Gallery, North-
ampton. City Museum, Sheffield. Windsor Castle,
Windsor.

DEALERS
Bluett and Sons, 48 Davies Street, London w1.
M Hakim, 4 Royal Arcade, Old Bond Street,
London w1. Spink and Son Limited, 5–7 King Street,
London sw1. Syndey L Moss Limited, 51 Brook
Street, London w1. Wells, 37a Crawford Street,
London w1. Collectors Treasures Limited, 91 High
Street, Amersham. Grammar Galleries Ltd, Peter
Street, Shepton Mallet, Somerset. Collectors Trea-
sures Limited, 8–9 Church Street, Windsor.

Snuff boxes

Romano Pane, a Franciscan Friar who accompanied
Columbus on his first voyage to the West Indies,
records the curious custom of the Indians who

derived great enjoyment from a golden leaf, by grinding it to powder and sniffing it up their nostrils. Snuff-taking was presumably established in Europe at the same time as tobacco smoking. By the middle of the 17th century snuff-taking was wholly acceptable in polite society and the small boxes designed to contain the powder were attracting the skill and attention of the goldsmith, the jeweller and the miniaturist who combined to produce an object which, at its best, has been hailed as "an elegant epitome of an age of elegance".

While richly jewelled or enamelled gold snuff boxes have been known to fetch thousands of pounds in the sale-room, there are many examples of this kind of box, made in humbler materials, which can still be picked up for a pound or two. Boxes made of wood, ivory, tortoiseshell or pinchbeck can be found in a wide variety of shapes and sizes and are usually reasonably priced. Silver boxes, on account of their intrinsic value, are normally more expensive. All but the very small ones (which were exempt from assay) should bear hallmarks and thus be possible to date accurately. Those bearing an inscription, often of a commemorative nature, are particularly interesting if the background to the recipient and the presentation can be traced.

Early 19th century agate snuff box mounted in gold

READING

European and American Snuff Boxes, 1730–1830, Le Corbeiller (Batsford)
Silver Boxes, Eric Delieb (Barrie and Rockliffe)

A History of Gold Snuff Boxes, K & M A Norton
Eighteenth century gold boxes of Europe, Kenneth
Snowman (Faber)

TO VIEW

British Museum, London. Victoria and Albert
Museum, London. Wallace Collection, London.
Wellington Museum, London. Waddesdon Manor,
Aylesbury. City Museum and Art Gallery, Birming-
ham. Royal Pavilion, Brighton. National Museum
of Wales, Cardiff. Royal Scottish Museum, Edin-
burgh. City Museum, Hereford. Temple Newsam
House, Leeds. Museum and Art Gallery, Leicester.
Central Museum and Art Gallery, Northampton.
Ashmolean Museum of Art & Archaeology, Oxford.
Salisbury and South Wiltshire Museum, Salisbury.
City Museum, Sheffield. City Museum and Art
Gallery, Stoke-on-Trent. Royal Tunbridge Wells
Museum and Art Gallery, Tunbridge Wells.
Windsor Castle, Windsor. City Museum and Art
Gallery, Worcester.

DEALERS

Antiques Corner Limited, 104 Mount Street, Lon-
don w1. N Bloom and Son Limited, 39 Albemarle
Street, London w1. M Hakim, 4 Royal Arcade, Old
Bond Street, London w1. Hancocks and Co Limited,
9 Vigo Street, London w1. J Lipitch, 10a, 25 & 26
St Christopher's Place, Wigmore Street, London w1.
D M and P Manheim, 69 Upper Berkeley Street,
Portman Square, London w1. S J Phillips Limited,
139 New Bond Street, London w1. Tessiers Limited,
26 New Bond Street, London w1. D & M Davis
Limited, 3 Livery Street, Birmingham. Owen's
Antiques, 86–88 Salisbury Road, Cathays, Cardiff.
Richard H Everard, Woodhouse Eaves, Nr Lough-
borough, Leicester. Staplegrove Lodge Antiques,
Taunton, Somerset. Also – most general dealers.

Spinning wheels

The spinning of thread by means of a spindle dates back to prehistory, but the earliest record of the use of such a mechanical refinement as a wheel is in a European illustrated manuscript of the 14th century, though it is believed that some form of spinning wheel was used in India at a much earlier date. This primitive wheel was known in Britain as a bobbing wheel and remained in use until the early 19th century. As early as 1533, however, a German invented the treadle which allowed the spinner to manipulate the fibres with both hands, and this, with modifications, is the type of spinning wheel used by hand spinners to this day. The size and style of spinning wheel differs considerably, not only from one country to another, but within the same country. Hand-spinning was, until very recently, a common pastime in the Western Highlands and islands of Scotland and the remoter districts of North Wales. As hand· spinning is dying out spinning wheels are being acquired by antique shops, even although there are still manufacturers turning them out.

READING

Chats on Cottage and Farmhouse Furniture, A Hayden (Benn)
Cottage Antiques, Therle Hughes (Lutterworth)

TO VIEW

Geffrye Museum, London. Science Museum, Kensington, London. Victoria and Albert Museum, London. Waddesdon Manor, Aylesbury. Museum and Art Gallery, Brighton. The Royal Pavilion, Brighton. National Museum of Antiquities of Scotland, Edinburgh. Royal Scottish Museum, Edinburgh. City Museum, Hereford. Temple Newsam House, Leeds. Museum and Art Gallery, Leicester. Central Museum and Art Gallery, Northampton. Blithfield, Rugeley, Staffordshire. City Museum,

Sheffield. City Museum and Art Gallery, Stoke-on-Trent. Elizabethan House, Totnes, Devon. City Museum and Art Gallery, Worcester. Snowshill Manor, Worcester.

DEALERS
Gordon Hand & Company, 18 Chepstow Mansions, Westbourne Grove, London w2. Ivar Mackay, 4 Kensington Church Walk, London w8. Graham Pontet Limited, 102 Mount Street, London w1. John Bell, 56–58 Bridge Street, Aberdeen. Roger Warner, High Street, Burford, Oxford. Dunnings Antiques, 58–62 Holywell Hill, St Albans, Herts. Christopher Clarke, The Square, Stow-on-the-Wold, Glos.

Spode

Josiah Spode (1733–1797) who took over a pottery at Stoke in 1770, has given his name to one of the aristocrats of English ceramics. Spode manufactured printed earthen ware and then progressed towards bone china and later imitated the jasper and basaltes pioneered by Wedgwood. The company was acquired by William Copeland in 1833 and later products are therefore marked "Copeland Spode". In the later period Spode's produced excellent blue and white earthen ware reproducing landmarks and scenery. Particularly prized are those depicting scenes in Italy – popular with the upper classes of the period who had undertaken the Grand Tour. The firm of Copeland-Spode is still active and many of its modern productions – dinner services, plates, figures and plaques – would be worth considering as antiques of the future.

READING

Spode and His Successors, A Hayden (Cassell)
Antique Blue and White Spode, S B Williams (Batsford)

TO VIEW

British Museum, London. Victoria and Albert Museum, London. Museum and Art Gallery, Brighton. Royal Scottish Museum, Edinburgh. City Museum, Hereford. Central Museum and Art Gallery, Northampton. Scone Palace, Perth. Salisbury and South Wiltshire Museum, Salisbury. City Museum, Sheffield. City Museum and Art Gallery, Stoke-on-Trent. Spode-Copeland Museum and Art Gallery, Stoke-on-Trent (most important collection). Windsor Castle, Windsor.

CLUB

English Ceramic Circle, 8 Church Row, London NW3

DEALERS

Albert Amor Limited, 37 Bury Street, St James, London SW1. The Antique Porcelain Company Limited, 149 New Bond Street, London W1. D & M Manheim Limited, 69 Upper Berkeley Street, Portman Square, London W1. Jean Sewell Limited, 3 & 4 Campden Street, Kensington Church Street, London W8. Spink and Son Limited, 5–7 King Street, London SW1. Andrew Dando, 4 Wood Street, Queen Square, Bath. The Old Black Horse, Burnham Market, Norfolk. Silver Cottage Antiques, The Green, Datchet, Bucks. The Ship's Wheel, 2 Traill Street, Thurso, Caithness.

NOTE—See china marks on page xx at the beginning of the book.

Spoons

These table implements have come a long way from the primitive shells and splinters of wood used in prehistoric times. The Egyptians used spoons carved from ivory, flint, slate or wood, while the Greeks and Romans favoured spoons in bronze or silver. In the Middle Ages spoons for domestic use were usually made of horn or wood, though pewter and latten (a form of brass) spoons are known from the 18th century. Early silver or gold spoons are excessively rare, being confined more or less to royal households.

The practice of giving spoons at christenings in Tudor times gave rise to a special type of spoon, known as the Apostle Spoon (q.v.). The earliest English spoon handles terminated in an acorn, plain knob or diamond. At the end of the 16th century the baluster and seal ending became common. At the Restoration the handle became broad and flat. In the early 18th century the bowl became narrow and elliptical, with a tongue or "rat's tail" down the back, and the handle was turned up at the end. The modern form, with the tip of the bowl narrower than the base and the rounded end of the handle turned down, appeared around 1760.

In modern times spoons have been produced for many specialised purposes, from cruet and coffee spoons to table spoons and serving spoons. In between there is a vast range of sizes and types. Collectors may specialise in certain fields – such as crested tea-spoons, or ornamental caddy spoons. Or they may collect loving spoons, carved and presented as a token of affection (hence the expression "spooning").

READING
Old English Plate, W J Cripps (Spring Books)
The Old Silver Spoons of England, N Gask (Herbert Jenkins)

Small Antiques for the Collector, Therle Hughes (Lutterworth)
The Spoon and its History, C J Jackson
Old Base Metal Spoons, F G H Price (Batsford)

Staffordshire figures

Probably the best known example of English folk art is the Staffordshire pottery figure which, at one time, could have been found in profusion in every cottage in the country. They were produced by the lesser potteries and even formed a substantial 'cottage industry' in which the whole family participated. The best-known examples of this *genre* are what are known in Scotland as "wally dugs", but in England are more accurately described as spaniels. They come in matched pairs, vigorously coloured in brown, black and white, with naïve expressions on their faces.

Apart from the dogs there are cows and other farmyard animals, milkmaids, sailors and highlanders. The famous and the not so famous were commemorated by figures and busts. What the portraiture lacked in sensitivity was more than compensated in their quaintly appealing character. Staffordshire figures range in value from a few shillings for a dog to about £100 for one of the rarer portrait groups such as Prince Albert and Queen Victoria at the time of their wedding. The literature on this popular subject is extensive.

Staffordshire figurine of
Benjamin Franklin, 1840

READING

Staffordshire Portrait Figures of the Victorian Age, T Balston (Faber)
Staffordshire Pottery Figures, J Bedford (Cassell)
English Ceramic Figures, G Bernard Hughes (Lutterworth)
Victorian Staffordshire Portrait Figures, B Latham (Tiranti)
Collecting Staffordshire Pottery, L T Stanley (W H Allen)

TO VIEW

British Museum, London. Fenton House, London. Victoria and Albert Museum, London. City Museum and Art Gallery, Birmingham. Museum and Art Gallery, Brighton. Museum and Art Gallery, Bootle. Royal Scottish Museum, Edinburgh. City Museum, Hereford. Temple Newsam House, Leeds. Museum and Art Gallery, Leicester. Wernher Collection, Luton Hoo. Stapleford Park, Melton Mowbray. Central Museum and Art Gallery, Northampton. Salisbury and South Wiltshire Museum, Salisbury. City Museum, Sheffield. City Museum and Art Gallery, Stoke-on-Trent.

CLUB

English Ceramic Circle, 8 Church Row, London NW3.

DEALERS

John Hall and David MacWilliams, 17 Harrington Road, London SW7. The Lion and the Unicorn, 11 Bute Street, London SW7. A J Reffold & Partners Limited, 1 Pont Street, London SW1. Them and Theirs, 17a St Christopher Place, London W1. Lionel Young, 93a Crawford Street, London W1. Benjamin Sims, 39 Upper North Street, Brighton. Tom Jones Antiques, The Mill, North Road, Bourne, Lincs. Antiques Unlimited, Canton, Cardiff. The Skip, 10 Barclay Terrace, Edinburgh. White Horse Antiques, 14 Gloucester Road, Ross-on-Wye, Hereford. The Old Forge, Pilgrim's Way, Hollingbourne, Kent. Long Farthing Antiques, West Burton, Nr Aysgarth, Leyburn, Yorks. Bown's Antique Store, Pontypridd, Glamorgan. Evaline Winter, Wolseley Road, Rugeley, Staffs. Wolseley Bridge Antiques, Staffs. The Treasure Chest, Taunton, Somerset. Brooks of Winchester, St Thomas Street, Winchester, Hants.

Stamp boxes

Small boxes designed to contain postage stamps became necessary soon after the introduction of adhesive stamps in May 1840. Perforation was not invented till 1854 so the earliest stamps had to be cut apart with a knife or scissors. These little boxes were useful for keeping a stock of stamps ready-cut. The earliest ones were probably those shaped like pill boxes – indeed, it is possible that pill boxes themselves were often used as a handy receptacle for the new stamps. Particularly prized are the small, flat, circular boxes, about 1½″ in diameter, covered with tartan and the name of the appropriate Scottish clan. Stamp boxes were also a favourite with the manufacturers of Tunbridge ware (q.v.), thousands of tiny tesserae being used to make a mosaic replica of the contemporary Queen's head postage stamps.

Stamp boxes may be found in wood, cardboard, ivory, bone, porcelain and a variety of metals, including silver and gold. The elegant silver stamp boxes dating around the end of the century consisted of one, two or three compartments and the lid had a glass top into which specimens of the various denominations were inserted for added decoration. Some of the later boxes have a spring-loaded base and an attachment which dispensed one stamp at a time. Of particular interest are the boxes which have contemporary (and very cheap!) postal rates inscribed on them; these tables of rates are a useful aid to dating a box correctly. Stamp boxes may be recognised by a sloping interior (though not all boxes had this feature) while an actual postage stamp was not infrequently stuck to the lid and varnished over. With the introduction of stamp booklets in the 1900's the use of stamp boxes, either for the pocket or the writing desk, gradually declined.

READING
All Kinds of Small Boxes, J Bedford (Cassell)
Silver Boxes, Eric Delieb (Herbert Jenkins)

Stevengraphs

This is the trade name given to silk pictures woven by Thomas Stevens of Coventry from 1863 onwards. At a time when the weaving of fancy silk ribbons was hit economically by the removal of the government embargo on imported silk goods from Europe, Stevens devised his silk pictures to meet the Continental challenge. By adapting the Jacquard loom to produce little multicoloured pictures he established a market for his novelties which endured till the First World War. Interest in Stevengraphs dwindled in the 1920s but the factory continued in operation till the Blitz of 1940. During the past few years interest in silk pictures has revived and Knight, Frank and Rutley in London have held several auction sales devoted entirely to Stevengraphs.

Until recently it was possible to buy good examples for a few shillings; now they fetch as many pounds, while individual rarities have fetched as much as £450 at auctions.

The subjects of Stevengraphs are many and varied. Royalty, politicians and celebrities of the sporting world were particularly popular. Sporting scenes, such as the trio entitled "The Meet", "Full Cry" and "The Death", or pictures of famous jockeys and racehorses, are now in great demand and fetch high prices. Also worth looking for are historical tableaux ("Death of Nelson" or "Christopher Columbus") or any Stevengraphs showing early locomotives. Among the commoner items are the many representations of Lady Godiva and "Ye Peeping Tom".

READING

The Silk Pictures of Thomas Stevens, W L Baker (Exposition Press Inc., U.S.A.)

TO VIEW

Victoria and Albert Museum, London. Rothesay Museum, Bournemouth. Herbert Art Gallery and Museum, Coventry. Elizabethan House, Totnes. City Museum and Art Gallery, Worcester.

CLUB

Stevengraph Collectors' Association, Irvington-on-Hudson, New York, USA.

Stone ware

This name is given to a particularly hard earthen ware fired in the kiln at a higher temperature than normal. It should not be confused with stone china, also a type of earthen ware, glazed to simulate porcelain.

Stone ware was usually glazed by the ingenious method of throwing common salt into the kiln during firing. The salt vapourised and acted on the stone ware in such a way as to give it a durable glaze. Salt glazed stone ware ranges in type (and value) from the late 18th century Staffordshire vases, dishes and teapots to the stone ware bottles of the early 19th century, used for rum, gin, brandy and whisky. Many of the latter were gaudily decorated or were shaped in many fanciful forms, to serve as ornaments as well as useful vessels, decorating the gantries in inns and pubs. The repeal of the Glass Excise in 1845 led to them being rapidly superseded by glass bottles. They are seldom seen nowadays, having been collectors' items for over a century now.

READING

The ABC of English Saltglaze Stoneware, J F Blacker (S Paul)

TO VIEW

British Museum, London. Victoria and Albert Museum, London. Wallace Collection, London. Museum and Art Gallery, Brighton. Royal Scottish Museum, Edinburgh. City Museum, Hereford. Central Museum and Art Gallery, Northampton. City Museum, Nottingham. Salisbury and South Wiltshire Museum, Salisbury. City Museum, Sheffield. City Museum and Art Gallery, Stoke-on-Trent. Spode-Copeland Museum and Art Gallery, Stoke-on-Trent. Wedgwood Museum, Stoke-on-Trent. City Museum and Art Gallery, Worcester.

DEALERS

Jean Sewell Limited, 3 & 4 Campden Street, London w8. Tilley and Co Limited, 2 Symons Street, Sloane Square, London sw3. Arthur West Antiques, The Strand, Dawlish, Devon. Runnymede Galleries, Egham, Surrey. S M Collins, 105 Leeds Road, Ilkley, Yorks. Evaline Winter, 1 Wolseley Road, Rugeley, Staffs.

Straw marquetry

Inlaid work on wooden articles, using pieces of straw which were often dyed in colour, was a speciality of the French prisoners-of-war interned at Peterborough in Northamptonshire during the Napoleonic period. They eked out their miserable allowances by decorating boxes, trays, fire-screens, etc with this intricate straw-work, either in geometric patterns or in ambitious pictorial designs. Straw marquetry was also carried on in traditional straw plaiting centres such as Luton, and a great deal of this kind of work was done in France and Austria until fairly recently.

Early examples, particularly genuine articles produced by the French prisoners, are extremely rare, since straw marquetry has not stood up to the rigours of time as well as conventional wood marquetry.

READING

Prisoners-of-War-Work, 1756–1815, J Toller (Golden Head Press)

TO VIEW

Bethnal Green Museum, London. Victoria and Albert Museum, London. City Museum and Art Gallery, Birmingham. Museum and Art Gallery, Brighton. Royal Scottish Museum, Edinburgh. Snowshill Manor, Worcester.

Stump work

The name, given to a form of raised needlework, is derived from the "stump" of wool used to fill out the figures. This distinctive style of needlework had come into use in England by the time of Queen Elizabeth and was the sort of work to which children graduated after they had produced an acceptable sampler.

The figures would often be worked separately, like little dolls, and then sewn on to the background, usually of satin. These figures were made of old pieces of material sewn together and stuffed with wool or horse-hair. The "three dimensional" effect was heightened by the use of wooden limbs and wax faces. The background might include patches of real moss, pieces of fur, feathers or straw, all neatly sewn into place in what would nowadays be termed a collage.

Stump work, being a far more tedious process than straightforward needle work (q.v.) was never as popular, yet endured fitfully till the general decline of such pursuits in the late 19th century. Favourite subjects were historical or religious scenes. Stump work pictures were usually mounted and framed for hanging on walls. Good examples are rarely seen nowadays outside museums, though the somewhat artificial late Victorian stump work, with its extravagant use of silver thread, lace and sequins, may still be found occasionally.

TO VIEW

Victoria and Albert Museum, London. Royal Scottish Museum, Edinburgh. Museum and Muniment Room, Guildford. Museum and Art Gallery, Leicester. Salisbury and South Wiltshire Museum, Salisbury. City Museum, Sheffield. City Museum and Art Gallery, Stoke-on-Trent. Snowshill Manor, Worcester.

Tea caddies

These are boxes, jars, canisters or other receptacles
for keeping tea. The word is thought to be derived
from *catty*, a Chinese unit of weight, equal to about
$1\frac{1}{3}$ lb. avoirdupois. The earliest examples imported
into England were of Chinese porcelain, in the blue
and white style with lids or stoppers of the same
material. They were soon imitated in pottery and,
later, in English porcelain. During the latter part of
the 18th and early 19th centuries, when tea drinking
was an elegant pastime, caddies were often made of
rosewood, satinwood, walnut or mahogany. These
caddies contained two or more boxes, for different
varieties of tea, and a mixing bowl, usually of glass or
porcelain. These wooden caddies, complete with
bowl and cannisters, vary from simple country
craftsmanship to the sophisticated articles produced
by the fashionable cabinet makers of London.

Silver tea caddy, English,
1773/4

Tea caddies may be found in silver, copper, pewter, enamel ware, ivory or even papier maché (q.v.).
Although they were mass-produced, tea caddies
embellished with pictures and inscriptions com-
memorating Royal occasions (Queen Victoria's
Jubilees, and coronations from Edward VII to
Elizabeth II), are highly prized on account of their
association with historic events.

239

READING
Small Antique Furniture, Bernard and Therle Hughes
(Lutterworth)

TO VIEW
Geffrye Museum, London. Sir John Soane's Museum,
London. Victoria and Albert Museum, London.
Royal Pavilion, Brighton. Royal Scottish Museum,
Edinburgh. Museum and Art Gallery, Leicester.
Central Museum and Art Gallery, Northampton.
Salisbury and South Wiltshire Museum, Salisbury.
City Museum, Sheffield. City Museum and Art
Gallery, Stoke-on-Trent. Wedgwood Museum,
Stoke-on-Trent. Elizabethan House, Totnes.

DEALERS
Michael Kenyon, 183 Fulham Road, London sw3.
Thomas Hudson, 4 Dollar Street, Cirencester, Glos.
B & R Elliott, 61 West Street, Farnham, Surrey.
James Brett, 100 Pottersgate, Norwich, Norfolk.

Tea pots

In a letter dated June 27, 1615, Mr R L Wickham,
the Honourable East India Company's agent at
Firando, Japan, wrote to his counterpart at Macao,
"I pray you buy for me a pot of the best *chaw*". This
was not only the first traceable reference in English
to the Chinese *ch'a* but to the vessel in which it was
infused.

The tea pot had its origins in the Chinese wine jug
and, bearing in mind the cost of tea (it varied in price
from £6 to £1 per pound, 1660–1760) it is hardly
surprising that the tea pots of the 17th and 18th
centuries were expensive articles in themselves.
Exquisite silver tea pots were produced in this

period, while the great porcelain factories of the 18th century manufactured tea pots which are now very expensive indeed. It was not until 1858, when the Honourable East India Company's tea monopoly was abolished, that the price of tea dropped sufficiently to put it within reach of all classes of society. From this date onwards tea pots are increasingly found in cheaper materials – earthenware, pottery and enamelled metals. Some interesting glass tea pots have appeared in recent years on the Continent.

A collection of 450 tea pots, formed by Thomas Williams of Newquay, was sold for £1,553 at Puttick and Simpson in 1968. The largest tea pot in the collection weighed 15 lb empty and held four gallons of tea. Reputedly manufactured in South Wales in 1840, this splendid tea pot was sold for £110, but interesting and unusual examples can still be picked up in antique shops for under £5. (See also Barge Tea Pots.)

Silver teapot, 1833/4

READING
Talking about Teapots, J Bedford (Parrish)
Small Decorative Antiques, Therle Hughes (Lutterworth)
Teapots, Pottery and Porcelain, F Tilley (HMSO)
Teapots and Tea, F Tilley (Ceramic)

TO VIEW
British Museum, London. Geffrye Museum, London. Victoria and Albert Museum, London. Museum and Art Gallery, Brighton. Royal Scottish Museum,

Edinburgh. City Museum, Hereford. Wernher Collection, Luton Hoo. Central Museum and Art Gallery, Northampton. Salisbury and South Wiltshire Museum, Salisbury. City Museum, Sheffield. City Museum and Art Gallery, Stoke-on-Trent. Spode-Copeland Museum and Art Gallery, Stoke-on-Trent. Wedgwood Museum, Stoke-on-Trent. Elizabethan House, Totnes, Devon. The Sharp Collection, Green Place, Wonersh, Surrey. City Museum and Art Gallery, Worcester. Windsor Castle, Windsor.

DEALERS
Most antique dealers.

Terra cotta

The Latin words for "baked earth" are used to describe unglazed earthen ware of a fine texture, varying in colour from yellow–brown to deep red. It is the oldest form of earthen ware known to mankind and ranges from the primitive clay figures found all over the world from ancient Egypt and China to pre-Columbian America. The Greeks produced finely modelled statuettes in terra cotta, not to mention urns and vases. It was universally popular in Europe till the end of the Renaissance, but the advent of porcelain, first imported from China and subsequently manufactured in Germany, France, Italy and England, led to a decline in terra cotta. There was a brief revival in the manufacture of terra cotta figures at the Sèvres pottery between 1792 and 1801, when the finest sculptors of France produced some exquisite pieces. Names to look for include Pajou Pagalle, Clodion, La Rue, Caffieri, Falconet and Boizot. Little in the way of modern sculpture is done in terra cotta since it involves the personal retouching by the artist of the detail of each piece, whereas casting in bronze can be relegated to skilled workmen.

Apart from figures, however, terra cotta tiles are more plentiful and many attractive designs in this medium can still be picked up for a pound or two.

TO VIEW

British Museum, London. Sir John Soane's Museum, London. Victoria and Albert Museum, London. Wallace Collection, London. Waddesdon Manor, Aylesbury. Museum and Art Gallery, Brighton. Royal Scottish Museum, Edinburgh. Central Museum and Art Gallery, Northampton. City Museum, Sheffield. City Museum and Art Gallery, Stoke-on-Trent. Wedgwood Museum, Stoke-on-Trent. Windsor Castle, Windsor.

DEALERS

Frank Partridge and Sons Limited, 144 New Bond Street, London w1. Arthur West Antiques, The Strand, Dawlish, Devon. Runnymede Galleries, High Street, Egham, Surrey. S M Collins, 105 Leeds Road, Ilkley, Yorkshire. Evaline Winter, 1 Wolseley Road, Rugeley, Staffs.

Tiles

Thin, flat slabs, usually of baked clay, glazed or unglazed, have for many centuries been used structurally or decoratively in building. We are here concerned with the latter type used either for floors or walls and arranged in decorative patterns or as individual ornaments. Decorative floor tiles in Europe date from about the 12th century. Wall tiles, however, have been recorded as far back as the Third Dynasty in Egypt while faience wall tiles were used in Minoan Crete from the 18th century B.C. The Moors reintroduced decorative tiles to Europe, the 14th century Alhambra at Granada being resplendant with tile decorations. Simultaneously glazed earthen ware tiles, often colourfully decorated, were produced in Germany and the Low Countries to ornament the large stoves used for heating purposes. In this way the Dutch tradition of tile-work was originated and raised to a high degree of technical and artistic perfection in the 17th and 18th centuries. Examples of early delft ware tiles are now highly regarded and very expensive. Popular motifs included nautical and biblical subjects. In Holland these tiles were used to decorate wainscotings but elsewhere they were used on stoves, hearths and fireplaces. Blue and white decoration is traditional, though some later examples were decorated in manganese purple. Modern tiles often have low-relief or embossed effects in addition to a greater versatility in colour and design.

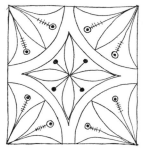

French tinglazed tiles of the early 14th century

READING

Tiles: A General History, A Berendson (Faber)
The Collection of Pottery Tiles in the Victoria and Albert Museum, A Lane (H.M.S.O.)
Hispano-Moresque ware of the XV century, A van de Put (H.M.S.O.)
Guide to Collection of Tiles (H.M.S.O.)

British Museum, London. Geffrye Museum, London. Guildhall Museum, London. Victoria and Albert Museum, London. City Museum and Art Gallery, Birmingham. Museum and Art Gallery, Brighton. Royal Scottish Museum, Edinburgh. City Museum, Hereford. Museum and Art Gallery, Leicester. Central Museum and Art Gallery, Northampton. Salisbury and South Wiltshire Museum, Salisbury. City Museum, Sheffield. City Museum and Art Gallery, Stoke-on-Trent. Elizabethan House, Totnes. Dyson Perrins Museum of Porcelain, Worcester.

Tobacco jars and boxes

Not so common as they once were, when pipe smoking was in its hey-day and tobacco was cheap, are the jars and boxes used by pipe smokers. The jars are found in a variety of earthen ware, stone ware and porcelain, usually gaily decorated around the sides and with ornamentation on the tight-fitting lid. Various metals were also used, from lead and pewter to silver, and they range in size from the small circular boxes, designed for carrying in the pocket before the advent of the tobacco pouch, to large containers which graced many a mantelpiece in days gone by.

Tobacco boxes, in a larger format than the small pocket boxes, were intended either for the table or mantelpiece, or were given as troop comforts in time of war. The latter are particularly fascinating, ranging from the Crimean and the Boer War to the two World Wars. These must have been produced by the thousand, yet fine specimens of Queen Mary's tobacco gift box of the First World War are highly prized today and relics of the earlier campaigns are correspondingly esteemed. There were also boxes with regimental badges or ship's crests and these are likewise in great demand with collectors of militaria.

READING

Tobacco and the Collector, Amoret and Christopher Scott (Parrish).

TO VIEW

Victoria and Albert Museum, London. City Museum and Art Gallery, Birmingham. Museum and Art Gallery, Brighton. Royal Scottish Museum, Edinburgh. City Museum, Hereford. Museum and Art Gallery, Leicester. Central Museum and Art Gallery, Northampton. City Museum, Sheffield. City Museum and Art Gallery, Stoke-on-Trent. Wedgwood Museum, Stoke-on-Trent. City Museum and Art Gallery, Worcester.

DEALERS

Smaller country antique shops, general dealers and markets.

Toby jugs

When the Rev. Francis Hawkes published his *Original Poems and Translations* in 1761 he could not have imagined that one of his pieces was to inspire that once common and now highly prized object, the Toby Jug. One of his poems, a translation of the "Metamorphosis" by the Italian, Geronimo Amalteo, was sub-titled "Toby Reduced" and told of the life and death of a hearty toper named Toby Fillpot. The last verse ran:

"His body, when long in the Ground it had lain,
And time into Clay had resolv'd it again
A potter found out in its Covert so snug
And with part of fat Toby he form'd this brown
    jug . . ."

This poem inspired an engraving of Toby Fillpot published by Carington Bowles after a design by Robert Dighton. This in turn inspired Ralph Wood of Burlsem to manufacture jugs in Toby's image about 1765.

Other potters were not long in producing their own versions of Toby and as the popularity of these jugs increased, they extended the range by creating new characters. Some, like Martha Gunn, the female Toby, were based on real people; she was a well-known bathing attendant at Brighton. The jug known as Bluff King Hal (distinguished by the three feathers in his hat) alludes to the fancy dress worn by the Prince of Wales at a Brighton masquerade. There are many other Toby characters: the Thin Man, the Parson, the Snuff-taker and the Sailor for instance. Toby Jugs vary considerably in size, style and colouring and they have been produced down to the present time. Modern Toby Jugs, like the modern imitations of the 18th century jugs, usually lack the artistic quality and vigorous colouring of the originals. Genuine 18th century Tobies may cost anything from £40 to £400.

READING
Toby Jugs, John Bedford (Cassell)
Good Sir Toby, D Eyles (F. Lewis)

TO VIEW
British Museum, London. National Maritime Museum, Greenwich, London. Victoria and Albert Museum, London. Museum and Art Gallery, Brighton. City Museum and Art Gallery, Birmingham. National Museum of Wales, Cardiff. Royal Scottish Museum, Edinburgh. Ashmolean Museum of Art & Archaeology, Oxford. Central Museum and Art Gallery, Northampton. Salisbury and South Wiltshire Museum, Salisbury. City Museum, Sheffield. City Museum and Art Gallery, Stoke-on-Trent.

19th century Staffordshire
Toby Jug

Most dealers in china should have a few Toby Jugs in stock; also, one can buy them in small antique shops and markets.

Toys

Until the end of the 18th century the transition from babyhood to adulthood was short and sharp. Children were dressed in miniature replicas of adult clothes and were expected to follow adult behaviour patterns. In this atmosphere there was little room for playthings, so that toys did not exist to any large extent. Such toys as there were consisted of things intended for the child's moral or educational improvement – lettered building blocks, dissected puzzles (see under jig-saws) and, in the Catholic countries, miniature altars and religious accessories.

Among the earliest toys were Noah's Arks, complete with sets of wooden animals in pairs. These originated in South Germany where the woodcarvers have long been famed for their realistic figures. Apart from dolls, dolls' houses, model soldiers, and automata (which are treated elsewhere in this book) there were paper toys, constructional toys, puzzles, clockwork toys and models of ships, trains, coaches and, in more recent years, aircraft and spacecraft.

The variety of toys is endless. From a collector's viewpoint it seems incredible that any toys should have survived generations of rough usage; this accounts for the rarity of early mechanical toys in working condition.

READING

Toys in the Victoria and Albert Museum (H.M.S.O.)
Toys and Games in the London Museum (H.M.S.O.)
Children's Toys Throughout the Ages, L Daikin (Hamlyn)
A History of Toys, A Frazer (Weidenfeld and Nicholson)
Japanese Toys, Sakamoto (Prentice-Hall)

TO VIEW

Bethnal Green Museum, London. British Museum, London. London Museum, London. Pollock's Toy Museum, London. Victoria and Albert Museum, London. Grange Art Gallery and Museum, Rottingdean, Brighton. City Museum and Art Gallery, Birmingham. Museum and Art Gallery, Brighton. Blaise Castle Folk Museum, Bristol. Museum of Childhood, Edinburgh. Museum and Art Gallery, Leicester. Central Museum and Art Gallery, Northampton. Pitt Rivers Museum, Oxford. Salisbury and South Wiltshire Museum, Salisbury. City Museum, Sheffield. Blithfield, Rugeley, Staffordshire. City Museum and Art Gallery, Stoke-on-Trent. Elizabethan House, Totnes. Royal Tunbridge Wells Museum, Tunbridge Wells. Windsor Castle, Windsor. City Museum and Art Gallery, Worcester. Snowshill Manor, Worcester.

CLUB

Antique Toy Collector's Club, 8110 Frankford Avenue, Philadelphia, Pa 19136, USA.

DEALERS

Gordon Hand and Co Limited, 18 Chepstow Mansions, Westbourne Grove, London w2. Pleasures of Past Times, 11 Cecil Court, Charing Cross, London wc2. The Victorian Cottage, High Street, Attleborough, Norfolk. Petersfield Bookshop, Chapel Street, Hants.

Trade cards

Two distinct subjects are classed under the heading of trade cards. The first, in terms of antiquity, consists of cards bearing printed advertisements for various trades and professions. The second consists of small pictorial cards given away with many products (principally cigarettes) and collected in sets and series.

Trade cards for advertising purposes shed valuable light on contemporary social and commercial history. Our knowledge of the early pottery and porcelain industry has been greatly enhanced, for example, by the existence of such cards, giving useful information about the potters, the range of their wares, their prices and methods of sale. In addition early trade cards shed a valuable light on the styles and technique of printing and the graphic arts over the years. Because they were regarded only as ephemeral, these cards were never systematically preserved and are thus very rare today. If interest in printed ephemera were ever to increase (and the indications are that this has already happened in America) they would rise astronomically in value. At present, however, they can still be picked up for shillings rather than pounds.

Cigarette cards became popular in the 1890s and were universal till the Second World War when they were discontinued as an economy measure. Since then they have been revived sporadically by the tobacco companies, but have been utilised more enthusiastically in other consumer industries, and are an increasingly frequent feature of tea and confectionery packets. Prices vary from 1d to several pounds for rare items in the early sets.

READING

Trade Tokens of the 17th Century, W Boyne (Stock)
British Trade Marks, Ambrose Heal (Tiranti)

TO VIEW
Blaise Castle Folk Museum, Bristol. Museum and
Art Gallery, Leicester. Central Museum and Art
Gallery, Northampton. Salisbury and South Wilt-
shire Museum, Salisbury.

DEALERS
Pleasures of Past Times, 11 Cecil Court, Charing
Cross Road, London WC2.

Tunbridge ware

This highly distinctive form of wood mosaic was
produced by craftsmen in the Tunbridge area on the
Kent–Sussex borders in the first half of the 19th
century. While everything from an egg cup to a
table may be found in Tunbridge ware the most
usual articles were boxes of all sorts and sizes. Boxes
for snuff, stamps, writing materials, cribbage and
dominoes, needlework and matches were turned out
in large quantities, decorated with tiny wood mosaic
patterns applied cunningly in a thin veneer. This took
the form of either rigid geometric patterns or a mosaic
picture, thousands of tiny *tesserae* being used in the
latter case.

The mosaic was produced from a solid block composed of countless thin rods of different coloured
woods glued together. A thin slice of this block was
sawn off, presenting a cross section, and then applied
to the article as a veneer. The best examples were
highly polished, but later varnishing was substituted,
with an inevitable lowering in standards of quality.
The production of genuine Tunbridge ware died out
before the end of the century although spurious
examples appeared in the 1920s and 1930s.

251

READING

All Kinds of Small Boxes, J Bedford (Cassell)
More Small Decorative Antiques, Therle Hughes
(Lutterworth)
Treen, W T James (Pitman)

TO VIEW

Victoria and Albert Museum, London. Museum and
Art Gallery, Birmingham. Museum and Art Gallery,
Brighton. City Museum, Hereford. Central Museum
and Art Gallery, Northampton. Salisbury and South
Wiltshire Museum, Salisbury. Royal Tunbridge
Wells Museum and Art Gallery, Tunbridge Wells.

DEALERS

Coxson Antiques Limited, 63 Cadogan Place,
London sw1. Brian R Verrall, 48 Maddox Street,
London w1. Trinkets and Treasures, 29 Barns Street,
Ayr. J Hutton, 108 High Street, Berkhamsted,
Herts. Avon Antiques, 26–27 Market Street,
Bradford-on-Avon, Wilts. Jan Struther, 13 Randolph
Place, Edinburgh. Charles Toller, 51 High Street,
Eton, Bucks. Wilkinson's Cottage Antiques, 27/28
Charnham Street, Hungerford, Berks. John Eddy,
22 Etnam Street, Leominster. Georgian House,
Halseworth, Suffolk. Elizabeth Hughes, Market Hall
Antiques, Towyn, Merionethshire. Vincent Wood,
Audley House, Osbournby, Lincolnshire.

Valentine cards

Why St Valentine's Day, 14th February, should be
celebrated by lovers is obscure, although it would
appear that this festival has an older, pre-Christian
origin, in the Roman feast of Lupercalia dedicated to
the god Pan. At any rate, since the Middle Ages at

least, it was customary for lovers to exchange tokens of their affection on this date. By the end of the 18th century these tokens were taking the form of written missives, with verses either composed by the sender or extracted from poetry books. These letters and cards were usually lavishly decorated by hand. Commercially produced Valentines were in existence by the 1820s and were handsome articles often adorned with lace, embossed and die-stamped paper in several layers, feathers, tinsel and ribbon. An appropriate verse or motto was printed on them and attractive pictures of lovers in rustic scenes were often incorporated. Special Valentine envelopes, embossed to simulate lace, were also produced but these are now very rare, as much as £50 being paid for one.

Valentines declined in the 1870s as Christmas cards, with their much wider appeal, grew in popularity. In the latter years of the 19th century and the period up to the First World War Valentines degenerated into a bad joke, with spiteful messages and malicious jokes which were sent to one's enemies rather than one's sweetheart. Since the Second World War, however, there has been a revival of the sentimental Valentine, largely inspired by America where card sending is a highly organised business nowadays.

READING
The Valentine, Frank Staff (Lutterworth)

TO VIEW
British Museum, London. Victoria and Albert Museum, London. City Museum and Art Gallery, Birmingham. City Museum, Hereford. Museum and Art Gallery, Leicester. Central Museum and Art Gallery, Northampton. Salisbury and South Wiltshire Museum, Salisbury. City Museum, Sheffield. Blithfield, Rugeley, Staffordshire. Elizabethan House, Totnes. Royal Tunbridge Wells Museum and Art Gallery, Tunbridge Wells. City Museum and Art Gallery, Worcester.

DEALERS
John Hall & David MacWilliams, 17 Harrington Road, London SW7. Pleasures of Past Times, 11 Cecil Court, Charing Cross Road, London WC2.

Vinaigrettes

Dutch vinaigrette in silver, about 1680

Vinaigrettes or vinegarettes, despite their French name, were an English invention though their origin has been fancifully traced to the medieval pomander and the spiced oranges carried by persons of rank to avoid infection from plague or pestilence. Isolated examples of these small silver boxes have been recorded as early as 1720, but great impetus to their popularity came from a series of lectures given in the 1780s by Dr William Henry on the subject of prophylaxis. He advocated the use of an aromatic liquid which became known as Dr Henry's Vinegar. Small silver boxes, their interior heavily gilt to prevent erosion, were produced to contain small pieces of sponge soaked in the liquid. The sponge was held in place by a perforated grille and the presence of this grille is a sure way of identifying a box as being a vinaigrette.

Many of them in the earlier period were not hallmarked since they were exempt from assay, so it is difficult to date them. The later vinaigrettes bore a hallmark and can thus be dated accurately. They seem to have survived until the end of the 19th century. Their purpose changed imperceptibly from being an antidote to infection to being a remedy for swooning and attacks of the vapours. Tight corseting, the stuffy, candle-lit atmosphere of the ballroom and drawing room, and the generally insanitary atmosphere everywhere must have been conducive to fainting fits, thus making the vinaigrette a social necessity. When these evils were removed the vinaigrette waned in popularity, though now it is avidly sought by collectors. Prices vary from £5 for a small, plain box to £300 or more for a "Trafalgar" vinaigrette bearing a portrait of Lord Nelson.

READING

English Vinaigrettes, E Ellenbogen (Golden Head Press)
Silver Boxes, Eric Delieb (Barrie and Rockliffe)

Small Decorative Antiques, Therle Hughes (Lutter-worth)

Watches

The earliest watches were no more than miniaturised clocks and date from the latter half of the 15th century. They consisted of tiny, spring-driven plated clocks encased in boxes. A rather later development was the so-called Nuremberg Egg, a splendid watch made in the early 16th century. Watches from the later 16th century were usually housed in gilt metal cases with decoratively pierced lids to protect the single hand from damage. By the end of the century watches were not only becoming smaller and slimmer but the conventional circular type was giving way to ovals or octagons. Rock crystal was occasionally used to cover the dial, but glazing did not become general till the mid-17th century. Enamelling, originally confined to the dial, extended to the inner and outer sides of the case and exquisite examples of polychrome pictures found on these watches are highly regarded by collectors, boosting the value of such items considerably. In the 18th century watch-cases were often decorated with transparent enamel over an engine-turned (*guillochèe*) background. Highly prized are the watches of the late 18th and early 19th centuries with enamelled pictures on them. It should be noted that watch-cases are collectable items in their own right, and, conversely, interesting "movements" (as the working parts are known) are also highly regarded. Combinations of watch and chatelaine, especially those which are elaborately ornamented with jewels, are in great demand.

READING

The Book of Old Clocks and Watches, Ernst von Basserman-Jordan (Allen & Unwin)
Clocks and Watches, E Bruton (Barker)
The Country Life Book of Watches, T P Camerer Cuss (Country Life)
It's About Time, P Chamberlain (Holland)
Investing in Clocks and Watches, P W Cumhail (Barrie & Rockliffe)

TO VIEW

British Museum, London. Guildhall Museum, London. London Museum, London. Science Museum, London. Victoria and Albert Museum, London. Wallace Collection, London. Waddesdon Manor, Aylesbury. Victoria Art Gallery, Bath. City Museum and Art Gallery (Department of Science), Birmingham. Gershom-Parkington Memorial Collection of Clocks and Watches, Bury St Edmunds. Royal Scottish Museum, Edinburgh. City Museum, Hereford. Museum and Art Gallery, Leicester. Usher Gallery, Lincoln. Central Museum and Art Gallery, Northampton. Ashmolean Museum of Art and Archaeology, Oxford. Salisbury and South Wiltshire Museum, Salisbury. City Museum, Sheffield. City Museum and Art Gallery, Stoke-on-Trent. Royal Tunbridge Wells Museum and Art Gallery, Tunbridge Wells. City Museum and Art Gallery, Worcester. Snowshill Manor, Worcester.

National Association of Watch and Clock Collectors
Inc, PO Box 33, Columbia, Pennsylvania 17512,
USA.

Aubrey Brocklehurst, 124 Cromwell Road, South
Kensington, London sw7. Camerer Cuss and Company, 54–56 New Oxford Street, London wc1.
Charles Frodsham and Company Limited, 173
Brompton Road, London sw3. Garrard and Company Limited, 112 Regent Street, London w1.
M Hakim, 4 Royal Arcade, Old Bond Street, London w1. Montefiore Antiques, 118b Cromwell
Road, London sw7. Wartski's, 138 Regent Street,
London w1. Beryl Birch Antiques, 89 Elmfield Road,
Castle Bromwich, Birmingham. Wilson & Sharp
Limited, 139 Princes Street, Edinburgh. Reid &
Sons Limited, 23–27 Blackett Street, Newcastle.
Bracher & Sydenham Limited, 26–30a Queen
Victoria Street, Reading. John E Davis, 14 Wokingham Road, Reading. Dunnings Antiques, 58–62
Holywell Hill, St Albans, Herts. Malcolm Gardner,
Bradbourne Farmhouse, Bradbourne Vale Road,
Sevenoaks, Kent. A T Silvester and Sons Limited,
2 and 4 High Street, Warwick. G H Bell, 32a The
Square, Winchester.

Wax fruit

Glass domes, known as "shades", containing three
dimensional "still life" in the form of flower arrangements or fruit, were very popular in Victorian times
and although they have long been despised and
neglected there are signs that they are coming back

into favour again. Similar in appearance are encased groups of flowers in variously coloured cloth, paper ware and shell work, or fruit groups moulded in pottery. All of them, available not so long ago for a few shillings, now cost as many pounds.

TO VIEW
Central Museum and Art Gallery, Northampton. City Museum, Sheffield. Snowshill Manor, Worcester.

DEALERS
Those specialising in Victoriana.

Wine coasters

These circular vessels, usually made of fretted or gadrooned silver, were used for containing decanters of port and madeira as they were passed around the table after the ladies had withdrawn. The underside of these shallow containers was flat and covered with felt to protect the surface of the table. They first appeared in the middle of the 18th century and continued to be manufactured for about 100 years.

The early coasters, or "slides" as they are sometimes known, were extremely light, with intricate designs pierced round their sides. The bottoms were made of turned wood inlaid with a thin covering of silver. Towards the end of the century solid silver became fashionable and the type of fluted pattern known as gadrooning was popular till the close of the Regency period. The early 19th century also saw the emergence of double coasters, usually mounted on wheels to form a sort of decanter waggon. These are sometimes found in polished hardwood but most of them were produced in silver or even silver-gilt.

Prices vary from £40–£50 for coasters in Sheffield plate (q.v.) to well over £1,000 for the extravagantly decorated coasters made by the great Regency silversmiths such as Paul Storr and Hester Bateman. The market in antique silver has been rising so rapidly, however, that it is impossible to give more than a relative idea of values.

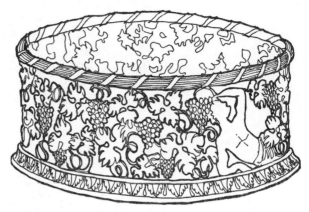

Gold wine coaster, 1814/15

TO VIEW
Victoria and Albert Museum, London. Waddesdon Manor, Aylesbury. The Royal Pavilion, Brighton. National Museum of Wales, Cardiff. Royal Scottish Museum, Edinburgh. City Museum, Sheffield.

DEALERS
Jack Christie, 36 St George Street, Hanover Square, London w1. London Silver Vaults, Chancery House, Chancery Lane, London wc2. Spink and Son Limited, King Street, St James, London sw1. D & M Davis Limited, 3 Livery Street, Birmingham, Warks. Harry Chernack, 85–87 Rose Street, Edinburgh. H A Davis, 10 Duke Street, Hove, Sussex. Bracher & Sydenham Limited, 26–30 Queen Victoria Street, Reading.

Wine coolers

This term covers a wide variety of objects, from the simple ice-bucket to the elaborate wooden cooler mounted on legs and castors. Their object, however, was similar; to chill those wines and beers which ought to be drunk below room temperature. While metal ice-buckets (ranging from silver-gilt to electroplate) are still being manufactured and are widely used at the present time, the old-fashioned wooden wine-cooler is now an antique. With their circular or octagonal tops they make ideal coffee or occasional tables and the elaborate examples, with marquetry inlay and brass mountings, are most attractive ornaments. Their capacious interiors, formerly packed with ice, are often utilised nowadays merely as a small wine or spirits cupboard – the prototype, perhaps, of the cocktail cabinet.

TO VIEW

British Museum, London. Victoria and Albert Museum, London. Waddesdon Manor, Aylesbury. The Royal Pavilion, Brighton. Royal Scottish Museum, Edinburgh. Temple Newsam House, Leeds. City Museum, Sheffield. City Museum and Art Gallery, Stoke-on-Trent. Spode-Copeland Museum and Art Gallery, Stoke-on-Trent. Wedgwood Museum, Stoke-on-Trent. Windsor Castle, Windsor.

DEALERS

Phillips Harris, 54 Kensington Church Street, London W8. Simon Kaye Limited, 1b Albemarle Street, Piccadilly, London W1. William Walter Antiques, London Silver Vaults, Chancery Lane, London WC2. Hare and Elyard, 48 Market Street, Hove, Sussex. Withers of Leicester, 142a London Road, Leicester.

Sheffield plate wine cooler

Wine glasses

For anyone wishing to form a representative collection of glass ware wine glasses provide a good cross-section of the various periods and styles. The earliest examples of modern European glass were produced by the Venetians whose goblets and wine glasses were delicately blown and beautifully ornamented. In the last decades of the 17th century George Ravenscroft of London evolved a new and heavier type of glass containing lead oxide. This "flint" glass is exceptionally rare, fewer than a dozen wine glasses by Ravenscroft being in existence.

Being darker and heavier than the Venetian ware and taking a relatively long time to cool, flint glass was unsuitable for the light ornament so beloved of the Venetians. The English glassmakers, however, made the most of its dark beauty and produced wine glasses which possess a simple charm and elegance. The earliest glasses (1690–1730) are huge by modern standards, with large bowls whose generous capacity reflected the drinking habits of the times. From the plain, straight-sided funnel evolved various fluted shapes, bell, waisted and trumpet-bowls. See page 263.

These shapes were retained well into the 19th century, so the stems of wine glasses are more important for the purpose of dating them. Predominant in the Queen Anne period was the baluster stem, upright or inverted. From about 1720 variety was added by the inclusion of knops, or shaped enlargements which gave strength and beauty to the stem. Highly prized are drawn-stem glasses and those in which air bubbles were drawn out and twisted to form an internal "rope" of fine air lines. Other rare examples had a "tear", or elongated air bubble in the baluster. See also "Jacobite Glasses".

READING

How to Identify English Drinking Glasses and Decanters,
D Ash (Bell)

Collector's Dictionary of Glass, E M Elville (Spring Books)

TO VIEW
British Museum, London. Guildhall Museum, London. Victoria Art Gallery, Bath. City Museum and Art Gallery, Birmingham. Museum and Art Gallery, Brighton. Royal Pavilion, Brighton. Museum and Art Gallery, Bristol. Royal Scottish Museum, Edinburgh. City Museum, Hereford. Museum and Art Gallery, Leicester. City Museum, Liverpool. Central Museum and Art Gallery, Northampton. Ashmolean Museum of Art and Archaeology, Oxford. Pilkington Glass Museum, St Helens, Lancs. Salisbury and South Wiltshire Museum, Salisbury. City Museum, Sheffield. City Museum and Art Gallery, Stoke-on-Trent. Windsor Castle, Windsor. City Museum and Art Gallery, Worcester. Snowshill Manor, Worcester. The Yorkshire Museum, York.

CLUB
The Glass Circle, 50a Fulham Road, London sw3.

DEALERS
W G T Burne Limited, 11 Elystan Street, London sw3. Arthur Churchill Limited, Marjorie Parr Gallery, 285 Kings Road, London sw3. Cecil Davis Limited, 3 Grosvenor Street, New Bond Street, London w1. Thomas Goode and Son, 19 South Audley Street, London w1. A Henning, 61 George Street, Portman Square, London w1. Howard Phillips, 11a Henrietta Place, London w1. Spink and Son, King Street, St James', London sw1. R Wilkinson and Son, 11 High Street, Wimbledon Common, London sw19. M Sainsbury, 35 Gay Street, Bath. D & M Davis Limited, 3 Livery Street, Birmingham. John Fileman, Ravenscroft, 4 Powis Villas, Brighton. Jan Struther, 13 Randolph Place, Edinburgh. Esme Dunn Antiques, 2 Paigle Road, Aylestone, Leicester. The Antiquary, 50 St Giles, Oxford. Collectors Treasures Limited, 8–9 Church Street, Windsor. A V Harrison, 61 Sidbury, Worcester. Robert Morrison, Adams House, Petergate, York.

(*1*) Double ogee bowl, 1715 (*2*) Mid. 18th century with opaque twisted stem. (*3*) Mid 18th century with red white and blue opaque twisted stem. (*4*) 18th century stem-bladed knob. (*5*) 18th century with air twist stem and double ogee bowl. (*6*) Late 18th century with bell shaped bowl and baluster stem. (*7*) Late 18th century bucket bowl. (*8*) Late 18th century, dark green glass, ovoid bowl. (*9*) Early 19th century, engraved with straight sided bowl.

Wine labels

The practice of cutting the glass sides of decanters in an all-over pattern from about 1770 onwards precluded the earlier fashion for engraving the name of the particular wines on them and led to the invention of a label which could be hung round the neck of the vessel. Originally parchment tickets were used, but something more substantial, in keeping with the elegance of the decanter, was required. The earliest silver wine labels are enveloped in mystery, although the experts seem to agree that among the first were those manufactured by Isaac Duke some time after 1743.

(*1*) French enamelled wine label of the 17th century. (*2*) Tinglazed wine label of the early 18th century. (*3*) Claret label, late 18th century. (*4*) Silver sherry label, 1877/8.

Early wine labels are difficult to date since silver articles under 10 dwt were exempt from hallmarking before 1790. Silver wine labels are still being made, but, as collector's pieces, the best of them were made in the late 18th and early 19th centuries. They vary greatly both in design and the style of lettering adopted. Popular motifs were the vine-leaf or bunch of grapes, which are found in many different forms. Scallop-shells and scrolls, sometimes incorporating heraldic devices, were also fashionable, while wine labels in the shape of animals such as bulls or pigs are comparatively rare.

While silver and silver-gilt were the most popular materials used, wine labels may be found in Battersea enamel (q.v.), close-plate or Sheffield plate (q.v.) (not to be confused with the later, and relatively worthless, electro-plate). Examples are also known in earthen ware or porcelain. Few wine labels worth collecting can be picked up nowadays for less than £5, while some of the animal-shaped rarities will fetch £100 or more.

READING
Book of the Wine Label, N Penzer (Horne & Van Thal)
Wine Labels, E W Whitworth (Cassell)

TO VIEW
Victoria and Albert Museum, London. National Museum of Wales, Cardiff. Royal Scottish Museum, Edinburgh. Central Museum and Art Gallery, Northampton. City Museum, Sheffield. Wedgwood Museum, Stoke-on-Trent. City Museum and Art Gallery, Worcester. The Yorkshire Museum, York.

CLUB
The Wine Label Circle, The Rectory, Hook Norton, Nr Banbury, Oxon.

DEALERS
B L Merriday, 10-12 Station Parade, Chipstead, Surrey.

Worcester

The Royal Worcester Porcelain Company is the oldest established pottery of its kind in Britain still in production. It was founded in 1751 by Dr. John Wall whose name is familiarly used by collectors and ceramics historians to describe the soft paste porcelain produced in the period 1751–83. The company passed successively through the hands of the Flights and the Barrs (in various combinations) (1783–1840), the Chamberlains (1840–52), Kerr and Binns (1852–62) and has been known by its present name since the latter date.

The products of this factory include both domestic and ornamental wares and range from the chinoiserie dishes decorated by Robert Hancock, to the celebrated bird figures modelled by Dorothy Doughty in recent years. The range of wares is so vast that it would be impossible within the scope of this book to mention them in detail. Suffice it to say that the literature on Worcester is equally prolific and some of the more readily obtainable books, dealing with various aspects and periods, are listed below.

READING

Worcester Porcelain, F A Barrett (Faber)
Old Worcester China, J Bedford (Cassell)
Caughley and Worcester Porcelain, G A Godden (Jenkins)
Worcester Poreclain, F S MacKenna (F Lewis)
Illustrated Guide to Worcester Porcelain 1751–1793, H Sandon (Jenkins)

TO VIEW

British Museum, London. Victoria and Albert Museum, London. City Museum and Art Gallery, Birmingham. Art Gallery and Museum, Brighton. National Museum of Wales, Cardiff. Royal Scottish Museum, Edinburgh. Littlecote House, Hungerford. Wernher Collection, Luton Hoo. Central Museum

and Art Gallery, Northampton. Ashmolean Museum of Art and Archaeology, Oxford. Scone Palace, Perth. Salisbury and South Wiltshire Museum, Salisbury. City Museum, Sheffield. City Museum and Art Gallery, Stoke-on-Trent. City Museum and Art Gallery, Worcester.
The finest and most comprehensive collection of Worcester Porcelain is to be seen at:
Dyson Perrins Museum, Worcester.

CLUBS
The English Ceramic Circle, 8 Church Row, London NW3.

DEALERS
Antique Porcelain Co Limited, 149 New Bond Street, London W1. Filkins and Co, 175 Old Brompton Road, London SW5 (by appointment only). Gordon Hand and Co, 18 Chepstow Mansions, Westbourne Grove, London W2. Newman and Newman, 156 Brompton Road, London SW3. Royal Worcester China Company's Showrooms, Worcester House, 30 Curzon Street, London W1. Spink and Son Limited, 5–7 King Street, London SW1. Tilley and Co Limited, 2 Symons Street, Sloane Square, London SW3. Andrew Dando, 4 Wood Street, Queen Square, Bath, Somerset. Stanley Fisher, 25 High Street, Bewdley, Worcester. Trevor Antiques, 14–15 Ship Street, Brighton. The China Corner, 22 Chequer Road, Doncaster, Yorks. Cothill Antiques, Kincardine O'Neil, Aberdeen. Collector's Treasures, Amersham, Bucks. Mrs Araxie Love, Newbiggin, Richmond, Yorks. Elizabeth Sumpter & Margaret Douglas-Home, Burnham Market, Norfolk. Lt Col Workman, Tetbury, Glos. Philpotts, 34 Sidbury, Worcester, Worcs.

NOTE—See page xx for china marks.

Workboxes

These are relics of the days when it was one of the principal domestic virtues to be adept at needlework, tatting and embroidery; workboxes have now come back into fashion and not so much for utilitarian purposes but for decorative reasons. Workboxes in lingwood, satinwood or other exotic hardwoods, mounted on pedestals, make elegant occasional tables and vase stands. They are found with intricate marquetry tops and sides, or with attractive walnut veneering. Workboxes of the portable kind were made not only in wood but in papier maché (q.v.) and these are now keenly sought after by collectors, particularly if still complete with their contents.

TO VIEW

London Museum, London. Victoria and Albert Museum, London. County Museum, Aylesbury, Bucks. Museum and Art Gallery, Brighton. The Royal Pavilion, Brighton. Royal Scottish Museum, Edinburgh. Guildford Museum, Guildford. City Museum, Hereford. Temple Newsam House, Leeds. Museum and Art Gallery, Leicester. Central Museum and Art Gallery, Northampton. Salisbury and South Wiltshire Museum, Salisbury. Blithfield, Rugeley, Staffs. Elizabethan House, Totnes. Windsor Castle, Windsor. City Museum and Art Gallery, Worcester.

DEALERS

Gordon Hand & Company, 18 Chepstow Mansions, Westbourne Grove, London w2. Ivar Mackay, 4 Kensington Church Walk, London w8. Graham Pontet Limited, 102 Mount Street, London w1. Ivy House Antiques, Abbots Bromley, Staffs. John Bell, 56–58 Bridge Street, Aberdeen. Roger Warner, High Street, Burford, Oxford. Dunnings Antiques, 58–62 Holywell Hill, St Albans, Herts. Christopher Clarke, The Square, Stow-on-the-Wold, Glos.